"Kirsten Foot has tackled the most important aspects of how to achieve effective collaboration in the complex and multifaceted efforts to end the slavery of human beings. She has identified the factors that must be addressed for different sectors to understand their contributions to accomplishing the common goal. May the book bring forth understanding among government offices, law enforcement, social service agencies, advocates and others to press on in this important effort together—to save many precious lives from this horrific crime." —**Donna M. Hart**, former District Director, U.S. Department of Labor, Wage and Hour Division

"Provocative, sensitive, and deeply reflective. This insider's account explores what it takes to combat human trafficking—together. Foot aptly describes the challenges of partnering and the complex interplay of interpersonal dynamics, cross-sector norms, social forces, and competing values. She calls for the thoughtful cultivation of partnerships based on respect, trust, and perseverance. For those who are 'in it to end it,' this is a valuable and timely contribution; for those interested in productive collaboration to combat human trafficking, it is a must-read. But be warned: Looking into this mirror upon our very human interactions may invoke discomfort." —**Dr. Luke Bearup**, consultant, former Child Protection and Research Development Specialist, Asia Pacific Region, World Vision

"Foot provides a rich and constructive review of the potential for public and private partnerships to combat human trafficking, including numerous examples of cross-sector initiatives led by NGOs, government agencies, foundations, grassroots volunteers, and even the president's cabinet. She utilizes deep research and firsthand accounts to eloquently outline why best intentions at collaboration sometimes succeed, sometimes fade, and sometimes fail, as well as the reasons why power, funding, and competition can interfere. *Collaborating against Human Trafficking* offers hope and direction on how these necessary cross-sector partnerships can work at scale." —**Karen Olcott**, Strategic Development & Innovation, T-Mobile USA; founder of Partnerships for Global Impact and The Freedom Movement

"This book brilliantly documents the trials and tribulations that law enforcement and NGOs experience. In addition to insightfully identifying

collaboration challenges, it will help improve partnerships by educating participants of any human trafficking task force—whether it is just starting or has already been working together—on what it takes to work together well. I highly recommend Foot's work for everyone embroiled in or researching the issues surrounding collaboration to end human trafficking."
—**Detective Sergeant Jon Daggy**, Indianapolis Metropolitan Police Department, Human Trafficking Vice Unit

"This book does an excellent job explaining some very real tensions that exist in collaborative anti-trafficking work, such as the tensions between faith-based and areligious organizations, or between those who are survivor-activists and those who are not. It captures the complex dynamics present in interorganizational collaboration in response to a social problem, including a discussion of power, race, gender, and value orientations that inform collaborator perspectives, yet are often missing from the discussion. Drawing from her own experiences and those of many others in the field, Foot has pulled together a resource of tremendous value to professionals, practitioners, and activists who are engaged in this work." —**Dr. Katherine R. Cooper**, associate director of the Network for Nonprofit and Social Impact, Northwestern University

"Foot has given the anti-trafficking community a monumental gift with this book. It is a powerful tool to guide more effective collaboration as well as catalyzing more coalitions and networks locally, regionally, and globally."
—**Alex Sum**, cofounder of Seattle Against Slavery and Founder of Human Rights Society

"As a program officer for a family foundation that invests in counter-trafficking efforts, I have heard—and made—numerous appeals for more partnership and collaboration among counter-trafficking stakeholders. However, until reading this book, I had not encountered much helpful insight or advice for making collaboration actually work. Kirsten Foot's in-depth research uncovers and explains the inevitable tensions and dynamics that make collaboration so difficult; instead of naively wishing those difficulties away, she challenges anti-trafficking stakeholders to reflect on why these tensions exist and recommends attitudes and practices necessary to overcome them in pursuit of more effective solutions. Practitioners, policymakers, and donors serious about improving collaborative efforts will benefit from reading this book." —**Jeremy Floyd**, program officer, Equitas Group

"This is a must-read for any person or agency who is engaging, about to engage, or ready to disengage in an anti-trafficking collaboration. Foot provides a deep, rich, and realistic analysis of the many challenges, pitfalls, opportunities, and rewards that come with multisector collaboration in counter-trafficking efforts. This book underscores the necessity of these partnerships and, through her analysis, provides an array of tools, resources, and insights that can help make these challenging partnerships more dynamic, powerful, and successful." —**Maria A. Trujillo**, former executive director of United Against Human Trafficking

"Based on my experience managing several multisector partnerships for Microsoft, I find that Dr. Foot's suggestions for improving collaborations are spot on. Since every business has a role to play in ending human trafficking, everyone in the private sector—and especially technology companies engaged with this issue—should read this book." —**Rane Johnson-Stempson**, director, Microsoft Research Outreach

"A unique and crucial perspective on anti–human trafficking efforts. Collaborations are the key to effectively addressing human trafficking domestically and internationally, as well as for securing funding for new and existing anti-trafficking coalitions. Foot replaces what has seemed like a mix of magic and luck with a more tenable roadmap for initiating and sustaining multijurisdictional alliances. Applying the insights from this book in new or existing collaborative efforts will enrich these partnerships and will mature coalition-building from magic to art form. This book serves as a practical reference for crafting more effective and sustainable collaborations against human trafficking —and making the end of slavery a more achievable reality." —**Derek Marsh**, deputy chief (Ret.), Westminster Police Department, CA, and cofounder of the Orange County Human Trafficking Task Force

"*Collaborating against Human Trafficking* gave me greater insight into the forces at play that both foster and disrupt the partnerships I work with on a daily basis. Dr. Foot's nuanced examinations about race, gender, and survivor leadership are of vital importance for everyone working in this field." —**Dr. Mar Brettmann**, executive director of Businesses Ending Slavery and Trafficking

"Foot has done a great service to the anti-trafficking movement here in the United States and around the world: She compellingly articulates what we've done right and where we've failed in using collaboration to end slavery. She calls out the inherent and often self-defeating power dynamics that emerge in collaborative settings—in particular, the pervasive and often systemic marginalization of trafficking survivors. This book invites leaders in the anti-trafficking movement to acknowledge and challenge the power dynamics, embrace the collaborative tensions, and seize the massive opportunities inherent in collaboration to achieve the outcome of advancing lasting human freedom. It is an essential read for everyone dedicated to ending modern day slavery." —**Jesse Eaves**, policy director, Humanity United; former senior child protection policy advisor, World Vision U.S.

"Leaders will agree that multisector collaboration is crucial to combating human trafficking, yet most are unaware of the inherent challenges and tensions that make collaboration efforts so difficult. Foot shows us the way forward with careful research and analysis to improve communication and organization. Experts, policymakers, researchers, and practitioners will find this book essential." —**Dr. Mark Latonero**, research director, Center on Communication Leadership and Policy, the University of Southern California Annenberg School; fellow, Data and Society Research Institute, NYC

"Incredibly well written and beautifully organized; this exploration of collaboration in the anti–human trafficking space is the kind of book that every academic should write, but that very few *do* write. Foot's narrative is logical and intuitive, with incredible signposting throughout. She interjects interesting real-world examples that excite even the expert reader. It won't simply be a classroom tool, but also a guide to making the world a better place. It will make a huge difference to those trying to end human trafficking: real-world activists, journalists, policymakers, police associations, survivors, church groups, women's rights groups, and so on. It is empowering because it lays out the 'what' of effective multisector partnerships, but also and more importantly, the 'how' and the 'why.'" —**Dr. Greg Goodale**, associate dean, College of Arts, Media and Design, Northeastern University

"For a donor, the anti-trafficking space can feel like a confusing maze of organizations and networks doing inspiring work on some slice of the problem. Well-intended efforts to collaborate all too often hit invisible walls that feel overwhelming to surmount. Dr. Foot takes the reader beyond the platitudes and good intentions of collaboration to look with an open mind and heart at the all-too-familiar obstacles, differing underlying values and objectives, and structural patterns that invisibly stymie effective partnership. Her painstaking research is impressive from a social science perspective, yet is deeply accessible to a nonacademic practitioner in the field. This is a worthy read for anyone seeking to do the hard yet critically important work of moving beyond the rhetoric and good intentions of collaboration to truly build effective human and organizational bridges, to heal our world, and to free it from the grip of enslavement." —**Emily Nielsen Jones**, cofounder and president of Imago Dei Fund

"In the anti-trafficking world, the stakes are high. If we do not find effective paths to cooperation, victims will not be found and resources will be squandered. This book is like the map for a video game that shows all of the obstacles along the way. It is useful for students in the classroom who will gain a deeper understanding of principles before entering the field, as well as for veteran practitioners who will nod their heads with recognition. The insight and tools will guide communities in building stronger networks that better serve the very people that need us to work together—victims of modern day slavery and trafficking." —**Dr. Sandra Morgan**, director, Global Center for Women and Justice at Vanguard University; host of the *Ending Human Trafficking* podcast series

"If we wish to come to grips with the multifaceted, multidimensional, and multisectoral global crime of trafficking in human beings, we will do well to consider the key elements addressed in this book: collaboration, cooperation, and coordination. Foot's study of collaboration dynamics reveals the underlying causes that combine to shape approaches and responses in combating human trafficking. Her analysis of collaboration and coordination is relevant in many places beyond the United States and her insights and recommendations should be read by everyone involved in countering human trafficking." —**Dr. Helga Konrad**, coordinator of the Regional Implementation Initiative on Preventing and Combating Human Trafficking; executive director of Anti-Trafficking at the Institute for the Danube Region and Central Europe IDM

"This book gives insights, models, and tools for success in crafting strong partnerships to end modern slavery. While we must serve with compassion at the margins, we must also work together to recreate community. I highly recommend the book and what it is calling us to do—and how to be—in collaboration." —**Rev. Kevin Austin**, director of the Set Free Movement, Free Methodist Church, Wesleyan Holiness Consortium Freedom Network

"I'm inspired! The ideas in this book are very timely for the deep review we are giving our organization after seven years of collaborating to stop human trafficking. Foot's discussion of motives and values and how they affect collaboration are especially helpful. She provides good examples from which to learn." —**Betty R. Edwards**, chair, Human Trafficking Task Force of Southern Colorado; recipient of the 2015 Jane Addams Award for Outstanding Service from the Midwest Sociological Society

"This book is long overdue for the anti-trafficking movement! A well-researched, deeply thoughtful, and practical framework for collaboration which offers insights for all those working in this movement and beyond. After more than a decade of running a coalition with collaboration as a central value and daily activity, I have seen that some of the most challenging partnerships have turned out to have some of the most strategic and significant results. Successful collaboration not only affects the lives of those we work with, but in the process also challenges and changes us—as people and as professionals—for the better. This book is an excellent resource for those looking to explore and understand more fully the pitfalls and potentials of building robust partnerships." —**Helen Sworn**, founder and international director, Chab Dai Coalition, Cambodia

Collaborating against Human Trafficking

Collaborating against Human Trafficking

Cross-Sector Challenges and Practices

KIRSTEN FOOT

ROWMAN & LITTLEFIELD
Lanham • Boulder • New York • London

Published by Rowman & Littlefield
A wholly owned subsidiary of The Rowman & Littlefield Publishing Group, Inc.
4501 Forbes Boulevard, Suite 200, Lanham, Maryland 20706
www.rowman.com

Unit A, Whitacre Mews, 26-34 Stannary Street, London SE11 4AB

British Library Cataloguing in Publication Information Available

Library of Congress Cataloging-in-Publication Data

Foot, Kirsten A.
  Collaborating against human trafficking : cross-sector challenges and practices /
Kirsten Foot.
    pages cm
  Includes bibliographical references and index.
  ISBN 978-1-4422-4692-8 (cloth : alk. paper) — ISBN 978-1-4422-4693-5 (pbk. : alk.
paper) — ISBN 978-1-4422-4694-2 (electronic) 1. Human trafficking—Prevention.
I. Title.
  HQ281.F656 2016
  306.3'62—dc23

                                                                    2015018993

♾™ The paper used in this publication meets the minimum requirements of
American National Standard for Information Sciences—Permanence of Paper
for Printed Library Materials, ANSI/NISO Z39.48-1992.

Printed in the United States of America

Contents

Acronyms

(All government agencies in this list are U.S.)

4Ps	Prevention, Protection, Prosecution, and Partnership
ATEST	Alliance to End Slavery and Trafficking
gBCAT	global Business Coalition Against Trafficking
BJA	Bureau of Justice Assistance
CAST	Coalition Against Slavery and Trafficking
CBP	Customs and Border Patrol
DHS	Department of Homeland Security
DOJ	Department of Justice
DOT	Department of Transportation
FAAST	Faith Alliance Against Slavery and Trafficking
FBI	Federal Bureau of Investigation
FBO	faith-based organization
FUSE	Force to End Human Sexual Exploitation
ICE	Immigration and Customs Enforcement
LCHT	Laboratory to Combat Human Trafficking
LE	Law enforcement
MANGO	mobilization and advocacy nongovernmental organization
MOU	memo of understanding
NGO	nongovernmental organization
NSN	National Survivor Network
OVC	Office for Victims of Crime
PFF	Partnership for Freedom

PITF   President's Interagency Task Force to Monitor and
              Combat Trafficking
SAP   Strategic Action Plan
SIB   social impact bonds
TIP Report   Trafficking in Persons Report
TTAC   Technical Training and Assistance Center
TVPA   Trafficking Victims Protection Act
US   United States of America
USAO   United States Attorney's Office
VSP   victim service provider
WARN   Washington Anti-Trafficking Response Network

1

The Collaboration Dilemma

We must show new energy in fighting back an old evil. Nearly two
centuries after the abolition of the transatlantic slave trade, and more than
a century after slavery was officially ended in its last strongholds, the trade
in human beings for any purpose must not be allowed to thrive in our
time. . . . The founding documents of the United Nations and the founding
documents of America stand in the same tradition. Both assert that human
beings should never be reduced to objects of power or commerce, because
their dignity is inherent.

—President George W. Bush, September 23, 2003[1]

[Human trafficking] ought to concern every person, because it's a
debasement of our common humanity. It ought to concern every
community, because it tears at the social fabric. It ought to concern every
business, because it distorts markets. It ought to concern every nation,
because it endangers public health and fuels violence and organized crime.
I'm talking about the injustice, the outrage, of human trafficking, which
must be called by its true name—modern slavery.

—President Barack Obama, September 25, 2012[2]

Slavery may be something we associate with other times and places we
consider more primitive than our own. Yet it continues to be a worldwide
problem on an almost unimaginable scale, and one that is not confined to
less economically developed areas of the globe. Human trafficking is defined
by the United States and the United Nations as compelling someone into any
form of work or service through force, fraud, or coercion. The essence of hu-

1

man trafficking is enslavement—that is, the control and exploitation of one person by another. In human trafficking situations, some victims coerce others while under coercion themselves. Money may or may not be exchanged when a person is trafficked, and victims may be commercially exploited or used as a personal slave by the trafficker. In short, human trafficking takes myriad forms. In our contemporary world, human trafficking crimes are sometimes intertwined with human smuggling and sexual exploitation, yet human trafficking crimes are legally distinct from both. They are defined by the fact that victims' agency and other human rights are violated through force, fraud, or coercion.

Human trafficking occurs at all levels of society, within local settings as well as between countries. Often referred to as modern slavery, it is recognized as a widespread "dark side" of globalization and an extreme form of exploitation of the weaker and poorer by the stronger and richer. The possession of a person by another person, the "control over a person by another such as a person might control a thing," is enslavement, whether that control is exercised through physical, verbal, or psychological forces and whether or not it involves the geographical movement of the controlled person.[3] Some victims are enslaved within their own country, while others are forced to work in another country.[4] Cases of human trafficking have been documented in most countries and in a diverse array of industries. In the United States, such cases have been documented in restaurants, technology companies, domestic services, nail salons, agriculture, carpet installation businesses, construction companies, massage shops, and magazine sales, to name just a few.[5]

Since well before the United Nations' 2000 adoption of the Palermo Protocol to Prevent, Suppress, and Punish Trafficking in Persons,[6] people working in a variety of sectors in many countries have been striving to stop the trafficking of persons and help those who have been trafficked. Most agree that the complexity of the problem and the many forms of harm to victims require collaboration across sectors. Many are convinced that "the power of a successful anti-human trafficking collaborative effort can transform the limitations of a singular agency or organization into a strong, strategic multidisciplinary team with substantially improved capacity to impact the problem."[7] This widespread belief in collaboration was evidenced in the 2012 survey of nearly two hundred US anti-trafficking organizations and government agencies conducted by the Laboratory to Combat Human Trafficking, which found that two-thirds were participating in at least one interorganizational alliance against trafficking, and most of those participated in two to four alliances. However, challenges that hinder collaboration against trafficking were also prevalent in the survey findings.[8]

The US federal government has sought to catalyze interagency coordination and cross-sector collaboration since the early 2000s.[9] To underscore the necessity of collaboration, in 2009 the U.S. Department of State added "Partnership" to the "3P" framework of prevention, prosecution, and protection employed by many governments. The intent of that addition was explained thusly: "The 'fourth P'—partnership—serves as a pathway to achieve progress on the 3Ps in the effort against modern slavery."[10] The 2010 *Trafficking in Persons Report*, issued annually by the U.S. State Department since 2000, included partnership as the fourth "P" for the first time. It articulated an expansive conceptualization of multiple forms of partnership. Here is the report's rationale for that inclusion:

> Combating human trafficking requires the expertise, resources, and efforts of many individuals and entities. It is a complex, multifaceted issue requiring a comprehensive response of government and nongovernment entities in such areas as human rights, labor and employment, health and services, and law enforcement. It requires partnerships among all these entities to have a positive impact.
>
> Partnerships augment efforts by bringing together diverse experience, amplifying messages, and leveraging resources, thereby accomplishing more together than any one entity or sector would be able to alone. Examples of existing partnerships governments use to facilitate prevention, protection, and prosecution include:
>
> - Task forces among law enforcement agencies that cooperate to share intelligence, work across jurisdictions, and coordinate across borders;
> - Alliances between governments and business associations that seek to craft protocols and establish compliance mechanisms for slavery-free supply chains; and,
> - Regional partnerships among nations, such as the anti–human trafficking efforts of the Organization of American States (OAS) or the European Union (EU).

Outside the government, partnerships include coalitions of nongovernmental organizations (NGOs) coming together for purposes of advocacy, service provision, information sharing, and networks of survivors, whose experiences inform the broader trafficking movement.

The concluding statement from the overview of partnership in anti-trafficking efforts quoted above is telling. It acknowledges that collaborating against trafficking entails challenges:

> While there is broad agreement on the purpose and benefits of a partnership approach to human trafficking, there is less agreement on and documentation of proven, successful strategies,—*something all should endeavor to create and share in the years ahead.*[11] (Emphasis added)

What effective collaboration entails, then, is not so easily delineated. We must figure out how to work together well in prevention, protection, and prosecution. This book is my contribution to the State Department's call: an analysis of the dynamics of collaboration designed to illuminate what it takes to build robust partnerships across sectors to counter human trafficking.

During both the Bush and Obama administrations, the US government made many attempts to foster partnerships to counter human trafficking. Under the mandate of the US Trafficking Victims Protection Act (TVPA), passed originally in 2000, multiple federal agencies have funded and facilitated collaboration against human trafficking in many ways. I highlight three very significant ones here. First, the 2000 TVPA's creation of the President's Interagency Task Force to Monitor and Combat Trafficking (PITF), a cabinet-level entity chaired by the Secretary of State, has been foundational in coordinating the efforts of federal agencies against human trafficking.[12]

Second is the use of TVPA funds to offer multiyear, renewable grants to support counter-trafficking efforts and services for victims, an effort begun in 2004 by the U.S. Department of Justice (DOJ) through its Office of Justice Programs, Bureau of Justice Assistance (BJA), and Office for Victims of Crime (OVC).[13] Initially, the BJA grants supported multiagency law enforcement anti-trafficking task forces in selected cities across the country. Correspondingly, between 2003 and 2009, the OVC offered grant funds to qualified victim service provider organizations in some cities that had a multiagency law enforcement task force. The purpose of the OVC funds during those years was to provide services to foreign nationals whom service providers believed to be victims of trafficking. Beginning in 2010, BJA and OVC began to jointly fund grants via an "enhanced collaborative task force model" that included support for victim service agencies and law enforcement agencies to take a comprehensive approach to investigating all trafficking crimes and providing services to trafficking victims regardless of citizenship or age.[14] The aims of these task forces are "identifying, rescuing and restoring victims . . . investigating and prosecuting trafficking crimes; and building awareness about trafficking in the surrounding community."[15] Proposals for "Enhanced Collaborative Model to Combat Human Trafficking" grants must be developed collaboratively between at least one law enforcement agency (LE) and one victim service provider organization (VSP) that have "an established working relationship"; grantees are also expected to work "in close collaboration with the local U.S. Attorney's Office."[16] At the peak of this grant program, task forces in forty-two US cities received DOJ funding. As of 2014 the number of cities with DOJ-funded multisector task forces had been reduced to thirteen.[17]

Third, the US government's significant investment in collaboration was evidenced in its landmark first five-year federal "Strategic Action Plan" (SAP) on services for people trafficked in the United States, released in early 2014.[18] The development of the eighty-page plan itself required major collaboration between the three entities that cochaired the plan development process (the Departments of Justice, Health and Human Services, and Homeland Security) and the seventeen other federal agencies that contributed to it. In addition, input from other stakeholders including nongovernmental organizations and trafficking survivors was elicited at several points during the process beginning in 2012. Public comments on the draft plan were invited during a 45-day period in mid-2013. The plan ambitiously details many ways that federal agencies will partner with stakeholders in a diverse array of sectors in the future.

The primary catalyst for the development of the SAP was a statement by President Obama to the PITF in March 2012, which broadened the collaboration mandate for federal agencies to include partnership with civil society and the private sector. Obama explained:

> The United States is committed to eradicating trafficking in persons, and we
> will draw on tools ranging from law enforcement and victim service provision,

to public awareness building and diplomatic pressure. Because we know that government efforts are not enough, we are also increasing our partnerships with a broad coalition of local communities, faith-based and non-governmental organizations, schools, and businesses.

To bring all these elements together, and to be sure we are maximizing our efforts, today I am directing my cabinet to find ways to strengthen our current work, and to expand on partnerships with civil society and the private sector, so that we can bring more resources to bear in fighting this horrific injustice.[19]

In September 2012, Obama announced his initiative to create "the first-ever federal strategic action plan to strengthen services for trafficking victims," in the process further elaborating the multiple forms of cross-sector collaboration the federal government was to help catalyze.[20] The broadened collaboration mandate—that federal agencies partner with a wide array of civil society organizations and businesses—was significant because previously, the primary federal program for stimulating collaboration against human trafficking was the DOJ's task force grants. By awarding the task force grants largely to law enforcement and service provider organizations, the government in effect defined those sectors as the primary, if not the sole, sectors necessary for countering human trafficking. Meanwhile, the social movement against human trafficking, which grew immensely since the early 2000s through successful awareness-raising efforts, had been informing people from many other sectors about the complex problem of human trafficking. Leaders in sectors beyond law enforcement and victim services were beginning to see ways their sectors could, and should, contribute to counter-trafficking efforts. However, the DOJ grants' definition of the primary sectors as law enforcement and victim services left a legacy. Task force leaders in many cities have been overwhelmed by, and unsure of how to respond to, requests to include such other entities as state agency officials, healthcare professionals, educators, leaders of business associations, faith-based organizations, and mobilization and advocacy NGOs (MANGOs).[21]

THE US GOVERNMENT'S GUIDE TO ENHANCING COLLABORATION IN ANTI-TRAFFICKING TASK FORCES

In 2011, the DOJ's Office for Victims of Crime Training and Technical Assistance Center published on its website the "Human Trafficking Task Force e-Guide," coproduced by the BJA and the OVC with input from law enforcement and victim service providers. Updated substantially in 2014, the second edition contained much more material on collaboration. The focus of the updated e-Guide continued to be collaboration between law enforcement and victim service providers. But it also acknowledged additional anti-trafficking activities and framed their importance in relation to their support of the primary functions of the law enforcement and victim services sectors:

> This Guide refers to all multidisciplinary, collaborative, anti-human trafficking efforts as "task forces." Multidisciplinary teams may also be referred to as coalitions or networks. *For the purposes of this Guide, task forces are those which focus on identifying human trafficking, serving victims and investigating and building cases.* These are the primary activities; however, others such as training, technical assistance and community awareness/education are viewed as activities that contribute to a task force's ability to perform the three core functions. The principles and advantages of the task force model apply to all multidisciplinary teams, regardless of funding sources or government affiliation.[22] (Emphasis in the original)

The updated e-Guide also acknowledged a wide array of organizations from diverse sectors that could be sources of referrals and support for law enforcement and service providers:

> Increased public awareness of the existence of human trafficking within communities often generates the interest and the benevolence of nontraditional supporters of law enforcement and service provider partnerships. Members can increase human trafficking case referrals from, and improve public awareness within, local faith-based groups, homelessness organizations, migrant farm worker groups, pro bono and immigration attorneys, sexual assault and domestic violence advocates, civic and cultural groups, restaurant and hotel employees, school and medical officials, as well as regulatory inspectors, routine patrol officers, truck drivers, and utility workers, among others. By providing outreach specifically tailored to the needs and circumstances of each group, the stakeholders learn how to contact the task force for help.[23]

Elsewhere in the e-Guide, a more detailed list of potential partners includes victim/survivor impact consultants, academics with expertise on human trafficking and low-wage workers' rights, sex-workers' rights groups, and immigrant advocacy groups, along with others.[24] Despite the anti-trafficking efforts of some businesses and industry associations (to be discussed further in chapter 3), the private sector was largely missing from this list of potential partners.

The e-Guide suggested expanding partnerships, though not to a degree that would diminish the original sectors' centrality in the task forces. While encouraging law enforcement and victim service provider organizations to consider reaching out to potential partners in other sectors, the e-Guide simultaneously cautioned against wandering from or diluting commitment to the DOJ's aims for task forces:

> *The primary goals of outreach and awareness-raising should be to increase victim identification, identify new resources, and generate political will and support for the issue.*
>
> Within many communities, there are networks, coalitions, and groups that can be approached to share information, create new partnerships, and identify resources, skills, and good practices for enhancing a community response to human trafficking. Task forces can collaborate with such groups to create effective communitywide strategies to combat human trafficking. Participation in a network of supporting partners does not necessitate participation in the primary task force group. Consistent with the necessary vetting of all task force partnerships, these relationships should be evaluated for conformance to the task force's core mission and purpose. For example, ensure that partners are supporting one or more of the core task force functions in a victim-centered manner and are not engaged in practices that may put a victim in harm's way, like underground rescue missions or any rescue missions that are not coordinated with law enforcement.[25] (Emphasis in the original)

This shows the particular perspectives of the law enforcement and victim services sectors on the aims of anti-trafficking work. The e-Guide recommends that potential partners from other sectors be assessed in terms of whether and how they can support the "core task force functions," which are defined as identifying and supporting victims and bringing perpetrators to justice. Clearly, these are good and important aims—for law enforcement and victim service providers. But taking a broader view of the multifaceted phenomenon of human trafficking and the many sectors that could be involved in countering it, we can see other goals that are equally worthy and important. Consider, for example, aims such as changing business norms and practices to make monitoring supply chains for forced labor a routine task, or effecting cultural shifts such that the sexual exploitation of others is presented in popular media as repulsive rather than glorified, or ensuring that every schoolchild in the United States is taught that no human should be bought or sold for any purpose. Such anti-trafficking efforts are equally worthwhile despite the fact that they are far outside the mission of the law enforcement and victim services sectors. So while the forms of collaboration encouraged by the e-Guide are essential, they are not sufficient. I will delve deeper into that. But first, I provide a brief summary of how the e-Guide addresses the processes of collaboration and the advice it provides on how to form and operate a task force, how to support victims, and how to build cases against perpetrators.

The e-Guide makes clear that disagreements between partners are to be expected in the process of collaboration. There are references to conflicts and collaboration difficulties throughout the 2014 version of the e-Guide, with many practical suggestions for addressing them. Within the section on operating task forces, the e-Guide assures readers explicitly that collaboration challenges are normal and manageable:

> Operational challenges are very common across multidisciplinary collaborations. Challenges can arise due to agency protocols that inhibit certain forms of collaboration, while others are about communication or sustainability. Some common barriers to collaboration that seem insurmountable at first can be solvable. Effective collaboration is built over time. Regardless of the specific issue causing trouble, other practitioners have been there before and have overcome these barriers successfully.[26]

The e-Guide also provides the following overview of conflict in collaboration, suggesting that it can develop interpersonally and interorganizationally:

> The challenges to collaboration are usually found in the group dynamics. Conflict will arise among agencies and organizations as well as among individuals. It is a predictable interpersonal human dynamic and organizational reality. Multidisciplinary groups can be very susceptible to conflict, with passionate individuals working together in intense, emergency situations.[27]

The e-Guide acknowledges "common cultural gaps" and some reluctance to share information between investigators and prosecutors, and between federal and local authorities. It also acknowledges historically patterned forms of competition between different law enforcement agencies, between state and federal agencies, and between service provider organizations. Within every sector funding increases status, and status increases influence. The e-Guide identifies each of these sectors as suffering from anti-collaborative dynamics that must be overcome. Long-standing tensions between the law enforcement and victim services sectors are also acknowledged; these are characterized as impeding collaboration. In naming these internal and cross-sector tensions, the e-Guide is remarkably forthright, and its honesty establishes an authentic foundation. Its recommendations regarding task force leadership and strategies for managing conflicts between law enforcement and victims service providers are well grounded in the experiences of task forces from across the United States, and they are generally consistent with current thinking on interorganizational collaboration. However, the e-Guide's usefulness in handling the challenges of multisector collaboration is limited not only by its primary focus on the law enforcement and victim service sectors, but also by the absence of attention to an array of other systemic tensions in interorganizational anti-trafficking efforts.

CHALLENGES IN COLLABORATING AGAINST HUMAN TRAFFICKING

I concur with most of the e-Guide's recommendations on strategies for advancing collaboration. However, this book differs from the e-Guide in three ways. First, I incorporate perspectives from other sectors involved in anti-trafficking efforts, such as businesses, donor foundations, mobilization and advocacy NGOs, faith communities, and survivor-activists. Second, I address a wider range of the systemic tensions that make collaborating challenging, including differences in power, race, gender, beliefs, and values. Third, I explain how interpersonal and interorganizational or multisector tensions are intertwined: Collaboration is a complex interaction between human agency, interpersonal dynamics, and the wider social, political, and economic contexts in which it takes place.[28]

The e-Guide's section on managing conflict in task forces has many useful elements, but it also includes some statements that are contradictory. For instance, consider this statement:

> Success is usually based on personal relationships and personalities and a willingness to communicate openly and overcome obstacles. The best organizations grow from a respectful and purposeful confrontation of differences, not the avoidance of them.[29]

Then read this:

> With a focus on the mission, the core purpose, and how issues will impact the
> ability of the task force to meet that mission, well-intentioned and respectful
> input among members of the group can help to resolve the differences and
> strengthen the group relationship. The common adage "focus on the issue,
> not on the individual" holds true. In a task force setting, that may need to be
> expanded to "focus on the issue, not on the agency or organization."[30]

The first statement acknowledges the importance of individual-level behavior and interpersonal relations for successful collaboration and recommends discussing differences. The second suggests the opposite, proscribing
the discussion of certain kinds of differences. The meaning of "the issue" is
ambiguous outside of the assumption that it lies among (not within) an individual, agency, or organization. Of course, avoiding accusation is constructive. But sometimes a focus on "the issue" on which there is disagreement
or conflict is a way of avoiding larger or more foundational differences that
contribute to the disagreement at hand. Differences in financial resources,
status or profession, race, gender, values, or beliefs are individual-level attributes. However, these also often correspond with sector-level patterns. Those
who perceive themselves as having less power due to any of these differences
can feel disenfranchised by collaboration norms that discourage discussion of
them. The e-Guide's advice to "focus on the issue" is a case in point.

Looking beyond law enforcement and victim service providers, leaders
from every type of agency and organization involved in countering human
trafficking agree on the importance of multisector collaboration, and they
also report that tensions and conflicts constrain their efforts to collaborate.[31]
Tragically, many attempts at collaboration have failed. As I conducted research for this book, I witnessed many interactions that highlighted the
necessity of collaboration while illustrating the difficulty of building and
sustaining such partnerships. The roots of the challenges included, but went
beyond, those addressed by the e-Guide. One such interaction that I observed
happened this way:

> Today I accompanied two people on a short walk along a barely lit, concrete-
> tiled hallway. The hallway connected the highly secured entrance of a drug
> rehabilitation hospital to the wing of the hospital that had been leased by an

underfunded, overworked nongovernmental organization dedicated to helping survivors of domestic minor sex trafficking, directed by an older, very smart, politically savvy survivor. The director, "Joan," had much expertise, but lacked the formal credentials that would make her an eligible applicant for government grants. A girl in her young teens, "Abby," was hobbling after the director as the latter walked briskly down the hall on her way to a court hearing for yet another prostituted youth who needed a safe place to heal. Abby, using a crutch to support herself because her foot was in a cast after having been stomped in a scuffle with police, struggled to keep pace with Joan, and made several bids for her attention. "You know, there are only three days left that I can stay here; the court said so. What's the plan for me after that? What is the plan?" Abby asked repeatedly. Joan, having just confided to me that she had no funds to extend anyone's stay in the trafficking recovery center/rehab hospital, seemed to be fighting back tears, but she steeled her expression as she kept her gaze focused forward. "I don't know yet, but I'm going to talk with some folks and see what we can do." At the end of the hallway, where Abby had to turn around, Joan said goodbye to Abby, then motioned for me to exit the hospital with her. Outside, she exhaled deeply and turned to me to explain, "All these kids think that I can make anything happen, but I need help; I need partners." (Fieldnote)

On another day, I witnessed the same director, a woman of color with a penchant for street slang, attempting to network with other participants in a meeting of organizations that offer services to victims of human trafficking. Most of the other participants were white women dressed in understated suburban styles, including several in pastel twinsets and pearl necklaces. Joan's bright outfit and jauntily wrapped scarf contrasted with the sea of pastels around her, as did her gregarious manner. From the participant list I saw that most attendees are licensed social workers; Joan is not.

Joan seemed to know most people's names. She worked the room, greeting and shaking the hand of everyone she knew, and introducing herself gregariously to a few she didn't recognize. The meeting agenda included a presentation on the potential for collaboration between the city's juvenile justice system and advocates for trafficked youth. Joan nodded vigorously, agreed or disagreed audibly with several of the speaker's points, and raised her hand a few times—but was not acknowledged by the speaker. When the meeting ended, the room buzzed as participants moved in and out of small clusters of conversations, but no one approached Joan and after a few minutes she left without saying goodbye to anyone. (Fieldnote)

Interactions such as these raised questions for me about many aspects of collaboration attempts in counter-trafficking efforts. I began to wonder whether there were patterns of differences in the racial, class, and gender demographics of people who work on human trafficking in each sector and how such differences shape interactions. I noticed that perceptions of differences in power and money between sectors cropped up in conversations about who did what and why. And I became curious about the sometimes conflicting motivations and values that influence how organizations approach counter-trafficking efforts in general and collaborations in particular.

It is well established that the kinds of societal changes that are necessary to counter problems like human trafficking require the engagement of leaders from every part of society, every sector.[32] Communication scholars Michael Papa, Arvind Singhal, and Wendy Papa summarize this point well, noting that "organizing for social change is a complex process that requires the coordinated and individual actions of many people—the poor and the privileged, outsiders and insiders, and expertise and local knowledge."[33] But how can such differently situated people, working within differently oriented and variously structured organizations and sectors, work together against human trafficking? Answering that question is one of the goals of this book.

AIMS

There are plenty of excellent books already written on many aspects of collaboration within and across sectors; I list several in the section on resources.[34] In contrast, the overarching purpose of this book is to help change the way leaders in every sector—including policy, business, healthcare, civic organizations, advocacy groups, and faith communities, as well as law enforcement and victim service providers—approach collaboration in counter-trafficking efforts by providing them with insights and tools with which to (re)think about partnering. This is especially important because in some realms, counter-trafficking efforts are evolving rapidly.

I demonstrate how and why certain tensions between sectors involved in anti-trafficking work are not only inevitable, but also necessary in order to foster reflection among leaders of anti-trafficking efforts in every sector on their own organization's hopes, fears, and contributions to collaboration opportunities, and to point to particular practices for leading, communicating, and organizing that can catalyze collaboration-building within the inescapable tensions of the anti-trafficking movement. Moreover, I aim to encourage everyone who has struggled with attempts at collaboration around human trafficking, everyone who has wondered whether robust collaboration is possible or worth the effort, and everyone who is considering giving up on multisector collaboration. Based on my research, these three categories include everyone involved in anti-trafficking efforts. Finally, I aim to contribute a well-grounded analysis of multisector collaboration to students and researchers of human trafficking, collaboration, or social change. The need for multisector collaboration against human trafficking is great, and the challenges are many, deep-rooted, large-scale, and systemic. It is true that these challenges, common to all who endeavor in this field, make collaboration difficult and costly. To assume that this makes collaboration impossible, however, would be an even more costly mistake. Collaboration can work well, and this book encourages and supports that process.

APPROACH

Before I began to study collaboration in anti-trafficking efforts, I knew some things about interorganizational and multisector relations and how people negotiate collaboration. I learned much more through the course of this research. Human trafficking is just one of many issues that requires sustained, coordinated efforts from multiple sectors, and multisector collaboration is a growing area of study for some scholars in the fields of organizational studies in general and organizational communication in particular. Because of the complex nature of human trafficking, though, efforts to counter it require engagement by many branches of the public, private, and civil society sectors. This creates a "perfect storm" of challenges for collaboration. In his fascinating book, *Freeing God's Children: The Unlikely Alliance for Global Human Rights*, Allen Hertzke detailed many of the contestations and collaborations between faith-based organizations, human rights organizations, feminist organizations, and government agencies that sparked and shaped the emergence of the contemporary anti-trafficking movement in the United States from the mid-1990s through some watershed events in 2003.[35]

To leverage current knowledge about collaboration, I drew on several strands of scholarship as the bases for the analyses I present in this book, and I have woven ideas and insights from this scholarship throughout the book. I used the definition of "interorganizational collaboration" developed by Joann Keyton, Debra Ford, and Faye Smith:

The set of communicative processes in which individuals representing multiple organizations or stakeholders engage when working interdependently to address problems outside the spheres of individuals or organizations working in isolation. The outcomes of these processes have the potential to benefit or harm the parties to the collaboration, as well as others.[36]

The fact that Keyton, Ford, and Smith worked as a multidisciplinary team (from the fields of communication, nursing, and business) to develop this definition is not why I chose it, but that does make it all the more appropriate for this book. They recognize that collaborations are loosely coupled and nested systems that continually change. Their definition specifies collaboration as communication; it identifies individuals who function as organizational representatives as those through whom interorganizational collaboration takes place, and it acknowledges that collaboration does not necessarily have beneficial outcomes for participants or anyone else. It makes clear that interorganizational collaboration is risky, including for those on whose behalf collaborative efforts are attempted.

Beyond defining interorganizational collaboration, Keyton, Ford, and Smith developed a model for it that "problematizes communication in collaborations, acknowledges that collaborations cross public–private boundaries, and recognizes that collaborations are loosely coupled and nested systems that continually change."[37] Put simply, their model is a useful lens for thinking through the complexities, contingencies, and evolving nature of multisector collaboration. For these reasons it was foundational to my thinking about collaboration against human trafficking.

Because I knew more about collaboration and organizing processes than human trafficking when I began this research, I started by learning everything I could about how each sector was attempting to counter human trafficking around the world. I began by analyzing systematically the websites of over 150 organizations representing nine sectors and operating around the world, for each year from 2008 to 2011. A team of research assistants inventoried the online reports of this panel of organizations to assess the prevalence of eight general kinds of anti-trafficking activities such as prevention, advocacy, and restoration, and the specific types of actions that comprise each category of activity.[38] This four-year series of assessments of anti-trafficking activities provided a good sketch of both the diversity of forms of anti-trafficking efforts and patterns in such efforts to counter human trafficking—that is, which activities are engaged in most frequently and most robustly by which sector. The most relevant findings for this book are that two-thirds of the anti-trafficking organizations claimed to be involved in some effort to build coalitions, and that around one-third reported that they were part of a named, multi-organization coalition, network, or alliance with at least three member organizations. Further, those proportions increased over time. Clearly, a large and growing number of anti-trafficking actors are involved in interorganizational collaboration.[39] My fieldwork revealed that many of the interorganizational collaborative efforts against human trafficking are also cross-sector.

In 2009, I started attending the organizing meetings of two start-up grassroots nongovernmental organizations in the area where I live. I began volunteering in anti-trafficking efforts locally, both community-oriented, awareness-raising campaigns and fundraising for national and international efforts. These volunteer efforts led me deeper into multisector interactions around human trafficking and evoked a host of questions about what it takes to build and sustain robust collaborations.

The approach I took to answering those questions is participatory action research. Between 2009 and 2013, I observed hundreds of interactions between people who work on combating human trafficking in one way or another. I participated in over fifty multisector meetings and conferences on human trafficking, ranging from a few hours to three days in length, in five US states, and I made multiple trips to each state over the course of the project in order to observe how meetings in each location evolved over time. In addition, I conducted in-depth interviews with nearly fifty individuals who work against human trafficking in business, law enforcement, victim service provision, prosecution, healthcare, faith communities, and/or civic and advocacy groups. They resided in ten cities in seven US states and in Austria, Cambodia, Denmark, and the Netherlands as well. Five of the ten cities in which my interviewees were based had DOJ-funded task forces during the period of this research; most interviewees in those cities were involved in those task forces.

Of the people I interviewed, six who were participating in counter-trafficking efforts were themselves survivors of human trafficking. With fifteen anti-trafficking leaders, I was able to conduct multiple interviews, which allowed me to learn how their perspectives changed over time. During interviews, I asked people about topics such as their organization's aims, their personal motives for working against human trafficking in their sector of choice, their perceptions of other sectors, the kinds of organizations with which they had attempted to collaborate, and both positive and negative experiences they'd had in collaborations. I also asked about their ideas of what kinds of things hinder or help advance interorganizational and multisector partnerships. Although most of the fieldwork and interviews on which this book is based were conducted primarily within the United States, interorganizational and multisector collaboration against human trafficking is happening in many countries.[40] The types of sectors, counter-trafficking organizations, and agencies represented in this study are active in most other countries as well, though they may operate differently. Collaboration dynamics outside the United States are likely to have both similarities and differences in relation to the dynamics analyzed in this book.

Along with observations of interactions and interviews, I continued to gain firsthand experience in the complexities of collaboration by participating in multisector anti-trafficking efforts, as a volunteer with local NGOs, as an advisor to local coalitions and national projects, and eventually as a speaker on interorganizational collaboration at anti-trafficking events. In doing so, I situated myself as a proponent of collaboration. Through these forms of participation in anti-trafficking efforts, I engaged in countless conversations with people from many sectors about the processes of collaboration. These personal experiences provided me with an intimate understanding of the consistently intense but differently oriented passions that those who work on human trafficking bring to their work. I have witnessed tears and complaints as well as congratulations between members of anti-trafficking coalitions, and moments of betrayal as well as expressions of sincere gratitude between professionals in different sectors who have been trained not to trust each other. These experiences, together with the forthrightness with which interviewees talked with me, were enormously helpful. They allow me to present my analysis of large-scale patterns and systemic contradictions in a way that I hope provides windows into the concrete situations—the very moments in which collaborations around human trafficking are strengthened or strangled. A foundational premise of this research is that every sector in society has a role to play for human trafficking to cease. I have sought to represent the perspectives of each actor and each sector respectfully as well as accurately, especially in my critiques.

To develop this book, I examined around one hundred instances of multisector interactions from my fieldnotes and interview reports and from descriptions of such interactions in other publications. In doing so, I identified communicative and organizing actions that contributed either to the advance or breakdown of collaboration, identified by the outcome (what happened next in the interaction), by actors' opinions (shared with me in conversations following the interaction), and by my own observations of subsequent interactions. I noticed that differences in profession and status, race and gender, beliefs and values were negotiated in recurring patterns during these interactions. These differences are evident at the organizational level as well as among individuals.

As other researchers of interorganizational relations have noted, what is possible to observe are groups of people talking. Through that, researchers can infer how organizations collaborate in ways that integrate individual, group, organizational, and sector levels.[41] I structured the book around patterns in these multisector interactions for two reasons. First, I aim to foster cross-sector thought and action; this was important because a sector-based analysis could reinforce sector-based thinking on the part of readers. Second, by focusing on instances of cross-sector communication, I could identify the inherent tensions between differing aims, values, and operating modes; the power dynamics related to profession, gender, and race; and sector structures and economics. In brief, the argument of the book is that these differences and power dynamics are systemic and therefore not readily changeable. Nonetheless, I have seen more robust collaboration across sectors through reflective attention to collective leadership, strategic planning, organizing processes, and communication practices.

SURVIVOR-ACTIVISTS AS A SECTOR

It is very important to note here that in multisector anti-trafficking efforts in the U.S., there are many survivors of human trafficking working alongside those who have never been enslaved. Some publicly identify themselves as survivors, while others choose not to do so. Several leaders in anti-trafficking efforts told me that they are survivors, but that they choose not to publicly disclose that information. In this book, I refer to survivors who contribute to anti-trafficking efforts as "survivor-activists." Three of the six survivor-activists I interviewed at length were among the sixteen survivor-activists who spoke publicly in multisector meetings about their efforts to counter human trafficking and their perspectives on what needs to be done (both additionally and differently). Other survivors are published authors, and I have cited insights from some of their publications. Most of the survivor-activists I encountered work in nonprofits or NGOs, though a few are employed by government agencies or in the private sector. As I will explain further in chapters 2 and 3, full-time, paid jobs in anti-trafficking nonprofits are rare, so many survivor-activists volunteer their time. Some work in what they term "survivor-led organizations"; others work independently or in other types of organizations. Some have reflected deeply not only on their own personal experiences, but also on the processes other survivors have undergone. Regardless of whether they have degrees or professional credentials, they have cultivated expertise on survivorship. I refer to this subset of survivor-activists as "survivorship experts."

All of the survivor-activists expressed the need for greater cooperation between survivor-activists and nonsurvivors, and for more survivors to be included in leadership of anti-trafficking efforts that have not been initiated by survivors. Although survivors hold differing views on many aspects of anti-trafficking efforts, they were unanimous that survivors often feel invisible and unheard, excluded from many anti-trafficking efforts and marginalized when they are included. My fieldwork both validated their perspective and complicated it, as I explain in subsequent chapters. Because of the complexity, there is no straightforward, perfect solution, but I want to avoid perpetuating the marginalization of survivors by explicitly including them in this book.

I refer to survivor-activists as comprising a distinct "sector" in this book because when survivors talk about anti-trafficking efforts, they tend to do so first and foremost from their perspective as survivors. Survivor-activists' perspectives are articulated in each chapter of the book, with attention to the patterns in their interactions with those from other sectors, as well as acknowledgment that there is diversity within the survivor-activist sector, as in every sector. However, referring to survivor-activists as a sector creates two interrelated risks that I hope to mitigate by making them explicit so that readers can avoid them.[42] One risk is that considering survivor-activists as comprising their own sector could result in a form of tokenism similar to the way that "diversity" initiatives sometimes marginalize "the diverse" rather than integrating them into a larger whole. Survivors could already be present—and should be welcomed—in every other profession-based sector. A second risk is that survivor-activists could be perceived solely as survivors, while other types of expertise they offer to anti-trafficking efforts could be disregarded. One way I sought to counter that risk in my fieldwork was to follow the verbal cues of survivors regarding the particular facet of expertise from which they were speaking at any moment. For example, when I witnessed survivors sharing insights or recommendations based on their professional expertise in a field such as social work, counseling, or business, I noted and reported those statements differently than I did the insights based on their trafficking experiences.

Due to the sensitive nature of collaboration interactions, I have taken several steps in this book to avoid damaging interpersonal dynamics in places where I conducted my research. Except when highlighting successes or when geographical information is critical, I do not name the cities in which I observed interactions or in which an interview or interaction took place, and the only statements I attribute to actual, specific individuals or organizations, other than government agencies, are ones that have been made publicly in open meetings or online. All other names I employ in this book are pseudonyms.[43]

As a participant-observer of the phenomena I studied, the fact that I am a middle-aged Caucasian female university professor certainly shaped the interactions I witnessed and participated in and my perspectives on them. Although I have lived through and recovered from some traumatic circumstances over the course of my life, I have never been enslaved, and thus in the parlance of some anti-trafficking activists I am a "nonsurvivor"—that is, not a survivor of trafficking. In several places in the book I reflect on the ways that various aspects of my identity, academic training, and professional position may have influenced the questions I raised, what was confided to me, and how I interpreted this research. At times I wished for what philosopher Thomas Nagel termed "the view from nowhere,"[44] but like Nagel, I do not think it exists in pure form. In keeping with the established practices of participatory action research, I establish the validity of this research not by distancing myself from those I have studied, but rather by taking into account the ways my characteristics might have influenced the process, by checking my analyses with leaders of anti-trafficking efforts from several sectors, and through other means.[45]

PARTNERSHIP HOPES AND FEARS

People who work on human trafficking approach potential and actual collaborations with both individual and collective or organizational hopes and fears. Overarchingly, everyone who invests time and energy in countering human trafficking (whether or not they are paid for this labor) wants their efforts to be effective. This is true regardless of what type of human trafficking they focus on, which sector they work in, and whether their primary role is identifying and helping victims, bringing perpetrators to justice, or preventing further trafficking in persons. In all cases, the individuals in the organizations, agencies, and businesses who work on human trafficking want to see it end. This shared aim is the motivation and foundation for nearly all attempts at collaboration. The slogan "In It to End It," employed by some breast cancer awareness advocates,[46] has become a rallying cry for many individuals and organizations devoted to stopping human trafficking.[47]

Many attempts at collaborative partnerships on human trafficking emerge organically, typically through the professional contacts and initiative of organizational leaders. Other partnerships begin through the stipulations of funders. For example, in the United States, not only the DOJ but also several private foundations have made structured collaborations a requirement for grant funding and have designated funds to support the coordination of interorganizational, cross-sector, and multisector partnerships.[48] Differences in the interaction dynamics within organic and funder-mandated partnerships will be explored in subsequent chapters. At this point it is sufficient to note that not all partnerships are initiated and structured by their member organizations.

Whether participation in a particular partnership is mandated or elected, the people representing any organization in an interorganizational partnership bring a bundle of hopes and fears about collaboration into their interactions. This creates a variety of tensions.[49] Based on my research, some hopes are fairly universal to all collaboration participants, such as advancing the aims and impact of one's own organization while contributing to the work of the partnership, persuading partners to get behind initiatives in which one's organization is invested, and being treated respectfully by partners. Other hopes correspond more specifically with an organization's role and position relative to other partner organizations and to power brokers outside of the partnership. For example, stronger organizations may enter partnerships with weaker organizations in order to establish themselves as leaders, and weaker organizations may enter partnerships to strengthen their organization's credibility and visibility.

Similarly, some fears are common to most people entering a potentially collaborative partnership, such as the fear of diminishing the autonomy of one's organization or of wasting time and energy on (in the words of several of my interviewees) "meetings that don't accomplish anything." Although common, such fears may be experienced to different degrees and in different ways depending on elements like an actor's status in the partnership, prior negative experiences with collaboration, and what is at stake for that actor. Stronger, well-established organizations tend to fear being "mooched on" by weaker organizations or having a less-reliable organization mar their hard-earned reputations. Smaller, newer, or weaker organizations fear being steamrolled by more powerful organizations. Some also fear having their ideas "stolen" by other organizations, especially those with better resources that have the capacity to implement initiatives more quickly and/ or more broadly.

Three brief examples from my fieldwork illustrate how hopes and fears about interorganizational relations create a dialectic that shapes attempts at collaboration on human trafficking. In the first, a small NGO with minimal funding planned a public event that they hoped would help catalyze more coordinated anti-trafficking efforts in their region. They waited until they had drafted the event for the agenda before approaching the larger, better-established NGOs in their area about participating, in part because they hoped to establish their organization as a peer leader, and in part because they feared being dismissed by the better-established NGOs. To their dismay, the better-established NGOs refused to participate: They had not been invited to help shape the agenda and feared that the event plan would reflect poorly on them. So although the small NGO successfully elicited participation from law enforcement and other government agencies and from some businesses, the effect on relations with some other NGOs was more detrimental than constructive.

In my second example, law enforcement agents whose job it is to find and investigate human trafficking cases have been engaging collaboratively with MANGOs with the hope of receiving useful tips on potential cases. Yet they fear being deluged with worthless and time-wasting bogus information.[50]

Conversely, MANGOs collaborating with the law enforcement agents hope to be useful in bringing cases forward, but at the same time they fear being dismissed as unreliable tipsters.

A third example of the dialectic of hopes and fears surfaced between a faith-based NGO that explicitly sought Christian volunteers and a self-described "areligious" NGO—in this case, an NGO that had been founded by Christians but strove to welcome participation by anyone. When the two attempted to collaborate, the leaders of the faith-based NGO hoped for the freedom to talk about human trafficking in spiritual terms and pray for collaborative efforts. The leaders of the areligious NGO, on the other hand, hoped that their religiously diverse volunteer base would feel welcome participating in collaborative efforts. At the same time, the faith-based NGO feared being denigrated for their religious beliefs, while the areligious NGO feared that proclamations of faith-based beliefs would offend those of their membership who did not subscribe to them. Since both hopes and fears are nearly always present within and between organizations attempting to collaborate, partnerships are fraught with tensions that are not resolvable. But better understanding of the kinds of tensions addressed in this book can facilitate better collaborations.

WHAT (NOT) TO EXPECT FROM THIS BOOK

This book does not promise that if an anti-trafficking organization does A, B, and C, the outcomes will be X, Y, and Z. As I explained above, my aim is to demonstrate how and why certain tensions between sectors are not only inevitable, but also necessary; to foster reflection among leaders of anti-trafficking efforts in every sector on their own organization's hopes, fears, and contributions to collaboration opportunities; and to articulate some general practices for leading, communicating, and organizing that are constructive for collaboration building.[51]

Chapters 2, 3, 4, and 5 each focus on a distinct set of differences that arise from and perpetuate perennial, systemic tensions in counter-trafficking alliances. Starting with two interrelated things that were brought up often in one-on-one interviews (but rarely mentioned in meetings), chapter 2 focuses on how multisector partnerships against human trafficking are shaped by power and money, and forms of power that are based on intangibles (that is, not on money). Perceived or actual differences in funding sources; legal mandates and constraints; and governance norms, protocols, and regulations for each organization and sector influence how those organizations and sectors function in interactions with others about human trafficking.

Chapter 3 explores the power dynamics of strategically positioning one's organization in relationship to others, positioning or "platforming" other organizations, and coleadership in collaboration. I explain how the kinds of roles in multisector collaborations that organizations either take, assign, or assume is influenced by, and often reproduces, their perceptions of their own and others' political power, funding, and latitude for action. In this chapter I also explore how education and class—meaning the status, as well as the general economic characteristics of various professions and the individuals working within them—shape collaboration. For example, when people who have not gone to college and people who have earned advanced degrees and various professional certifications attempt to collaborate, their perceived status differences affect their understanding of their interactions with each other. This chapter draws primarily on perceptions that were articulated by anti-trafficking leaders about such differences, because such perceptions shape interactions.

Moving from one set of touchy subjects to another, in chapter 4 I explore why race and gender matter in efforts to counter human trafficking. Although patterns in the demographic characteristics of the individuals involved in counter-trafficking efforts were rarely discussed in the interactions I observed, they were consistently apparent in the meetings I attended, and they surfaced in the one-on-one interviews I conducted. In interviews, those who were not Caucasian or male expressed concerns about power differentials between sectors and organizations that are largely populated by Caucasians or by men. In this chapter, I draw on demographic data along with insights from sociology, gender studies, and cultural studies, and on my fieldwork observations and interviews. I offer, based on these sources, exploratory interpretations of the influence of race and gender on interactions across sectors regarding human trafficking. Although I discuss aspects of class in chapters 2 and 3, and highlight facets of the influence of race and gender on collaborations in different sections of chapter 4, I do not seek to disentangle race, class, and gender. Rather, I view these as continually and mutually constituting each other.[52] In other words, this analysis is not just about the differences between professions of anti-trafficking actors, such as street cops versus federal agents. It is also about how the race and gender of cops or federal agents may affect their approach to collaboration, and how those same factors are perceived by others in the collaboration.

The focus of chapter 5 is the dynamics caused by aligned and conflicting motives and values in anti-trafficking efforts. Motives and values are held and enacted by both individuals and collectives in every line of work. They are often unconscious, shaped by a person's or an organization's history, culture, and beliefs. Collective attributes like the status of a profession, as well as the individual attributes of gender, race, and religious beliefs, shape the basic values and worldview of all the professions.[53] They can be powerful forces in multisector interactions: when actors align on them, they coalesce more easily; when they do not, collaboration may be more turbulent. In this chapter I analyze organizational and coalition texts and interactions I observed for how motives (including fears, hopes, and prejudices) and values (whether based on professional norms, religious beliefs, or other sources) manifest in multiple ways, such as in interorganizational planning processes, in coalition meeting agendas and facilitation, in public messaging about collaborative events, and in the terms by which other organizations and sectors are referred.

Finally, in chapter 6, after summarizing the reasons why multisector collaboration is both especially important and particularly difficult in counter-trafficking efforts, I suggest several ways that multisector collaborations can be started, repaired, and enhanced. Relatedly, I also provide positive examples of practices that catalyze counter-trafficking collaborations. These include the following: (1) acknowledging perceived power differentials, whether due to differences in political economic positions or in the demographics of the people who represent a sector in an particular setting, and agreeing explicitly on how these will be mitigated in collaborative work; (2) openly discussing ways that leadership structures and communication processes can be democratized in multisector coalitions; (3) collectively reflecting on the variety of motives and values that bring actors into counter-trafficking efforts, shape their aims, and influence how they work; and (4) developing shared norms for multisector interactions.

These practices require investments of time and resources to plan and to implement consistently from the beginning of a multisector coalition. However, such practices become even more costly when attempts at collaboration break down. Sustaining a carefully designed and well-led coalition is easier than mending one that has seized up or fallen apart. It is no simple matter to overcome disillusionment over failed collaborations, to reshape counterproductive patterns such as retreating into intrasector interactions, or to expand functional alliances that were built around "like-minded" organizations across sectors but wind up as exclusionary forces. By the end of the book I hope to have made a persuasive case that multisector collaboration against human trafficking is essential, that it is possible, and that it is worth the investment.

For those wishing to build the collaborations necessary for successful joint anti-trafficking work, the Collaboration Resources section at the end of the book pulls together additional promising approaches. First, I offer a few exercises that might be useful for collaborations against human trafficking in particular. Second, I suggest some tools for building, managing, and sustaining collaborations. Third, I provide pointers to some of the many resources available on interorganizational collaboration in general, and to publications by survivors that include discussions of their experiences with multisector efforts. In sum, those in ant-trafficking efforts have long known that it is necessary to work together to diminish the practices that demean and damage people, but they have lacked recommendations based on what actually happens when such organization try to effect those very collaborations. This book's goal is to address that need.

Power in Collaboration

FROM GAS STATIONS TO STATE REST AREAS

Late in the autumn of 2009, I co-organized an innovative distribution effort of posters designed to raise awareness of human trafficking via a regional coalition of grassroots organizations, faith communities, and concerned citizens. The winter Olympics would take place in Vancouver, British Columbia, in February 2010, and human trafficking experts in Seattle were cautioning that it was likely that vulnerable people from or traveling through the Seattle area could be coerced or tricked into various forms of forced labor before and during the Olympics in Vancouver. So my co-activists and I decided to try to mobilize volunteers to visit every gas station within a few blocks of Washington's I-5 highway, the main road connecting Portland, Oregon, with Vancouver, via Olympia, Seattle, Everett, Bellingham, and many other Washington cities. A local victim service provider told us we could probably obtain several hundred anti-trafficking posters and brochures at a minimal cost from the U.S. Department of Health and Human Services (HHS). Their materials were available in several languages, but with only one language per poster. In other words, there were no multilanguage anti-trafficking materials. We were also disappointed to find that the materials in circulation at that time were addressed to people who might encounter a trafficking victim, but not to victims themselves. We were surprised that we could not find any victim-addressed posters or brochures, despite calls to multiple government agencies and national NGOs. However, we decided to proceed with distributing the materials we had obtained from HHS.

Using highway exit lists from our state's Department of Transportation website and spreadsheets in Google Docs, I created a system that enabled volunteers to sign up for each exit along the 239 miles of I-5 that connected the northern and southern edges of Washington. My colleagues recruited dozens of volunteers to sign up, and we distributed materials through hand-offs at various meetups. As we embarked on this gas-station-postering campaign at the end of November, I described our goal this way to "Kerry," the leader of a trafficking victim service provider (VSP) network:

> We have two aims: encouraging and equipping gas station employees and customers to notice and report incidents they suspect might evidence trafficking, and providing trafficking victims with hotline numbers for the United States and Canada. Ideally, over the next six weeks we'll give the gas station owners at each I-5 exit a trafficking awareness brochure and receive permission from each gas station owner to tape a poster to the wall in both the men's and women's restrooms.

Kerry's response was enthusiastic: "Thanks for working on this. Projects like this are so very helpful in identifying victims, and we will be here to provide the services they need!"

A few days later, in an e-mail to an anti-trafficking lobbyist I wrote, "In addition to our aim of facilitating intervention in trafficking from and through WA, we're hoping that this kind of grassroots effort will demonstrate to the WA legislature how much WA citizens want the state to distribute anti-trafficking info." The lobbyist liked this idea, and she and her colleagues began working on a strategy to try to persuade the legislature to require anti-trafficking notices in public restrooms, in the same vein as anti–domestic violence notices. As an initial step, she would use her contacts in the state government to try to obtain permission from the Department of Transportation (DOT) for citizens to put up anti-trafficking posters in the restrooms of the state's rest areas along the two main north-south and east-west highways.

The next two months were a form of trial by fire for me, as I became immersed in attempts at cross-sector collaboration. One set of dynamics were between the MANGO (mobilization and advocacy NGO) volunteers and gas station personnel, but these were tame in comparison with the negotiations between the MANGOs, the legislative staff, and the DOT officials. Despite the fact that all of us were united in wanting anti-trafficking posters to be placed in the restrooms of state rest areas, the e-mail correspondence was sometimes torturous among "Virginia," the key legislator's assistant, "Sam," the director of "capital facilities" (including rest areas) for the DOT, and several MANGO leaders (including myself). I witnessed both daunting obstacles to collaboration and persistent communication and organizing practices that ultimately overcame the obstacles.

In brief, officials in Washington's DOT wanted to collaborate with the MANGOs that initiated the rest-area postering project, but in order for them to be able to allow citizens to post anything in a state rest area, a state law had to be changed. A small group of dedicated citizens sought and received help from a state legislator and her staff, and following several months of intensive work, the law was changed. In the meantime, because of the approaching Olympics, the DOT officials and the legislator agreed that a particular victim-addressed poster created by a local MANGO would be approved by the DOT officials for "temporary posting" in rest areas, one per restroom. However, Kerry, the leader of the VSP network, who had been enthusiastic about the distribution of posters from HHS, thought that the wording of the new victim-addressed poster was ineffective and recommended (to the MANGO leaders) that it be rewritten. The MANGO leader/lobbyist who had worked most closely with the legislator wrote, "It is three weeks until the Olympics. Could we agree to 'something is better than nothing' as this poster is temporary?" But other MANGO leaders hoped it might be feasible to get a VSP-approved poster approved quickly by the DOT as well.

After volunteers had begun postering the rest areas along I-5 (north-south highway), Robert Beiser, the MANGO leader who had been working closely with Kerry from the VSP network, sent the DOT a new poster design that VSPs had approved, requesting that it be used in the I-90 (east-west highway) rest areas. Apparently someone in the DOT talked (unhappily) to the lead legislator's staff member Virginia about it, because I received a private e-mail from Virginia, which was appreciative and politely worded but included this request:

> The Department of Transportation needs to be hearing from just one person regarding the rest area posters. Can that person be you? Robert Beiser asked DOT to post other signs that haven't been approved by the department. We need someone from the inside be in charge and make sure only approved signs go up in the approved areas.

Although I had been the primary spokesperson on behalf of the MANGOs with the DOT, I did not want to become the sole contact for the DOT, because three other MANGO leaders and I had agreed to each take responsibility for a different aspect of the initiative. Becoming the sole contact would require more work on my part (to relay messages), add another layer of interpretation to already-sensitive negotiations about poster design and content, as well as disrupt the distribution of work agreed upon among the MANGO leaders. So I responded with what I intended to be a similarly polite but firm refusal, cc'ing Robert and explaining that the division of labor agreed upon among the MANGO leaders (who represented three different organizations] meant that the DOT would be hearing from Robert:

> First let me assure you that Robert (cc'd) and I are working closely together, with additional help from [the two other MANGO leaders, whom I did not cc] and that we all know that volunteers should only post DOT-approved posters in DOT rest areas.

I understand why the DOT would prefer to have just one contact person for the poster campaign, but since all of us on the citizen side are volunteers and are working on this in addition to our regular jobs, we have agreed to divide responsibilities. Robert is coordinating the poster development/approval process, and I am coordinating the recruitment and instructing of volunteers. . . . Since Robert had told me that he was seeking approval from your office & the DOT for an improved version of the poster, I am holding off on distributing instructions for the I-90 rest areas until I hear from Robert whether the new version he (and [a leader of the state's trafficking victim service provider network]) are proposing is approved.

Virginia's reply did not include Robert, but was copied to two DOT officials:

Kirsten, again, thank you for all you do!!!! The Senator is so happy these posters are going up before and during the Olympics. A small group of us worked with DOT and agreed to only post the one poster that we approved. So, please only use that poster.

Once the Senator's bill becomes law, we will again work with DOT on maybe a better graphic and message . . . but for now—only the approved poster.

By not including Robert in her response, Virginia effectively rendered me as the sole contact for the DOT, despite my having declined that request, because the only way for Robert to get the message that the VSP-approved poster design he had sent to Sam could not be used prior to the Olympics was if I forwarded it to him.

Independently, that same day, Sam from the DOT wrote to the MANGO leaders (who were mobilizing dozens of volunteers from other community groups and congregations), that only the legislator-approved poster could be hung in state rest areas. Moreover, the posters would need to be laminated, and could only be affixed to the wall with easily removable, double-sided tape. My MANGO collaborators and I thought that these were reasonable stipulations, and I assured Sam that we would inform volunteers of them (which we did, repeatedly). In addition, Sam noted that "some rest areas have multiple buildings, where one is open and one is locked—coordination between us will be required to have staff on hand to open the standby buildings for access." In other words, volunteers could not simply show up and hang a poster; for each new location they would have to find out whether it would be necessary to make advance arrangements to meet a DOT staffer there. This was a more difficult hurdle for volunteers.

Anyone who has tried to direct a distributed network of volunteers, or herd cats, can imagine what happened next. Posters other than the one approved by the lead legislator and DOT were put up, using forms of adhesion other than the double-sided tape specified by the DOT, and volunteers made offline "swaps" between the rest areas they had signed up online to visit—which made it difficult to ascertain who had put up which poster, using which adhesive in any location. E-mails such as the following arrived complete with photographic evidence of unapproved and unlaminated posters, adhered with unapproved substances:

> Our statewide Safety Rest Area Program Manager stopped at the rest area #X yesterday and took the attached pictures of posters placed inside bathroom stalls. The pictures depict several things that need to be addressed immediately:
>
> - The posters being placed in some of the rest areas are not the approved version—the posters found at rest area #X were removed. Please make sure that your volunteers have the correct posters for placement. Furthermore, these were not laminated and included an option to remove a tab containing a phone number.
> - The method for attaching posters to the interior surfaces is not approved. The material used for affixing the posters has an extremely aggressive adhesive which will take our personnel considerable time to remove, and will probably result in damage to the painted surface.
>
> Please pass this information along to all volunteers immediately. The DOT has agreed to temporarily allow this very important effort to occur within specific parameters. However, continued unapproved postings may affect the duration of this campaign. (Fieldnotes and personal correspondence)

Apparently, some volunteers had used whatever posters and adhesives were on hand, not realizing that their renegade postering could compromise the whole effort. Fortunately, this wrinkle in the process was ironed out. In the end, although there were many misunderstandings, charged interactions, and setbacks along the way, the rest area temporary postering project was ultimately successful—and paved the way for additional DOT-MANGO collaboration both within in Washington state and elsewhere (I continue this story in chapter 6). The experience left me intrigued about the process through which the collaboration was brokered (and re-brokered) between the MANGOs, the victim service provider, the DOT, and the legislator's office. I wanted to figure out the power dynamics of multisector collaboration in anti-trafficking efforts.

Power is a complicated thing, especially in the context of interorganizational collaboration.[1] This topic is charged for many people, but it is particularly so for those who have survived any form of exploitative control by others, much less enslavement. In the words of a participant in a study of interorganizational collaboration conducted by Laurie Lewis and her colleagues, "Issues of power need to be addressed. They need to be said out loud. Often times it is not. It is just in the room and plays itself out."[2]

Dictionaries provide several meanings for the term "power," including the ability to act autonomously as well as to influence, have authority over, or have control over others. To understand how power dynamics reveal themselves in the practical workings of collaboration is to look at who makes the decision, who sets the direction, who gets the resources—and who gets left out in the process. When people consider collaboration, the commonsense understanding is that it consists of partnership, something that is thought to be characterized by relatively equal distributions of power.[3] The idea that equal distribution of power is endemic to collaboration, however, is a misconception. Power differences among collaborators, whether in anti-trafficking efforts or anywhere else, are unavoidable given the uneven distribution of power in society at large and organized representatives' differences in resources and authority.[4] Unsurprisingly, power inequities in collaborations are perceived most often and felt most keenly by those who experience themselves as having less power.[5]

The general subject of power dynamics in various kinds of multisector collaborations has been analyzed in detail from many perspectives.[6] My aims here are to help illuminate a few power dynamics that are particularly relevant to anti-trafficking efforts, discuss how they affect collaboration attempts, and invite reflection on ways that anti-trafficking partnerships can be effective despite persistent power differences. Perspectives articulated by survivor-activists both illuminate and complicate these dynamics, because of their experiences with exploitation.

Power is a complex subject to study in organizations because it manifests in so many ways. When sectors involved in countering human trafficking come together, the fact that they are made of different categories of professions and, not unrelatedly, have diverse forms and levels of power, results in innate differences that display themselves in interactions. Within sectors, organizations compete with and for power—often via competition for money—resulting in further structural differences in collaborations. The donor-funder sector, comprised of the private organizations and government agencies that fund anti-trafficking efforts, wields significant power because its decisions on resource allocation are very consequential to other sectors' and specific organizations' capacity to act against trafficking. Thus another power dynamic is introduced. Further, both particular organizations and the individuals who represent them bring their positions in societal categories (and the power associated with those categories) to the table. This introduces the power dynamics of each sector's historically rooted racial, gender, and status patterns and of each individual's profession, race, and gender.

In short, power takes myriad pathways through a variety of actors and associations. Because the enactment of power in collaborations significantly affects their outcomes, we would do well to enhance our understandings of its workings. Race and gender will be addressed in chapter 3. The foci of this chapter are the structural and economic power dynamics within and between the sectors involved in efforts to counter human trafficking. Here we will explore different sources and levels of funding and the boundaries between professions and various forms of expertise. These elements affect the status of those who represent particular professions within and between anti-trafficking sectors—and therefore enhance or diminish their participation in collaborative processes.

Let's return to the concept of power and consider some of its characteristics. From my perspective as a social researcher, wherever there are people, there is power at play. So power's primary characteristic is that we can neither avoid it nor eradicate it. The second thing to consider is where power emerges and flows. Because power is not tangible and its dynamics change over time, we need to look to where it plays out—that is, in social interactions. Third, to understand power we must realize that it is not intrinsically good or bad, but that it does enable and constrain action and influence. The use of power can result in good or harm. Fourth, the way power manifests itself changes. Although it accrues over time within and between societal structures, sectors and organizations, it is neither inherent nor static in any particular sector or organization. In other words, one cannot assume the degrees to which or ways in which power operates, nor can one assume that once discerned it will stay the same. Finally, power plays out on multiple levels as it is negotiated among individuals and among organizations through their representatives.

Although money is not necessarily the foundation of all forms of power, it is clear that economic relations are integral to power dynamics. For any individual, organization, or sector, the source, level, and stability of funding affects the ability to act autonomously or to influence others. We understand this well in the private sector, where businesses gain power through money, and where money gives or limits opportunity for individuals. Yet all organizations, including those that are not for profit, are empowered or constrained by their finances (or the lack thereof). In the power dynamics between sectors, organizations in sectors with historically and generally higher prestige sources of funding (e.g., government grants versus contributions from individual donors), greater amounts of funding, and/or more consistent levels of funding, typically are perceived to have more power than organizations in sectors with less prestigious, lower level, or less stable levels of funding. In sum, although money is not the only determinant of power, it is clearly a significant factor that merits examination.

MONEY AND POWER

During my fieldwork, representatives from government agencies, private foundations, and for-profit businesses usually appeared to have more power in multisector interactions than representatives from sectors such as academia, survivor-activists, and NGOs and nonprofits. Across many of the interactions I observed, the development, negotiation, and exchange of power tracked with the categories into which agents fall. At times, though, this hierarchy was not rigid; on some occasions it appeared inverted, and in some collaborations power structures changed over time. It is clear, then, that one cannot explain everything about power dynamics through tracking categories of actors and their access to monetary resources. This being said, it is evident that money matters in anti-trafficking efforts, as it does in most aspects of life, politics, and society.

Most nongovernmental organizations that work against human trafficking operate on shoestring budgets based on contributions from individual donors. Most state and local governments provide meager, if any, funds for preventing human trafficking, prosecuting traffickers, protecting victims, and helping survivors heal. As a result, a lot of anti-trafficking efforts in the United States are essentially unfunded. They are designed and implemented by individuals and organizations using whatever resources they have. For example, citizens who volunteered to participate in the gas station and rest area poster campaign described in the opening vignette for this chapter used their own funds to pay copy shops to print and laminate the posters they downloaded for distributing. Even some government-funded victim service providers spend tremendous amounts of time and energy soliciting donations of household items, clothing, and groceries from local businesses and community members and negotiating reduced rents from landlords on behalf of the trafficking victims they seek to serve. Moreover, the only way some law enforcement (LE) investigators I spoke with are able to conduct the lengthy investigations required to unravel human trafficking cases is by working unpaid overtime and covering expenses they incur out of their own pockets.

One major consequence of the widespread and chronic funding shortages for anti-trafficking efforts is that the costs of participating in partnerships are not prioritized. Except for the DOJ's Enhanced Collaborative Model task force grants discussed in chapter 1, funding for the level of coordinating leadership and support required for robust multisector collaboration is rare. I suspect the dearth of funding for partnership is not just related to budget constraints. It is also due to a lack of understanding of what it takes to build and sustain strong and impactful collaboration. However, there are signs of improvement that are cause for hope, and I sketch some of them below.

State Funding for Collaboration

State funding for coordinating partnerships to counter human trafficking is nonexistent in most of the United States. A few notable exceptions are encouraging. For example, in 2014 Colorado's legislature passed a law that mandated the creation of a state human trafficking council to be coordinated by the state's Department of Public Safety and composed of anti-trafficking leaders from a wide-ranging array of sectors.[7] The law requires the council to include between twenty and twenty-nine individuals representing twenty-two different state or county agencies (including departments of law, human services, and labor), investigators from multiple agencies, representatives of statewide district attorney and criminal defense attorney associations, and several categories of nongovernmental organizations. Some NGO categories, such as those that provide direct services to victims, are to be represented by more than one organization. The categories of organizations specified for council membership include a "statewide organization that provides services to crime victims," a "statewide immigrant rights organization," a "statewide organization that provides legal advocacy to abused, neglected, and at-risk children," and a "faith-based organization that assists victims of human trafficking." A "representative of a college or university department that conducts research on human trafficking" is to be part of Colorado's council, along with a person "appointed by the commissioner of agriculture," and three to five people who each represent "a regional or city-wide human trafficking task force or coalition." The council must also include "two persons who are former victims of human trafficking, one . . . for involuntary servitude and one . . . for sexual servitude." This latter clause underscores both the importance of survivors' input in counter-trafficking efforts and the fact that there are multiple forms of trafficking that need to be countered.

The legislature's mission statement for the council begins with catalyzing collaboration:

> *To bring together leadership from community-based and statewide anti-trafficking efforts, to build and enhance collaboration among communities and counties within the state*, to establish and improve comprehensive services for victims and survivors of human trafficking, to assist in the successful prosecution of human traffickers, and to help prevent human trafficking in Colorado. . . . The membership of the council shall reflect, to the extent possible, representation of urban and rural areas of the state and a balance of expertise, both governmental and nongovernmental, in issues relating to human trafficking.[8] (Emphasis added)

Along with the creation of the council, the Colorado legislature also appropriated funds for the Department of Public Safety to hire a full-time human trafficking program manager whose responsibilities include coordinating the council and helping its members implement its mission.

Similarly, in early 2015 the Washington state legislature authorized a statewide task force, with a multisector composition akin to Colorado's council, to advance coordination and improve counter-trafficking efforts.[9] The state Office for Victims of Crime was assigned the responsibility of providing "necessary administrative and clerical support to the task force," and a modest amount of funding was appropriated for this purpose. In effect, this was a re-creation of a previous task force. In 2002, Washington's legislature had been the first to create a statewide task force on human trafficking, comprised primarily of representatives from law enforcement, victim service providers, and government agencies, but the mandate for that task force had expired in 2004. In the 2015 legislation, the text added to the task force section stipulated seven additional state agencies and categories of NGOs that must be represented on the task force, including the Department of Agriculture, the state Superintendent of Public Instruction, the Attorney General, academic institutions, and faith-based organizations. Congruently with Colorado's, Washington's task force is to be composed of organizations that are "diverse in viewpoint, geography, ethnicity, and culture, and in the populations served."[10]

That Colorado and Washington authorized these task forces reflects a much-expanded understanding of the range of sectors that need to collaborate against trafficking. The commendable support they give to multisector collaboration against human trafficking should be replicated in every state. It is particularly significant that the very diverse array of entities identified by both these legislatures identifies those sectors as not merely useful, but integral to multisector counter-trafficking efforts. The key change here is that the proper involvement is seen as much broader than the three-sector core (law enforcement, victim service providers, and prosecutors) of the DOJ's task forces.

Private Foundations and Collaboration

Besides the DOJ's task force grant program, and a few states' legislatures or specific agencies, funding for counter-trafficking efforts in the United States comes from individuals' charitable contributions, from religious congregations, and from private foundations. In addition, a small but growing number of businesses make charitable contributions (sometimes in the form of sponsorship) to anti-trafficking programs. Although there has been no large-scale analysis to date on the amount of funding given to counter-trafficking efforts from each category of donor, my fieldwork, not surprisingly, indicated that most of the funds from nongovernmental sources go to nonprofit and nongovernmental organizations. Correspondingly, for the vast majority of anti-trafficking NGOs, funding comes only from individuals, congregations, and foundations.

Even some publicly administered counter-trafficking programs are funded at least in part by individuals and foundations. For example, in 2009, after several years of preparations, the Seattle city government had finalized plans for its first residential recovery facility with coordinated, holistic services for minors who had been victims of commercial sexual exploitation. Called the Bridge Continuum of Services for Sexually Exploited Youth (abbreviated as the Bridge), the facility was scheduled to open in mid-2010. From early in the planning, the Bridge was intended to be run via a partnership between the city, the county prosecutor's office, and an NGO with significant experience in providing shelter and services for vulnerable minors. However, the city's revenues plunged in the wake of the recession, and the funds allocated for the Bridge were cut drastically. As news spread that the opening of the Bridge would be postponed indefinitely due to the city's budget cuts, concerned citizens flooded Seattle's Human Services Department with offers of contributions. The city created a Prostituted Children Rescue Fund into which private donors could contribute by check or credit card. Community supporters spread the word, and in December 2009, the *Seattle Times* published an editorial that urged readers to donate.[11] Within a couple of months, individuals, congregations, community groups, and foundations had donated the remaining $200,000 needed. The Bridge opened as scheduled in May 2010 with this acknowledgment:

> The Bridge Continuum was established through a historic partnership led by the City of Seattle and including municipal and county authorities, health professionals and other service providers, foundations, and private donors. This community collaboration is supported by Seattle Public Schools, the King County Prosecuting Attorney's Office, the Seattle Police Department, and local juvenile justice systems.[12]

A second example of a private foundation catalyzing multisector collaboration is the Colorado Project to Comprehensively Combat Human Trafficking. This began when the Embrey Family Foundation supported a Denver-based nonprofit, the Laboratory to Combat Human Trafficking, in designing an extensive and intensive multisector, statewide, research-and-strategy development process around the question, "What would it take to end human trafficking in Colorado?"[13] The resulting Colorado Action Plan articulated far-reaching recommendations for ways every sector can help advance implementation of the 4Ps in Colorado, and advocated legislative changes as well. The plan advances the Embrey Family Foundation's mission to "catalyze action toward achieving systemic solutions [to counter domestic human trafficking], as well as serve as a model for innovative and impactful philanthropy."[14]

A third example of multisector collaboration against trafficking that involves strong participation by private foundations is the Partnership for

Freedom (PFF), launched in 2013.[15] Led by the Humanity United foundation together with the Department of Justice, the Department of Health and Human Services, and the Department of Housing and Urban Development, with additional private donors, the PFF aims to achieve the following:

> *Inspire communities to work together* to identify the most innovative and sustainable ways to address three major barriers facing trafficking survivors and the organizations supporting them. Those barriers include: (1) The lack of support for trafficking survivors, including sustainable housing, economic empowerment, and social services; (2) The lack of data needed to *build stronger national coordination mechanisms* to support and empower survivors; and (3) The practice of treating survivors as criminals instead of as crime victims.[16] (Emphasis added)

The PFF's vision statement articulates the need to involve "new actors" and stimulate collaboration in counter-trafficking efforts across differences in sectors, geography, beliefs, and demographics:

> We are looking for new ideas and new partnerships that lead to innovative and sustainable social services for human trafficking survivors in the United States. . . . We want to see new actors, new skills, new ideas, and new energy enter the anti-trafficking conversation. To solve this problem, we must find new ways to work together across traditional silos—among business and community groups; across regions and towns and borders; and between faith, class and neighborhood lines.[17]

Using private funds as prizes, PFF will offer a "challenge" contest to elicit novel ways of addressing each of the three barriers it identified. A critical question for any funder of anti-trafficking effort is how influential the perspectives of survivorship experts and victim service providers are in selection and investment decisions. To date the PFF has not made explicit whether or how it incorporates the hard-earned wisdom of leaders from those sectors in its proposal development and selection processes.

One of the two winners of the first challenge announced in 2014 was proposed by a three-way partnership between an anti-trafficking NGO (the Polaris Project), a state agency (the New Jersey Department of Children and Families), and an NGO that provides technology and other resources to the voluntary sector (Caravan Studios, a division of TechSoup Global). With PFF funding, this partnership, the Safe Shelter Collaborative, will develop and deploy technology that promises to "dramatically increase access to appropriate, supportive shelters for survivors" and to "increase the amount of shelter available by broadening the base of organizations who can provide quality assistance to trafficking survivors."[18] In selecting this project as a winner in its first challenge, the PFF both rewarded the multisector work it took to develop it and resourced the expansion of the network of organizations that can offer services to survivors, thereby catalyzing another form of interorganizational collaboration. The Safe Shelter Collaborative, as well as the PFF itself, are examples of some of the kinds of public-private partnerships that have become common in other arenas such as school reform and social service provision. We will consider power dynamics in such partnerships in more detail later in this chapter.

Foundations engage in interorganizational collaboration against human trafficking within their own sector via donor networks such as the multiple foundations that contribute to the PFF. Another form of alliance is demonstrated by the Justice and Mercy Philanthropy Forum, which describes itself as "a small community of funders, motivated by Christian faith, that invests in global social change."[19] Yet another example is the Freedom Fund. Launched in 2013 with commitments of $10 million each from Humanity United, Legatum Foundation, and Walk Free Foundation, the fund aims simply and ambitiously "to mobilize the capital and knowledge needed to end slavery."[20] During its first two years the Freedom Fund was joined by two additional "anchor donors," and it welcomes additional supporters. Its investments will undoubtedly have significant impacts, including the creation of new partnerships and expansion of existing collaborations. The Freedom Fund's leaders identify the costs of uncoordinated anti-slavery efforts in terms of lost opportunities:

> The Fund was founded on the premise that current philanthropic and programmatic efforts in the anti-slavery space are fragmented. Individual actors are often working in isolation and missing the opportunity to create scalable and lasting change. Consequently, the Freedom Fund's founding partners, some of the world's leading philanthropic organizations, have come together to create the world's first private donor fund dedicated to ending modern slavery.[21]

The high value that many foundations place on collaboration is evidenced in a variety of ways. One is the common requirement that funding applicants list the entities with which they collaborate in their applications. To illustrate, questions asked of prospective grantees by the Boston-based Imago Dei Fund include the following:

> Please indicate how you partner with other organizations to accomplish your [organizational] mission. . . . Will you be partnering with any organizations in this project? Will your project build on work that is being done by others, or are there others that will build on your work? Are there others doing work that will be a complement to your work on this project?[22]

In addition to encouraging or requiring grantees to engage in some form of partnership, it is not unusual for foundations to engineer collaborations among their grantees. The oldest donor-convened coalition of recipient anti-trafficking NGOs in the United States is the Alliance to End Slavery and Trafficking (ATEST). In 2006, Humanity United created the group that would become ATEST in 2009. By 2015, ATEST's fourteen member organizations included some of the largest human rights NGOs that address human trafficking in the United States as well as in other countries. Policy advocacy is the central aim of ATEST. It lobbies the U.S. Congress and offers recommendations to federal agencies on how to create "lasting solutions to prevent labor and sex trafficking, hold perpetrators accountable, [and] ensure justice for victims and empower survivors with tools for recovery."[23] Humanity United houses ATEST in its Washington, DC, office and provides salaries for ATEST staff. Members of ATEST help inform its policy objectives and strategies, and their reputations as leading anti-trafficking NGOs lend persuasive credibility to ATEST's advocacy work.

In this section we have considered how financial resources provide a form of power to organizations. We have examined the influences of funders on collaboration against trafficking, in terms of the prestige and dynamics of different types of funding and ways in which some funders support, shape, or lead partnerships. A critical question with which every funder of anti-trafficking efforts needs to grapple is how to incorporate the wisdom of survivorship experts and victim service providers in their funding strategies and investment decisions; without that funders risk causing harm as they attempt to do good. In the following section I explain three types of organizational power. Although each is influenced by funding, they all function independently of money as well.

TYPES OF POWER

Power typically manifests in and between organizations in one of the following ways: the power to act, the power to influence, and the power to control. I will unpack each of these briefly, describing some of the general economic influences and outcomes of each. I will also note ways that differences in organizations' level of access to each form of power shape relations between organizations as they strive to work together against human trafficking.

The Power to Act

The power to choose one's actions, sometimes called "agency," is highly valued in American culture, by organizations as well as by individuals. The essence of enslavement is the loss of this type of power—that is, the ability to act autonomously. For organizational leaders, the latitude to determine an organization's mission, goals, strategies, and procedures, much less to execute plans, requires the power to act. As with individual citizens, the agency of organizations is constrained by laws and resources. In every sector, evolving laws and fluctuating resource levels challenge the ability of organizational leaders to plan well and to execute the plans they have made. When there are substantial gaps between resource levels, whether financial or human, and actions to which an organization is legally mandated, morally obligated, or strategically committed, organizational leaders experience great stress, sometimes distress.[24]

During my interviews with people who work to combat human trafficking in various sectors, I was not surprised to hear them recount the sadness they experience as they see or hear about the abuses suffered by victims. However, I was surprised by how many expressed sadness about anti-trafficking actions they felt they should take, but could not due to resource constraints. In interview after interview, with police investigators, victim service providers, prosecutors, community mobilizers, survivor-activists, and others, faces fell and voices flattened when people talked about the gap between what they felt they and their organization should be doing, and what they perceived themselves and their organization to be capable of doing, often because of inadequate funds. Their sadness was rooted in a profound sense of impotence.

However, even leaders of well-funded organizations, such as private foundations and leaders of corporate social responsibility offices, expressed sadness over the gap between the resources they had to work with and the massive scale of the problem of human trafficking. But the sadness they conveyed was resignation, expressed in phrases such as "we can only do so much." This contrasted to the angst-filled sadness of leaders who work in organizations or agencies that are legally mandated or otherwise obligated to accomplish particular things but lack the funds to do so. From these observations we can conclude two things: first, those who work in the anti-trafficking realm are quite aware that the scope and complexity of human trafficking exceeds the resources they can bring to it; and second, although the money is not the only type of resource, and not the only source of power, it is an undeniably significant source.

The Power to Influence

A second form of power is the ability to influence others' actions. In contrast to the power to act (that is, having autonomous control), this form of power is essentially relational. Among organizations, influence can occur as organizational representatives interact directly, such as happens in a negotiation where representatives from one organization try to persuade their counterparts to do something. However, influence can also occur indirectly, for example, when one organization strives to emulate another by adopting the other's anti-trafficking policies or by implementing a program inspired by the other. The level of direct influence an organization has is often proportional to its resources, as when one organization can pay for what it wants another organization to do.

In contrast, an organization's power to influence others indirectly often stems from nonmonetary sources. For example, an organization can leverage its status—that is, the respect it commands from other organizations—to exert power. In a conversation I had with a law enforcement officer about the power exercised by government agencies in cross-sector partnerships, he noted that nongovernmental organizations gain power to influence other NGOs when they receive federal grants. In addition to increasing capacity (by hiring staff and expanding programs), such grants provide recognition by the federal granting agency. He made the following observation:

> An NGO that is federally funded to serve victims is right up there, power-wise, with government agencies. Overall, it comes down to the "money" side, but also the referent power they have simply by being the "grantee" and the go-to for victim services. For example, I've had other NGOs [in this area] call me and ask me to please put a word in for them with [a federally funded NGO], so they could get "under" their grant. Money equals employees and influence in every sector. (Interview)

In other words, funding from a respected source such as a federal agency increases the respect-based power of the recipient organization to influence, as well as its capacity-based power to act.

Many nonprofit anti-trafficking leaders I interviewed talked about how chronic underfunding and unstable funding in their sector have given rise to a dynamics of destructive competition between nonprofits. Some expressed feeling like they were in a struggle for survival that required them to guard their organization's plans and actions in order to keep them proprietary. On several occasions, when a nonprofit I was observing succeeded in obtaining a significant grant, other nonprofits in its relational network began to react in ways that were at best tepid toward the organization that had received the grant, and at times defensive or even hostile. Such reactions strained relationships and created divisions, negatively affecting collaboration within the interorganizational network. This kind of dynamic evidences that organizational leaders can exert influence for better or for worse within their organization's network of relations, with or without funding, because influence as a form of power is relational by definition.

The Power to Control

A third form of power that is relevant to anti-trafficking efforts is the power to control another organization's actions. The power to control affords an organization the ability to either mandate particular action or constrain action on the part of others. This power is not simply a stronger version of influence, which typically stems from resources or status. The power to control action by anti-trafficking organizations is derived from legal authority and held by government agencies, most especially law enforcement. We will consider some of the dynamics this form of power creates in multisector interactions in the next section.

HOW ANTI-TRAFFICKING ORGANIZATIONS DEVELOP POWER WITHOUT MONEY

The conventional wisdom that the greater an organization's financial resources, the more autonomy it has and the more influence it enjoys holds true generally in the anti-trafficking field for both organizations and individuals. But this does not entirely explain power relations in this realm. In order to more fully understand the dynamics of collaboration against human trafficking, it is important to explore forms of power that develop and function independently of money. In this section, I describe three: (1) power that is derived from authority or status in ways that are unrelated to the distribution of money; (2) power via the credentialing of a profession; and (3) power that is negotiated between sectors.

Power Derived from Authority or Status

While money confers authority and status, it is also true that authority and status can at least to some degree enhance power independent of economics. The most obvious example is in the sectors of government involving social service offices and law enforcement agencies (including investigators and attorneys). The power (that is, the authority) of these sectors is vested in them by government. Moreover, the continuation of law enforcement as a sector is virtually guaranteed in the United States and most other countries, giving them a secure position enjoyed by few other sectors. Obviously, funding levels for law enforcement and government agencies wax and wane over time, and those changes affect the capacity of these sectors to carry out their mandate. Because government funding for both law enforcement and social services is finite, and such agencies at every level operate under broad (some would say impossibly broad) mandates, there are always financial constraints on government agencies' ability to exercise the power of their mandates. We will explore those tensions and their effects on collaboration later in the chapter. My point is that the power of law enforcement and government service agencies does not disappear even when funding wanes.

Although NGOs have far less stable funding, from the perspective of some law enforcement agents, the distribution of power between NGO victim service providers and law enforcement is generally balanced. In the words of one federal investigator who recognized different types of power:

> Overall, I think this [power dynamic] evens out. While NGOs have power to encourage/discourage a possible victim from cooperating with law enforcement, we [law enforcement] have the power over, at least in dealing with victims who are illegally present, granting continued presence [a type of immigration status available to a non-US citizen enabling the person to temporarily remain in the United States and not be subject to removal]. Continued presence, in an immigration sense, doesn't mean much to us—we would never be deporting a victim anyway—but it means a lot to the victim to say "I'm legal" and it means a lot to both the victim and the NGO because continued presence opens up the door for funding similar to refugee funding that the NGO can provide. Without continued presence, the NGO or someone else is on the hook for providing the services out of their own pocket. (Interview)

Unsurprisingly, law enforcement agents and victim service providers tend to have different perspectives about the power relations between their sectors. Although some victim service providers (VSPs) articulated a sense of "balance" in the power dynamic between themselves and the LE officers with whom they work on trafficking cases, others within and outside of the VSP sector perceive VSPs to be subordinated by law enforcement. In the words of a non-investigatory government agency administrator who works closely with law enforcement and VSPs, "I see lots of law enforcement officers with an arrogant attitude of, 'we are here to investigate and you [VSPs] are here to pick up the pieces.'" Several VSPs noted that the fact that the LE sector is populated mostly by men, and the VSP sector is populated mostly by women, contributes to a sense of power imbalance. We will explore this gender gap further in chapter 4.

A booklet for victim service providers who work for law enforcement agencies (in contrast to those who work for NGOs) was put out by the International Association of Chiefs of Police. Entitled *Backing the Badge: Working Effectively with Law Enforcement*, it conveys the ambivalence on the part of some law enforcement toward service providers even as it ostensibly validates them.

There are few other professional positions within the law enforcement agency that require the level of collaboration with officers as that of the victim service professional. This level of collaboration was not achieved overnight. Instead, it represents a gradual but steady merger of concepts, objectives, practices and perspectives that continues today at a greater pace than ever before. Some of the greatest champions of this effort may now be found within the ranks of a profession once indifferent, if not reluctant, to this merger—the law enforcement officers themselves.[25]

Many victim service providers are also ambivalent about working with law enforcement, and do so gingerly, using a variety of strategies to communicate what they perceive to be necessary distinctions and boundaries between their aims and procedures and those of law enforcement agencies. For example, in the following excerpt from a policy statement addressed to representatives of the LE sector, an NGO victim service provider organization communicates its approach to collaborating with law enforcement:

Confidentiality and Collaboration: While we appreciate you making the referral/introduction, we have confidentiality with the clients we serve and it is our policy to meet with them without law enforcement (or anyone else) present. Please understand this when you make a referral to us.

- We have a professional responsibility and ethical obligation to the clients we serve.
- We will collaborate with you on cases you refer to us with clients' consent.
- We will work with you to access the services your agency has access to.
- We will support clients and advocate for their rights as they cooperate with your investigation and prosecution of their case.
- We would like to work with you and the client to explain roles and responsibilities so that it is clear who the client should contact for specific things. This will make everyone's job easier and help the client navigate the very strange world of investigation/prosecution and services.

Referrals to Law Enforcement: [We] will refer clients who choose to report to law enforcement to the U.S. Attorney's Office. The U.S. Attorney's Office will then work with the appropriate law enforcement agency to proceed with the case. [We] support clients to make informed decisions in this regard by thoroughly explaining victims' rights, the criminal justice process, and our relationship with and trust in our law enforcement partners.[26]

This statement explains the differences, from the victim service provider's perspective, in protocol when a client has been referred to the service provider by law enforcement cases versus when a client has come to the service provider through some other means. Most significantly, it articulates the right of the service provider to respect clients' choices rather than pressuring clients to report to law enforcement.

In addition to the authority that law enforcement generally holds over other sectors, there are also legally mandated lines of authority within the law enforcement sector that structure relations between the federal and local levels in general and between particular entities across those levels. A key example of this is the authority that the U.S. Department of Justice has over local police agencies. Since the 1980s, federal prosecutors (U.S. Attorneys, employed by the U.S. DOJ) have had the authority to investigate municipal police agencies on the grounds of suspicions that the local agencies have policies or practices that violate the U.S. Constitution, including gender bias in cases involving sexual assault and race-based discrimination. Whether such bias or discrimination is suspected of occurring internally within police departments or in patterns of police investigations and arrests, it is the responsibility of the Civil Rights Division of the DOJ to investigate.[27] Such investigations are typically conducted by the U.S. Attorney's Office (USAO) in the district in which the police department is located. According to the Police Executive Research Forum, "the DOJ's role in monitoring local police is a complex, controversial issue."[28] Although differences in perspective on this are to be expected, the authority of a USAO over a police department is an important structural element in relations between police and federal prosecutors. As I explained in chapter 1, active involvement by the USAO with local law enforcement is required by DOJ's Enhanced Collaborative Model grants. It is conceivable that tensions in other domains of interactions between the USAO and the police department could make collaboration on human trafficking cases more challenging.

The authority for enforcing laws extends beyond DOJ agencies. It is exercised by other kinds of government agencies as well, at federal, state, and local levels. This authority shapes collaboration between government agencies and businesses on human trafficking. For example, consider the potential influences of the overarching power structure between businesses and government on anti-trafficking collaboration attempts between representatives of the private and public sectors. Businesses are licensed by state agencies and expected to function according to federal and state laws. Many aspects of businesses' employment practices and working conditions are regulated by federal and state labor laws and monitored by inspectors from the U.S. Department of Labor and states' labor agencies. When businesses are asked to collaborate with government on anti-trafficking initiatives, they may be wary, fearful of increased costs and unwanted scrutiny.

To illustrate, on several occasions I attended panels in which a business leader had agreed to participate alongside labor investigators in a discussion of human trafficking. Each time, the business leader was asked by the panel moderator to describe the steps his or her business was taking to help counter human trafficking in its industry. On three of these occasions, the business spokesperson was subsequently asked civil, but very pointed, questions by audience members about forced labor within that business or in its supply chains. In the first instance, the spokesperson represented a medium-size, fruit-growing and distribution business. The second represented a multinational company involved in entertainment, clothing, and toys; and the third represented a multinational technology company. On each occasion, the labor investigators remained silent during these exchanges, but the business leaders were visibly uncomfortable and cast sidelong glances toward the government officials. These interactions, though stressful for the spokespeople, were relatively low-stakes for the businesses they represented in relation to government agencies. But they serve to demonstrate that the authority of government over businesses influences the content and modes of their communication in anti-trafficking efforts. When businesses in any industry stick their necks out to advance anti-trafficking efforts in multisector environments, they incur the risks of greater scrutiny—by government as well as by the public.[29]

The sector of nongovernmental and nonprofit organizations (which includes faith-based, community-based, and other types, and is sometimes collectively called the "civil society" sector), provides a quite different example of how power can function independently of money, through nonlegal authority or social status. In this sector, it is possible for organizations to exercise a high level of power even though they have relatively unstable funding levels. Leaders of nonprofits who are respected within their communities or social networks wield great influence because they can persuade large numbers of people to take certain actions against human trafficking regardless of their organization's finances. Organizations can trade on different kinds of status to influence people to donate money to advance the organization's anti-trafficking efforts, for example, when leaders of a faith-based organization use their spiritual authority, or when leaders of a community organization or professional association leverage their social status. When these efforts are successful, the financial standing of the recipient nonprofit may increase. But these can also operate independently: the power of many nonprofits is derived as much or more from social capital as from financial capital.[30] For some nonprofits whose leaders are well connected across like-minded communities and intersecting social circles, the power to act and influence has little to do with money.

CREDENTIALING A PROFESSION

Beyond deriving power from vested authority or social status, another way it is possible for anti-trafficking organizations to develop or exercise power without any increases to their financial base is through the creation or expansion of credentials and certification for a profession. There are a variety of ways that organizational leaders in every sector seek to improve the work conducted by professionals in their sector and to establish and enforce boundaries about who can claim legitimately to be affiliated with their profession or with their sector more generally. Such "boundary work" is a strategy employed by a profession to position and promote itself; it also develops a paradigm or framework for that profession's worldview.[31]

Strengthening and strategically positioning one sector (or subsector) often involves differentiating it from related sectors or subsectors and increasing its status relative to others. To begin unpacking the ways that the defining of a profession does this, let's consider an example from the healthcare realm: the establishment of medical schools for the training of would-be physicians by established doctors. The system by which people earn MD degrees also helps nonphysicians distinguish doctors with actual expertise from medical quacks. Not incidentally, the MD degree system also serves to distinguish one particular form of health-related expertise (medicine) from others that also grant doctorates (such as naturopathy and osteopathy) and to reproduce the professional boundaries between them. At the same time, it initiates, changes, or reproduces differences in status among the health-oriented professions.

In the same way, leaders of sectors involved in anti-trafficking work strive to improve the work and position of their sector. The relatively recent emergence of the profession of victim services is a useful example. The profession's development was described by the U.S. DOJ's Office of Victims of Crime Training and Technical Assistance Center this way:

> Out of the grassroots movement of the 80s, victim services has become a recognized profession that seeks to attract leaders with an appropriate mix of traditional credentials and experience with crime victims to guide the field into the future.[32]

The "grassroots movement" to which this sentence refers is the victims' rights movement. The profession of victim services is now widely understood as an interdisciplinary occupation associated with providing mental health, social services, and legal advocacy for victims. The kinds of credentials that have become "traditional" over the last thirty years include bachelor's and master's degree programs in social work, mental health, or a related field, plus specialized training in victim advocacy. The National Advocate Credentialing Program, launched in 2003, offers four levels of credentials; eligibility for each level is based on years of experience (0–8+ years) plus training in various facets of caring for victims of crime. The DOJ's Office for Victims of Crime offers several types of training and certification in victim services as well.[33]

The recent emergence of certification programs on trauma-informed care for social workers and health professionals is another variant in the positioning of victim services as a profession. Such certificate programs aim both to increase the competencies of those who provide direct care for trafficking victims and to create and promote a new kind of professional expertise that differentially positions those who are certified in it from those who are not. The following description of one multiphase certification program, which includes human trafficking as a setting in which trauma occurs, illustrates how increasing competencies and professional positioning are accomplished simultaneously:

> This first phase is for all practitioners and serves as an introduction to key elements of trauma-informed care perspective . . . A minimum score of 80% is required on all 3 exams [in the first phase] in order to be accepted by most state and national boards. Once you have completed all 3 tests we will mail you an elegant certificate suitable for framing.[34]

The fact that exams are required helps establish the legitimacy of the certificate program in terms of knowledge acquisition, while the "elegant certificate"—visual evidence of completing those exams and thus graduating from a credible program—is clearly designed to be publicly displayed by the certificate recipient as a marker of professional expertise. Such status indicators help leaders in the victim services sector position their sector as legitimate and differentiate that sector's expertise as valuable in collaborations with other anti–human trafficking sectors. It also functions as a differentiator among the individuals who seek to serve victims. As with any professional certificate, the holder of a trauma-informed care certificate may have some advantages over those who have not earned that certificate. It can help in getting a job in the victim services field, in the first place, and later in exerting influence in multisector deliberations on victim care protocols.

Because some survivorship experts work in victim services, and other survivors wish to do so, there is a double-edged quality to the professionalization of victim services. Of the trafficking survivors in the U.S. who seek to contribute to counter-trafficking work in public ways, most focus their efforts on reaching out to victims and providing services for survivors. They work (paid or unpaid) in the victim services profession within the nonprofit social services sector. Although some trafficking survivors in the U.S. have earned college degrees, many have not—and they face numerous obstacles to doing so. In contrast, their colleagues, counterparts, and their competitors for paid positions tend to be licensed social workers and mental health care providers with master's degrees.[35] Most of the survivors I interviewed or heard speak publicly about their anti-trafficking work described experiencing tensions in relation to service providers who were not also survivors. Their comments expressed a mix of feelings of inadequacy or regret regarding their lack of professional credentials and confidence that insights they had gained through their own journeys are valuable to other survivors. One articulated the tension this way:

> I know that I know a lot, even though I never made it to college. Maybe I will someday. But it's important to me to reach out to other victims because I can help them just by telling them what I've lived through and how I got out. It's one thing to have a social worker who has never been down and out tell you what to do. It's a whole other thing to be able to hear, "Here's what I did." That's what I can do for other victims. (Interview)

Some survivors with academic credentials are ambivalent about them. Two I interviewed were pursuing graduate degrees at the time we spoke, and a third had already earned a master's degree. All three described internal conflict over these credentials. On the one hand, their graduate studies helped them gain broader perspectives on their personal experiences and acquire much more knowledge; on the other hand, they view their journeys as survivors as their most important form of expertise. As one graduate degree–holding survivor told me in an interview, "I got my first degree to show myself I could do it, and I got my second degree to show other survivors what we are capable of." She values her degrees primarily because of the accomplishments they represent, and secondarily because of the expertise she gained by acquiring them.

I have discussed the relatively recent emergence and establishment of the victim services profession, and some implications for survivors who want to enter it in order to illustrate a form of strategic positioning through which power develops, a positioning that has direct bearing on collaborative efforts to address human trafficking. The dual aims of increasing competencies and advancing the position of a profession or sector can complement each other. As Dr. Dana DeHart, a social psychologist who specializes in victim services and consults regularly for the OVC, explained during an OVC service provider forum, there are two primary reasons for credentialing victim services: (1) promoting quality and accountability in services to those served; and (2) recognition of the accomplishment of victim service providers.[36] Victims benefit from increasing the competencies of those who care for them; therefore such benefits are not compromised by the strategic positioning of the sector by leaders who are advancing trauma-informed care certification. However, any form of professional credentialing authorizes some actors and excludes others within a sector. This tension empowers those who are able to earn professional credentials and disempowers those, such as survivor-activists, who either lack access to them or are vested in a different type of expertise. Returning to the healthcare example we began with in this section, the tension is obvious: the prominence of the MD degree affords status to those who earn it and can marginalize other forms of health expertise, such as naturopathy and nursing.

Each profession has a social history of patterns in the class, gender, and education of its members that shapes their interactions with people in other professions. Each profession has its own culture, which includes values, beliefs, attitudes, norms, and protocols that have evolved as the different professions developed. Educational experiences and the socialization processes that occur during the training of professionals reinforce the problem-solving approaches, language choices, and communication patterns of each profession.[37] In subsequent chapters we will explore further how differing professional cultures contribute to the challenges of effective multiprofessional teamwork, including within multisector collaboration.

NEGOTIATING POWER BETWEEN SECTORS

In addition to gaining power through authority or status (of which credentialing a profession plays a part), an organization's or a sector's power can also increase or diminish through negotiations among sectors. In these interactions, leaders from different sectors often seek to advance (or at least to preserve) the power of the organizations in their respective sector by negotiating the structure of the partnership, including the roles and responsibilities of participating entities. The creation of a "memo of understanding" (MOU) is a common way in which organizations in a formal, named partnership negotiate these elements of their relationships. But whether a partnership is formal or informal, the process of deciding who is going to do what, and when, involves discussion of the capacities, constraints, and operating modes of each organization, and many of these are sector-specific. Formal partnerships often develop more detailed protocols for processes in which they must coordinate closely together. For example, multisector task forces have found it important to develop a protocol regarding how the law enforcement, victim service providers, and healthcare providers will coordinate their actions and communication during the first few days after a trafficking victim is identified by or referred to any of them.

At times during my fieldwork I noticed organizations refusing to engage, much less negotiate, with those in another sector in an attempt to increase their power or to protect themselves from the risk of losing power through the process of negotiating a cross-sector partnership. As one example, some nongovernmental victim service provider organizations work intensively with populations who perceive greater risks of harm than potential help from law enforcement. Such VSPs sometimes refuse to engage with law enforcement agencies because they think they have more to lose than to gain for their clients by negotiating. A second example can be seen among some faith-based organizations that choose not to engage with government agencies or areligious nongovernmental victim service providers because they fear diminished autonomy to act against trafficking according to their beliefs if they collaborate with areligious entities.

Power relations between sectors are deeply rooted in broader political, societal, and economic forces and histories. This must be kept in mind as we consider the complex challenges of counter-trafficking efforts, such as providing services to victims. Many of the forms of assistance that are necessary for victims of human trafficking to recover fall within the general category of "social services." Thus, social service provider networks are a critical part of the larger context in which multisector collaboration against trafficking takes place—and a useful realm in which to examine power negotiations between sectors.

For decades, social services in many areas of the United States have been provided via public-private partnerships, a web of governmental agencies, nongovernmental nonprofit organizations, and nongovernmental for-profit organizations (that is, businesses).[38] Some NGO providers of social services receive government funding for the services they provide, including some businesses and some faith-based NGOs.[39] Government funding for social services comes with usage constraints and reporting requirements; because of this, some NGO providers of social services choose not to seek government funding in order to have greater autonomy. In addition to directly providing social services such as child care; job training; and mental health, drug, and alcohol treatment, the private sector also funds social services provided by nonprofit NGOs. One mechanism for private sector funding of social services is through corporate gifts and grants from private foundations. Recipients include both areligious and faith-based NGOs,[40] and long-lasting interorganizational relationships are often forged through social service grant-making. A second mechanism by which the private sector funds social services is social impact bonds (SIBs), also called "Pay for Success Bonds" or "Social Benefit Bonds." An SIB is defined as follows:

> [An SIB is a] social impact financing arrangement whereby funds are raised from private sector investors to provide social service agencies the funding necessary to deliver their services. The government enters into a contract with a private sector entity working as an intermediary and the private sector

entity's chosen social service providers. The private sector entity assumes the performance risk of the social services program and is repaid entirely or almost entirely based upon achieving performance or outcome targets.[41]

SIBs are designed to "combine nonprofit expertise, private sector funding, and rigorous evaluation to transform the way government and society respond to chronic social problems."[42] First initiated in the UK in 2010, proponents claim they encourage multisector collaboration and innovation on difficult social problems.[43] SIBs are examples of recent policy and financial developments in multisector collaboration around complex social problems.

Reputations and relationships in the social services realm have been developing for many years between some individuals and organizations in the public, private, and NGO and nonprofit sectors. They are part of the structural context in which many services for victims of human trafficking are negotiated, funded, and managed. Meeting the survival needs of trafficking victims (providing housing, food, and clothing) and supporting their recovery from the trauma of being enslaved often requires collaboration between many kinds of actors, including landlords, store managers, healthcare providers, and legal advocates. Especially because victim services are typically underfunded, a service provider organization's capacity to act by providing, directly or indirectly, the array of services its clients need depends on its ability to persuade many other entities to serve clients at below-market rates. For this reason, a victim service provider's visibility, credibility, and established relationships with other sectors are a form of nonmonetary currency. As these resources increase through negotiations with actors in other sectors, the power of the service provider both to act and to influence others increases.

SUMMARY

In this chapter, I have illustrated how power relations are structured and negotiated between sectors in the realm of anti-trafficking efforts in ways that shape multisector collaboration against trafficking. Although economics are foundational to some forms of power, other power relations are based in authority and professional status. Some cross-sector negotiations about anti-trafficking efforts are not primarily based in economics; rather, they are part of political and societal patterns of interactions among sectors. All of the bases of power discussed above reflect the larger political and societal structures in which multisector collaboration takes place. In turn, these power dynamics also contribute to shaping such structures and in influencing multisector and interorganizational relations in collaborations against trafficking. Unpacking the dynamics of power as deployed through money and status has provided us with a basis for understanding the context within which anti-trafficking collaborations function. With this broad context of cross-sector power dynamics in mind, we can go on to examine more specific strategies. In the next chapter, we will examine several strategies employed routinely by anti-trafficking organizations to bolster their status or to increase or limit the power of other organizations.

Leadership Strategies and Power Dynamics

THE LAUNCH OF AN ANTI-TRAFFICKING NONPROFIT

Festive sounds spill out of the trendy bar in the business district of a mid-sized city. Having made my way past the patrons in the front room, I'm greeted at the entry to the back room by a friendly volunteer holding a clip-board with a list of names. She checks mine off and hands me a drink ticket. The room feels full, but not uncomfortably crowded. About sixty people are milling around, enjoying appetizers and chatting. We are all here to celebrate the launch of an anti-trafficking NGO with an innovative focus—the first of its kind in the United States. It is the brainchild of a midcareer academic who decided he wanted to spend the second half of his career very differently than the first. He felt compelled to join the counter-trafficking movement and bring his expertise to bear in practical ways. Having obtained a small grant as seed funding from a private foundation, he worked within an established nonprofit for nearly a year, networking and researching current efforts and gaps in anti-trafficking efforts, both in his city and nationally. He sought input from leaders in business, law, and politics, as well as victim services and law enforcement, in crafting a plan for this new nonprofit, and most had encouraged him to proceed.

He wanted to leverage the launch of the nonprofit to position it both within the existing ecology of anti-trafficking organizations in his city and in relation to private sector and civic leaders whose organizations were not yet involved in anti-trafficking efforts. The program agenda for tonight's event evidenced his genuine respect for the people he had asked to speak; it also demonstrated his success in persuading them to support his nonprofit pub-licly. As I listened to city- and state-level elected officials, a well-respected survivorship expert, the director of another nonprofit, and an internationally known trafficking expert speak on behalf of the new nonprofit, I noticed that they each took the opportunity to say something about their own anti-trafficking efforts as well. Being "platformed" at this event expanded their audiences, boosted their visibility, and bolstered their reputations. And in the process it helped create an identity for the new nonprofit. (Fieldnote)

The event I described in the fieldnote above illustrates some of the leadership strategies that reflect—and shape—power structures and dynamics between organizations and across sectors. The new nonprofit described above planned its launch event as a way of both introducing itself to and positioning itself among other entities within its ecology of anti-trafficking actors. It invited particular other organizational leaders to share the platform of the launch event, and those who agreed to speak allowed their organizations to be platformed by the new nonprofit. The internationally known trafficking expert made it clear in her comments and in what she later wrote about the new nonprofit that she saw herself as having been a partner in the founding of the new organization, even though she did not have a titled leadership role. Positioning, platforming, and partnering to share leadership: we will explore several facets of each of these three strategies in this chapter.

STRATEGIC POSITIONING ACTIONS BY LEADERS

The strategy of positioning becomes evident when we examine how particular organizations establish themselves as industry or sector leaders against human trafficking. Positioning actions influence in more than one way; they affect how an organization is perceived by others in its sector, and they illustrate the power of an organization to influence others as well as to act in anti-trafficking efforts. In the private sector, a small but growing number of businesses (typically large businesses) have taken leadership roles within their respective industries and leveraged those effectively across sectors.[1] Some have subsequently become co-leaders of multisector efforts against trafficking. As global business consultant Alice Korngold explains in her book, *A Better World, Inc.: How Companies Profit by Solving Global Problems . . . Where Governments Cannot*:

> Some corporations working in partnership with NGOs are becoming potent players in addressing the complex problems of . . . supply chain issues, and human trafficking . . . and other human rights issues. . . . Many of the most effective business initiatives to address human rights are done through coalitions and partnership with NGOs.[2]

Such leadership expands a company's influence and also boosts its profits, according to Korngold. She contends that for the companies that are industry leaders in anti-trafficking efforts, "combatting trafficking is a moral issue and a business imperative, raising employee morale, engendering good will with customers, and protecting the brand."[3]

Examples of businesses taking strong anti-trafficking measures internally and leadership roles in anti-trafficking efforts within their industry and across sectors have become increasingly common since the mid-2000s. In 2006, the Manpower Group, a multinational employment services firm, was the first corporation to sign the Athens Ethical Principles that "declare a 'zero tolerance' policy for working with any entity benefiting in any way from human trafficking, including clients, vendors and business partners." The group issued invitations to 1,000 other multinational corporations across industries to sign as well.[4] In 2012, David Arkless, then–Global President of Corporate and Government Affairs at Manpower, cofounded the global Business Coalition Against Trafficking (known as the gBCAT) after persuading Manpower and eight other blue-chip multinational corporations, each from a different industry, to become founding members. Although the gBCAT is comprised solely of for-profits, its aims include "driving connections between businesses and governments, international organizations, non-profits and civil society for the purpose of knowledge- and idea-sharing on solutions to address human trafficking."[5] By the time the gBCAT was announced in 2012, at least three of the founding members of the gBCAT—Carlson, a global hospitality and travel company; LexisNexis, a global provider of online information services; and technology giant Microsoft—had already established strong corporate anti-trafficking policies and were coleading multisector anti-trafficking efforts in collaboration with governmental and civil society organizations.

Carlson is another example of businesses that have positioned themselves as sector leaders to counter human trafficking. Since the early 2000s, the Carlson conglomerate has led efforts within the hotel and travel industries to recognize and prevent the commercial sexual exploitation of children worldwide. Since 2004, the company has been proactively training its employees to be aware of the risks of child trafficking. Among the innovations it has introduced to anti-trafficking efforts (developed through collaboration between its Carlson Wagonlit Travel business and the U.S. State Department) is a statement that appears on electronic ticket itineraries educating travelers on the sexual exploitation of children and asking travelers to report any suspicious activity to the Human Trafficking Hotline. In an interview published by the U.S. Global Leadership Coalition, Marilyn Carlson Nelson, the company's recently retired CEO, explained the reasoning behind the company's early and sustained actions against trafficking:

> Traffickers often use the travel and hospitality industry as a facilitator. Airlines are used to transport victims and hotels can unknowingly be used as the settings for this illicit activity. We felt we had the tools and resources to make a difference. As a family-owned business, once we learned of the millions of children who are used for sexual purposes in the travel and tourism industry worldwide, we could not turn away. This became our focus.[6]

Carlson Nelson described explicitly her company's strategy of effecting change in its industry by accepting leadership positions in industry associations (the World Travel and Tourism Council, the Travel Industry of America, and the American Hotel & Lodging Association) and then using those positions as platforms to "consistently . . . urge our colleagues to become allies in this fight." She explained why multisector collaboration is essential:

> If we train our hotel employees but hotlines aren't answered promptly or law enforcement is complicit, it's to no avail. If the legal community won't prosecute the perpetrators, there is no *disincentive* to engage in this criminal activity. If there is no safe haven where victims can take refuge, it is unlikely that they will come forward and testify.[7] (Emphasis in the original)

In 2013, Marilyn Carlson Nelson became the inaugural recipient of the U.S. Presidential Award for Extraordinary Efforts to Combat Human Trafficking in appreciation of her leadership of her corporation's anti-trafficking initiatives, influence within its industry, and contributions to multisector collaborations against trafficking.[8] Carlson Nelson reflected on the award as follows:

> It was personally gratifying for me to know that we are successfully joining hands across sectors to bring our unique leverage, resources and expertise to bear on this problem. . . . Now that 10 years have passed since we first took up

the mantle to lead on this issue, we are pleased to see so many elected officials, business leaders, NGOs, academic leaders and citizens [who] are now aware of this problem and have joined in the fight against human trafficking.[9]

Clearly, the Carlson corporation's power to act and to influence increased as it pioneered company-wide anti-trafficking trainings, leveraged leadership positions within its sector, and collaborated with government agencies and nonprofit organizations against trafficking.

A second gBCAT member, LexisNexis, partnered with the US-based anti-trafficking NGO the Polaris Project in 2009 to develop a database of social service providers for the National Human Trafficking Resource Center. LexisNexis then developed an online library for attorneys who work with trafficking victims, and collaborated with the American Bar Association to support a training institute on civil remedies for victims of trafficking—initiatives for which it received kudos from the U.S. State Department in its 2012 *Trafficking in Persons Report*.[10] Around that time LexisNexis launched its Human Trafficking Awareness Index, which tracks and analyzes news articles on human trafficking published in 120 countries. The Index, which highlights "emerging trends and patterns of awareness [of trafficking] within and across national borders," was lauded by the United Nations Global Initiatives to Fight Human Trafficking office.[11] In 2011, Rob McKenna, then Attorney General of Washington state and president of the National Association of Attorneys General (NAAG), invited LexisNexis to be one of two corporate members on his leadership council for the NAAG's initiative against human trafficking.[12]

The other corporation on McKenna's multisector leadership council was Microsoft. Its inclusion was due to more than just being headquartered in McKenna's state. According to the Global Sourcing Council, Microsoft is known as a leader in corporate social responsibility. Its global Citizenship Program was launched in 2002; it has consistently addressed multiple facets of human trafficking as well as other human rights issues. Microsoft's anti-trafficking efforts have several prongs. Among them are the eradication of forced labor within its supply chains and the development of technology that can be deployed to disrupt trafficking. In statements regarding the latter, Microsoft acknowledges that because digital technologies are employed by traffickers as well as by law enforcement, they have had both positive and negative impacts on trafficking.[13] Microsoft aims "to advance public under-standing of human rights implications of ICT [information and communication technology] and explore the role business can play in driving respect for human rights" through its Technology and Human Rights Center.[14] The "PhotoDNA" software released by Microsoft's Digital Crimes Unit in 2009 and donated to the National Center for Missing and Exploited Children is arguably Microsoft's most significant contribution to date toward disrupting online sex trafficking. Using PhotoDNA, analysts can create a "fingerprint" of a facial image and use that fingerprint to identify additional instances of that image (including resized and recolored variants) in large datasets. Employed by law enforcement agencies and sublicensed by other technology companies (including Facebook), PhotoDNA has enabled the recovery of child victims of sex trafficking and disrupted the online distribution of child pornography.[15]

Together with the Digital Crimes Unit, Microsoft Research initiated a cross-sector, multidisciplinary research network in 2012 by offering grants via a request for proposals for studies on the role of technology in sex trafficking. Six of the submissions were funded, catalyzing research on such topics as the following:

- How networked technologies, including the Internet, mobile phones, and social media, are used in the recruiting, selling, and buying of victims of sex trafficking.
- How law enforcement takes advantage of the benefits—and overcomes the obstacles—of using technology to combat the trafficking of children for commercial sexual exploitation.
- How identifying the clandestine language that is used in web advertising of child sex trafficking and conceptualizing intelligent software can aid in identifying such online advertisements.[16]

In addition to supporting the development of knowledge about technology and sex trafficking, the leaders of this initiative in Microsoft Research, Rane Johnson-Stempson and danah boyd, aimed to create a multidisciplinary community of academic researchers that could become a resource for "practitioners and advocacy groups" working against trafficking.[17] Toward that end, in 2012 and 2013 Johnson-Stempson, boyd, and colleagues organized several events during which researchers presented their work. These events were attended by people from a mix of sectors. Findings from studies conducted by this network have also been presented at anti-trafficking conferences organized by other entities, such as the annual Interdisciplinary Conference on Human Trafficking at the University of Nebraska. Johnson-Stempson has also represented Microsoft on multisector committees convened by the White House Office of Science and Technology Policy to generate strategies for improving cross-sector information sharing with law enforcement and online outreach to trafficking victims.[18]

In describing his efforts to cofound the gBCAT, David Arkless acknowledged that "by publicly taking a stand on trafficking, many [businesses] feared that the public would assume they faced problems on this issue and 'were trying to cover something up.'" However, based on Arkless's experience with corporations in anti-trafficking efforts, his advice to business leaders is that "when you get involved in something like this your employees will love it, the public will love it and your shareholders will love it."[19] The track records of each of the companies discussed above confirm Arkless's advice. These companies also demonstrate that the power to act and influence increases as organizations develop strong anti-trafficking policies for themselves and in turn offer leadership within their industry or sector, as well as in multisector efforts. Their cases also illustrate how proactive, strategic positioning enables organizations to influence public understanding of the potential for their industry or sector to contribute to the prevention or disruption of trafficking.

PLATFORMING OTHER ORGANIZATIONS

In addition to increasing power by strategically positioning one's own organization within a sector, leaders in one sector have opportunities to help increase or diminish the power of other sectors, through platforming or marginalizing other leaders. Put simply, when a leader from a higher status sector, such as a business, platforms a leader from a lower status sector, such as a nonprofit, the power of the lower status sector increases, at least for the duration of the event. At times a lower status entity platforms a higher status entity, such as when academics persuade government officials to speak at a conference, or a nonprofit director gets a business leader to agree to join its board. This situation may also be a power boost for the lower status entity, though perhaps a lesser one. Both types of interorganizational platforming convey the respect of the inviter for the invitee, and both grant the invitee a modicum of power—that is, the opportunity to say yes or no. However, status differences between inviter and invitee organizations cast different meanings on invitations even when they are worded similarly. But either way, sector leaders that platform another sector's leaders often benefit from doing so. The potential gains are accessing a different form of expertise or perspective, combined with demonstrating the inviter's ability to persuade another sector to collaborate (a form of status in itself). Receiving such invitations is also a status boost; it validates the organization's or person's contributions to anti-trafficking efforts and boosts visibility. In cross-sector invitations, both the inviting and invited organizations stand to gain power to influence others, within their own sector and in the other sector.

Consider a brief instance of these dynamics at play. Let's say an attorney in private practice with expertise on how anti-trafficking laws affect businesses is asked to speak at an event organized by a nonprofit for business representatives. When the nonprofit nets a credible person from a high-status profession who has valued expertise, that nonprofit gains status both among other nonprofits and in the estimation of the businesspeople it hopes will attend its event. The attorney potentially gains visibility, credibility, and influence: Her practice is featured in public, which might bring in more clients. She is featured as an expert, which puts a stamp of legitimacy on her talents, and she is given a forum for persuading business leaders to act in the ways she recommends. This example demonstrates that while the benefits may not be equal, platforming a person or organization at a different status level can potentially enhance both high- and low-status players.

THE SPECTRUM OF COLEADERSHIP

We have seen how platforming someone from another sector, or being platformed, can be beneficial to both parties. However, it should also be noted that doing the inviting brings more power than being invited. For the initiator, there are significant differences between platforming a representative from another sector versus inviting that person to colead. In platforming as a form of collaboration, the initiator invites someone to carry out a particular function determined by the inviter. Think of interorganizational coleadership between two or more organizations as a spectrum of coleadership. Platforming can be seen as representing one end of the spectrum with consensus-based partnership at the other, with a variety of collaboration structures arrayed be-

tween those ends based on the power relations of each. When one organization or person platforms another, the initiator retains power over the invitee.
Typically, the invitee's contribution is limited to what has been requested by
the inviter. As the collaboration moves toward the center of the spectrum, the
initiator shares an increasing amount of power with the invitee; the invitee is
able to contribute more toward developing the overall plan for and structure
of the collaboration. At the far end of the collaboration structure spectrum,
opposite to platforming, the initiator asks another leader to partner equally
in coleading the collaboration. This kind of collaboration structure employs
a consensus-based decision-making model, where plans are developed jointly
with full agreement among the coleaders.[20]

Immediate consensus is rare because it requires alignments on values,
priorities, and modes of action—core precepts that are likely to differ across
sectors. A willingness to compromise is what makes possible the negotiation
of consensus between organizations. As an example of coleadership through
negotiated consensus, the leader of an anti-trafficking nonprofit contacted
the leaders of a statewide business association, offering to train their members
on human trafficking. The business association leaders agreed that training
on human trafficking would be beneficial, but they wanted the opportunity
to review the training materials developed by the nonprofit. The nonprofit
agreed, and what transpired was a collaborative editing process. The nonprofit leader characterized it this way:

> We had numerous meetings with [the business association's] representatives
> to hash out the best practices and training material. They held a lot of power
> in this relationship because at any point they could say, "No, we won't support
> this," and our project would immediately lose momentum and credibility. This
> [collaborative editing] wasn't the fastest way to do it or the way I would have
> chosen, but it was what they wanted and [the training materials] ended up be-
> ing much better in the long run. Far far higher quality and relevance. And much
> more engagement from [the people who attended the trainings]. (Interview)

One wrinkle was that the business association requested a substantial
revision: the removal of a section on a topic that the nonprofit thought was
important and that the association considered too sensitive to introduce in a
general training. Though the nonprofit had good reasons for wanting to keep
the sensitive section in the training, it agreed to the removal of that section.

Having agreed on the materials, negotiating the agenda for the initial training went relatively smoothly, and all of the collaborating leaders viewed the event as a success. The two organizations continued to collaborate, and the nonprofit was able to incorporate information on the sensitive topic into subsequent trainings. As the nonprofit leader explained:

> After that first training . . . we did add in a section [on the sensitive topic] and have continued to include this section without [the business association's] express "permission"—we just did it and informed them—and [the association] has continued to be a cohost for the trainings. It was just that initial training that was very difficult and scary for them, so we compromised to make sure it would happen. (Interview)

The nonprofit in this relationship demonstrated its willingness to respect limits of the association's comfort zone, and both entities demonstrated a willingness to persevere in working together. We will explore the importance of such respect and perseverance further in chapter 6.

Unsurprisingly, anti-trafficking leaders across sectors perceive significant differences between being platformed versus being invited to colead as partners. In interviews, I asked people from every sector how collaborations are initiated and about how they had responded to those invitations. Most expressed awareness of and sensitivity to differences in proposed collaboration structures and the power relations they manifest. In the course of my fieldwork, I witnessed many failed attempts at collaboration. In a significant number, the invitees turned down an invitation to participate in an event, campaign, or program because they wanted to co-organize rather than simply be platformed. Some who declined felt marginalized, resentful that their potential contribution was prescribed or otherwise constrained by the initiator. Invitees who saw themselves as more experienced or more professionally expert in anti-trafficking work than the initiator were sometimes offended by a platforming invitation that they perceived to disregard or disrespect their credentials. Some invitees told collaboration initiators that they would have preferred to be invited to colead; others simply declined. When invitees did not agree with the overall aim or strategy of the initiator, many declined platforming invitations, and would not have accepted the invitation to colead even if that had been offered. But a few interviewees said that they sometimes accept platforming invitations even when they disagree with the initiator's aim or strategy in order to try to influence the initiator. They explained that they were aware that their participation could be perceived as condoning that with which they disagree, but that they viewed the opportunity for influence as worth the potential cost of being misconstrued.

In sum, the spectrum of coleadership is broad, and there are many varieties of collaboration relationships that are possible within it. The strategy of platforming other organizations is important and can be affirming and beneficial to all involved. However, it can also be perceived negatively by invitees. So it is important, before issuing a platforming invitation, to consider the risks of platforming and the possible array of acceptable coleadership options.

SURVIVOR-ACTIVISTS' PERSPECTIVES ON PLATFORMING AND PARTNERING

Those who spoke most often and most intently about the differences between platformed or invited to partner were survivor-activists. They recounted occasions in which they were invited to participate in a cross-sector collaboration, but only within the narrowly prescribed form of "telling their stories" of exploitation and recovery. They explained that the problem with such platforming invitations is that they feel their other forms of knowledge and expertise, such as ones involving therapeutic insights, mobilization skills, and policy recommendations, were to be left behind the door. The only status gain possible would be to their roles as authentic experience-based spokespeople; their qualifications in other areas, in fact, would lose status by being ignored.

One might expect such stories to date from less enlightened times, but unfortunately, I witnessed some such instances in my fieldwork. At some of the multisector events on human trafficking that I attended, survivor-activists were slated to present together on a "survivors' panel" in which the moderator asked them to relate various aspects of their experiences, but not their recommendations on anti-trafficking efforts. In a few (but too few) instances, I witnessed survivor-activists platformed in broader ways. In these cases, even when the agenda was predetermined by event organizers, survivor-activists were encouraged to provide recommendations as well as to discuss their experiences.

To illustrate, organizers representing the National Association of Attorneys General planned an event on human trafficking in which they platformed as speakers both a representative of the U.S. Department of Homeland Security and a survivor-activist. The DHS representative spoke before the survivor-activist, stating, among other things, that "successful prosecution of traffickers requires the active participation of empowered victims to speak out about their abuse and trauma." (This kind of statement is common, and widely agreed upon across sectors, although many in the victim services and survivor-activist sectors challenge the implied prioritization of prosecuting traffickers.) For the purposes of this analysis, the key aspect of this statement is how it prescribes what is most important for "empowered victims" to do—that is, to "speak out about their abuse and trauma." When the survivor-activist spoke later on in the program, she went beyond that prescription and used the platform to make a case for empowering victims of trafficking in order to help them become activists and raise public awareness and understanding of trafficking. In doing so, she both called for and modeled a multifaceted role for survivor-activists.[21]

Survivor-activists have more to offer than the relating of their stories for the general expansion of the audience's conceptions of trafficking. Minh Dang is a survivorship expert who holds an MSW, has significant experience in service learning, and writes extensively about anti-trafficking efforts. In Dang's foreword to Laura Murphy's edited volume of survivors' narratives, she calls on nonsurvivors to invite survivor-activists to do more than raise awareness:

> I urge all of you to continue to partner with survivors—to ask survivors not just about their stories, but also about their policy recommendations, their ideas for improved intervention, as well as their hopes and concerns for the movement.[22]

Dang's charge is echoed in the federal government's Strategic Action Plan (SAP), which instructs federal agencies to "integrate survivor experiences *and* input" (emphasis added):

> Responses to victimization must retain a focus on the needs, beliefs, and interests of the victims. The Federal Government recognizes that engaging survivors in anti-human trafficking leadership and decisionmaking is imperative to providing effective services. This is a core value of the Plan, implicitly woven through each goal and often discussed in federal interagency meetings.

Feedback received during the public comment period reinforced the importance of this effort. Survivors expressed a desire to do more than share their stories to educate the public about human trafficking; they want to be included in the development of programs, policies, strategies, and materials. Federal agencies . . . will work . . . to develop a collaborative approach to explore partnerships with survivor groups in order to seek ongoing input from survivors on initiatives and policies.[23]

In various documents on anti-trafficking efforts from federal sources preceding the SAP, the inclusion of survivors and their perspectives was "encouraged" or "recommended." So the SAP's characterization of "engaging survivors in anti-trafficking leadership and decision-making" as "imperative" and the pledge to "seek [their] ongoing input . . . on initiatives and policies" marks a distinct shift toward coleadership.

In January 2014, representatives of the survivor-activist sector were invited to two events in Washington, D.C., to address audiences composed of U.S. Senate and White House staffers and representatives from five federal agencies. Nineteen survivor-activists participated in a first-of-its-kind "Human Trafficking Survivor Forum and Listening Session," developed in response to public comments received during the development of the SAP; symbolically, a White House representative announced the publication of the finalized version of the SAP during the survivor forum. Having selected a panel of survivors with geographic, gender, and experiential diversity from among those who expressed interest in participating, the DOJ's Office for Victims of Crime convened a daylong meeting attended by over forty representatives from the White House Domestic Policy Council, the DOJ's Attorney General's Office and Office of Justice, the Department of Health and Human Services, and the Department of Homeland Security. Survivors were invited to provide "input on a number of issues, including how Federal Government agencies can collaborate to engage survivor groups and incorporate their perspectives in federal anti-trafficking efforts."[24] The chief convener referred to the forum as a way for the federal government to bring life to President Obama's public pledge to survivors from September 2012: "We see you. We hear you. We insist on your dignity."[25]

Later in January 2014, five survivorship experts addressed the U.S. Senate with their views on trafficking-relevant laws. In addition to commenting on two bills under discussion in Congress at that time, the survivorship experts at the Senate briefing advocated for the following (survivorship-experts' names are shown in parentheses after each request):

- Stronger regulations on foreign labor recruiters, since fraudulent labor contractors lure desperate foreign workers to the United States with promises of better jobs (Shandra Woworuntu)
- US government training for law enforcers, community leaders, educators, and government officials to learn how to properly identify and profile trafficking victims (Ima Matul)
- Law enforcement officers' treatment of survivors of commercial sexual exploitation as victims and not criminals, because a prostitution arrest hurts the survivor's chances of finding a job (Beth Jacobs)
- An increase in services such as art therapy, psychological counseling, and medical care for survivors, and in school-based education on human trafficking (Margeaux Gray)
- Increased funding for the Labor Department so it can incorporate an anti-trafficking approach across its programs (James Kofi Annan)
- Quick implementation of the goals listed in the recently published Federal Human Trafficking Strategic Action Plan (Ima Matul)

Adding to these recommendations for policy changes within the United States, James Kofi Annan, a trafficking survivor who leads anti-trafficking efforts in Ghana, urged the US government to put pressure on Ghana's government to implement its own trafficking laws. He also praised the U.S. State Department's *Trafficking in Persons Report* for holding African leaders accountable for combatting slavery.[26]

Public statements by some of the participants in the survivor forum attested that it was a positive experience for them. Bukola Oriola, who describes herself as an advocate, entrepreneur, mentor, and author, as well as a survivor, wrote this about the survivor forum:

> When I received the official invitation to join 19 other survivors of human trafficking across the United States, to participate in a Survivors Forum and Listening Session, I did not know exactly what to expect in actual fact. I had a mixed feeling—I was happy on one hand to have been selected for this presti-

gious assignment; on the other hand, however, I was anxious. I was anxious to know whether the federal government really meant what it said about engaging survivors to provide expert opinions on how to better serve victims and survivors of human trafficking in the United States. . . .

Well, I was not disappointed. The session was great. The government officials did as promised. They listened to us speak. We bare[d] our hearts to these people, who showed great concern for change for the better for victims and survivors in the United States. They were willing to consider every suggestion and paid attention to every detail we provided. In fact, there were white pieces of paper on the wall where we were supposed to post our written suggestions on sticky notes. I was surprised that they even had a paper on the wall called, "The parking lot." *The Parking Lot* was for posting ideas that were not mentioned in the discussion but burning on our minds. The moderator said, "We are going to look and read every suggestion out there."

Another gesture from these passionate agencies' representatives was the fact that they thought about survivors who could not make it to the session. They even asked us to tell them what some survivors had told us that we could share, because the government is thinking about all survivors and victims at large. That gesture showed me that there is hope for victims and survivors of human trafficking in the United States. It was also interesting to know that the department of labor was represented in this discussion, in order to provide jobs for survivors.

Overall, it was a great forum and listening session.[27]

The ambivalence Bukola described feeling when she received the invitation to participate in the forum is not surprising; many survivor-activists have experienced marginalization by government representatives and others. The experience she conveyed in this post, of having been listened to well, was clearly a turning point for her.

A second participant, Harold D'Souza, who had earned advanced degrees in his native country before being deceived into enslavement in the United States, was similarly effusive about the forum:

The "Survivor Forum" was focused, informative and meaningful. It was simply amazing to experience the effort, detailing, networking and interaction with several top Federal Government partners at The White House Conference Center. The OVC staff is so passionate, dedicated and committed towards survivors and involved in anti-human trafficking efforts. They have been working over a year to partner with the White House, several top Federal Government officials and to engage survivors like us for an effective, positive, productive and meaningful outcome.[28]

These events demonstrate the federal government's intention to incorporate the insights of survivorship experts into government agencies' anti-trafficking efforts. While such steps are essential, they are not sufficient. For survivor-activists to feel fully integrated in the anti-trafficking movement, there will need to be more frequent and more robust experiments with co-leadership between them and leaders from other sectors.

There is a range of ways that the survivor-activist sector and other sectors have interfaced in the context of anti-trafficking efforts in the United States over the past decade. One of a handful of nongovernmental organizations whose leadership structures reflect the ideal of coleadership between survivor-activists and leaders from other sectors is the Sun Gate Foundation, which provides education support via scholarships to trafficking survivors. Although it was founded in 2013 by two nonsurvivors, it describes itself as a survivor-led organization, and in 2014 the nonsurvivor cofounders selected survivorship expert Shamere McKenzie to be its CEO. However, collaborations that reflect any form of shared leadership beyond platforming have been few, in part because of the status differential between legally defined or profession-defined sectors and the survivor-activist sector.

A successful example of shared leadership was initiated by the Coalition to Abolish Slavery and Trafficking (CAST), founded in Los Angeles in 1998. In 2003, nonsurvivor leaders of CAST helped survivor-activists organize a Survivor Advisory Caucus that has grown in scope and strength over the last decade. Together, members have had a direct impact in catalyzing stronger protections for trafficking victims, both in California where CAST is based, and, through the Caucus's input on federal laws, across the United States.[29] Leveraging the successes and lessons learned in the Caucus, CAST launched a National Survivor Network in 2011 that included, by the end of 2014, members from at least twenty-five US states and twenty-four countries.[30] The Network's aims are to "foster connections between survivors of diverse forms of human trafficking, in order to build an anti-trafficking movement where survivors are at the forefront and recognized as leaders" and to support and encourage "survivors to realize their own leadership qualities and to value their insight not just as survivors but as experts in the field."[31] The phrasing of these aims confirms the data from my study: that many survivors perceive themselves as having been marginalized by nonsurvivor anti-trafficking leaders rather than recognized as coleaders. One form of evidence for their perception comes from a systematic analysis of hundreds of US news articles about human trafficking, which found that the survivors (and their advocates) were the least frequently quoted sources.[32] The Network's aim of encouraging survivors to value the insights they have "not just as survivors but as experts in the field" points again to the pattern survivors have faced repeatedly—that of being asked to limit their talk to their stories of victimization and escape and leave behind views on how best to counter human trafficking or to care for victims.

FINANCES AND PARTNERING IN LEADERSHIP

The importance of wages to those who were once enslaved is difficult to overstate. It is not only a matter of principle to them that they be paid for their work. For many trafficking survivors who get by on a shoestring, compensation for time they spend on anti-trafficking efforts is a matter of necessity. It comes down to this: Survivors, like anyone else, need funds to support themselves and cover the expenses of activism to continue to act against trafficking. In every city where I conducted fieldwork and interviews, the people who participate regularly in anti-trafficking efforts are financially able to do so only when it is part of their jobs (that is, they get paid for it) or when their "day jobs" (which are typically salaried, not hourly) allow them to donate some of their discretionary time and money to countering human trafficking. For some, life circumstances—retirement, spousal support, or independent wealth—have freed them from the need to earn a wage. Among the survivor-activists I encountered in this research, most were unemployed or working in poorly paid, hourly-wage jobs. A few were paid to work against human trafficking; fewer still were in salaried jobs that enabled them to feel they could afford to volunteer some time on anti-trafficking efforts.

Of course, survivor-activists are not the only ones in the anti-trafficking movement constrained by hourly-wage jobs. The federal e-Guide includes an anecdote that illustrates that victim service providers are also sometimes constrained by the restrictions of their jobs:

One [salaried] law enforcement task force member became increasingly frustrated at the lack of availability of a case manager after hours. Once the case manager explained that she was paid hourly and had to receive permission to flex her hours, the two worked together to plan a weekly schedule [for joint work].[33]

Although there are many hourly-wage people in law enforcement as well as victim services and other fields who voluntarily work unreportable and unpaid hours to help counter trafficking, this anecdote also demonstrates the importance of communicating explicitly within a collaboration about the job schedules and constraints and volunteer capacity.

Since there are only twenty-four hours to each day, everyone who gives their time to work on a societal problem or to help others is giving up something in order to volunteer. Whether the sacrifice is time with family or friends, work, hobbies, or sleep, there is always a cost to volunteering. For many survivors (and for others who live with little financial cushion), the struggle to survive daily life precludes participation in anti-trafficking efforts. It is a manifestation of the old truism that "whoever can pay gets to play." In multisector collaborations against human trafficking, those from the survivor-activist sector are often absent from the table because they cannot afford the costs of getting there or of spending time on non-income-producing activities. As other researchers of interorganizational collaboration have noted, when actors with precarious power positions miss meetings, those absences further diminish their standing and influence in the collaboration.[34]

In view of this pattern, it can be maddening, if not outright insulting, when survivors are asked to volunteer their time in situations where nonsurvivors are getting paid to lead anti-trafficking efforts, provide services to victims, or to educate others about human trafficking. On the National Survivor Network's webpage on the availability of some survivors for consultations and trainings, there is a telling statement:

Several members of the National Survivor Network (NSN) regularly speak on the issue of human trafficking, as well as offer training and technical consultation to a variety of audiences and agencies. . . . Please note that every individual charges a speakers fee or honorarium, which will vary by individual. Travel and accommodations for speakers should be covered by the requesting organization.[35]

The fact that the NSN considers it necessary to make this statement suggests that the NSN speakers feel they have been taken advantage of previously by others in the anti-trafficking movement.

Despite recent efforts by leaders in several sectors to highlight the importance of survivor-activists to anti-trafficking work, there is still an ongoing and destructive cycle in which the marginalization of survivor-activists and lack of funding for their work disempowers them by constraining their capacity to act, much less to influence others' actions. The dynamics of that cycle look like this: When survivors are unemployed, they are necessarily focused on finding paid work and minimizing nonessential expenses, such as the bus fare or gas money it takes to get to meetings on anti-trafficking efforts. Those who hold full-time jobs with typically low hourly wages risk losing income and incurring additional expenses by participating in anti-trafficking efforts. In order to participate regularly in even local efforts, survivors, like everyone else, must have the kind of income that is not reduced by their participation in non-income-generating activities. In order to participate in higher-level anti-trafficking work, such as conferences, expert trainings, and advocacy on state or federal policies and programs, survivor-activists must have the funds to cover registration fees, train or airplane tickets, hotel rooms, and other travel-related expenses. On several occasions, after local anti-trafficking meetings during which some higher-level event or opportunity was announced, I casually and privately asked the survivor-activists who were present whether they intended to participate. Each time, the response I got was, "I wish I could, but I can't afford to." Their precarious finances constrained their ability to participate in the very events and efforts that could benefit most from their input. Informed by the concerns of survivor-activists and intent on including them in meaningful ways, some US government agencies and NGOs raise and allocate funds specifically for the purpose of supporting survivor-activists as participants—and occasionally coplanners—of higher-level anti-trafficking events. Such efforts need to be multiplied if survivor-activists are to take the participatory or formative roles in anti-trafficking work that their experiences and skills merit.

SUMMARY

As we have seen in this chapter, when individuals from different sectors come together to work against human trafficking, their positioning in larger sector and societal systems affects their interactions. The ways organizations lever-age their positions, and the collaboration structures they create, can either bolster or diminish the power of other organizations as well as their own. In addition to these systemic dynamics, individuals bring with them personal and embodied differences in perspective and power. Some of these, specifi-cally race and gender, we will explore in the next chapter.

4

Race and Gender in Multisector Anti-Trafficking Efforts

A BLACK MALE ABOLITIONIST'S PERSPECTIVE

At an anti-trafficking event one evening, the room was buzzing with conversations among about thirty leaders from the business and nonprofit sectors. I noticed an African American man who appeared to be in his late fifties working his way around the room introducing himself to other attendees. He was the only non-Caucasian in the room. When he came near, I initiated a handshake and introduced myself. After chatting for a few minutes, he mentioned he had recently relocated to the northern-US city in which this event took place. I asked where he had moved from, and he named a city in a southern state. After talking a while longer, I asked what had brought him to the northern city. Gazing intently at me, he said first, "Now I don't want you to change the way you're looking at me when I tell you this." I nodded, agreeing. He said, in slowly formed phrases, that he had lost his daughter, that she had been trafficked, that he got her back once, but that then she was trafficked again and killed. He maintained eye contact through all of those statements, despite the tears welling in his eyes. Trying to keep my promise to him, I willed the tears back from mine without looking away. "After that, I knew I had to spend whatever time I'm not working for my job, working against trafficking. But as a black man," and with those words he averted his eyes and looked down, "I couldn't do anything in my old city. People like me are not welcome in anti-trafficking work there. So I decided to move north, and see if I could find a way to volunteer against trafficking in a different kind of place." He met my eyes again, then looked around the room, then back at me, smiling gently. "So far it feels like this was the right move." I found myself hoping his sense of being accepted would persist as he became more involved in anti-trafficking efforts in his new city. (Fieldnote)

I did not set out to study race or gender in collaborative anti-trafficking efforts. That is because none of the books I had read from organizational studies of collaboration before launching this research mentioned either as even a potential influence on collaboration. Before writing this chapter, I double-checked ten prominent books on managing collaboration to see if any of them mentioned gender or race. None did. So I will hardly be shocked if seeing a chapter on gender and race in this book surprises you. Yet race and gender do influence the way collaborations function, and they do so in anti-trafficking efforts.

In chapter 1, I explained that individuals who represent organizations are those through whom interorganizational collaboration takes place. Obviously, every individual has a body that is raced and gendered, as well as a unique mix of cultural background, education, sector experience, and personal and professional beliefs and values. I have already mentioned that a field analyst of interorganizational collaboration examines what is observable—that is, groups of people talking. In the same way, every individual involved in interorganizational collaboration experiences that process through interactions with particular, embodied others. When organizations collaborate, it is these people who work together in ways that integrate the individual, group, organizational, and sector levels in which their work is situated. So the characteristics and sense of identity carried by individuals are consequential to interorganizational interactions at every level.[1]

Based on research about how such patterns affect communication between people in other contexts, we can expect race and gender patterns to matter in anti-trafficking collaborations. Starting in the 1970s, many studies have examined patterns of gender and race in teams, organizations, community organizing, and professional networks. Nearly all conclude that race and gender are among the factors that make a difference in how people think, feel, interact, work, and organize themselves and others.[2] Because multisector collaboration consists of practices of thinking, feeling, interacting, working, and organizing, we must examine how efforts to collaborate against trafficking can be affected by race and gender in addition to the sector-based economic, status, and professional power differentials we looked at in chapters 2 and 3, and the influence of differences in beliefs and values that we will consider in chapter 5. In this chapter, I first describe patterns in the race and gender demographics of anti-trafficking actors and trafficking victims. Then I explain how such demographic differences—in combination with attitudes and emotions about gender and race—can affect collaborative anti-trafficking efforts. Finally, I identify some gaps and redundancies in such efforts that can result from collaborating primarily with people who share our respective gender or race, and identify some ways to diversify collaborations without "tokenizing" people.

RACE AND GENDER PATTERNS

Although markers of professional and class distinctions are not always apparent, race and gender demographics are generally more obvious. Early in my fieldwork I had noticed that at most meetings and events, the rooms were disproportionately filled with women. After attending my first couple of anti-trafficking meetings, I decided that along with keeping track of the total number of attendees at each meeting and how many representatives there were from each sector, I would track the ratios of women to men. And since I would be counting male noses (assuming that there would typically be fewer of them), I would also count noses that were any color other than shades of Caucasian white. Since my purpose was simply to get a general sense of how numerically dominant white women are in anti-trafficking efforts, I erred on the side of underestimating by counting people with ambiguous gender or racial features as men and nonwhites.[3]

Across all the meetings and events I attended in seven racially diverse cities across five states, the ratio of whites to nonwhites among attendees was typically somewhere between four to one and nine to one, and sometimes higher. Since Caucasians comprise about 75 percent of the US population, these statistics mean that somewhat smaller proportions of people of color in the United States participate in anti-trafficking efforts as do Caucasians. There were always more women than men in attendance at the meetings I attended, but the ratio varied more than the ratio of whites to nonwhites; it depended on the type of event and the sectors involved in it. At meetings in which the nonprofit and NGO sector had the strongest presence, the ratio of women to men was sometimes as high as nine to one. Women far outnumbered men in nearly every nonprofit and NGO-centered meeting. At meetings that included representatives from the private sector or law enforcement, the ratio of women to men dropped to as low as three to two, coming closer to a proportional participation level. The only occasions I observed in which men were the majority were meetings focused on the law enforcement sector.

Although these were basic-level assessments, I am confident that the gender and race patterns I observed among the attendees of anti-trafficking meetings are representative of this period in anti-trafficking efforts in the United States. In a nutshell, white women constitute the largest demographic group involved in anti-trafficking efforts, especially in the MANGO (mobilization and advocacy nongovernmental organization) and victim services sectors.

My observations correspond with public data about the demographics of law enforcement and social service providers. In a national survey of more than 10,000 licensed social workers in the United States, 81 percent of respondents were female and 85 percent were white.[4] In the most recent analyses of US law enforcement demographics available, women represented 13 percent of sworn police officers and 15 percent of the agents working for the three federal agencies primarily involved in human trafficking investigations (Customs and Border Patrol [CBP], Immigrations and Customs Enforcement [ICE], and the Federal Bureau of Investigation [FBI]).[5] Racial minorities comprise 45 percent of CBP agents, 37 percent of ICE agents, and 18 percent of FBI agents.[6] In US municipal police departments, minorities make up one quarter of the police force on average. More significantly, in hundreds of police departments across the country, the percentage of whites on the force is more than 30 percent higher than in the communities they serve.[7]

In contrast, federal analyses of cases of trafficking in the United States show that across all forms of trafficking, victims who have been identified by law enforcement agencies or victim service providers are disproportionately non-Caucasian and female.[8] In recent US government data on the race and gender of people law enforcement agencies or victim service providers have identified as trafficking victims, the racial disparities are striking. In 2011, although Caucasians make up 75 percent of the US population, 98 percent of identified labor trafficking victims and 74 percent of the victims of commercial sex trafficking were non-Caucasians.[9] A closer look at the data shows that although African Americans represent 13 percent of the total US population, they made up 40 percent of the sex trafficking victims (and 10 percent of the labor trafficking victims).[10] Hispanics and Latinas were significantly overrepresented in both: they comprised 24 percent of the sex trafficking victims and 58 percent of the labor trafficking victims (while making up 16 percent of the US population). The percent of Asian American victims of sex trafficking victims was equivalent to their proportion of the US population (about 4 percent), but Asians were victims in 15 percent of the labor trafficking cases. Collectively these statistics demonstrate that non-Caucasians are disproportionately victimized at astounding levels in human trafficking crimes in the United States.

Moreover, trafficking crimes often involve egregious discrimination based on gender, race, or national origin as well. The US Equal Employment Opportunity Commission (which participates in investigations of some human trafficking cases) notes the following:

> Trafficking cases often involve discrimination on the basis of national origin or race. Even when employees are legally brought into this country, employers may discriminate on the basis of national origin or race through the use of force, fraud, or coercion. This discrimination may include harassment and setting different terms and conditions of employment. It also may include retaliation against workers for exercising their rights under the anti-discrimination laws by threatening them with or subjecting them to suspension from work, deportation, physical harm, or fraud. In trafficking cases, it is not unusual for employers to maintain segregated jobs, pay unequal wages, or deduct unreasonable amounts from paychecks in these situations. . . . Many labor trafficking cases involve sexual exploitation. Trafficked women are sometimes sexually assaulted or subjected to other severe sexual harassment.[11]

In other words, in addition to the traumas that victims endure from force, fraud, or coercion in trafficking, their exploiters often expressly use their race, gender, or national origin against them. This additional layer of victimization is triggered by the race and gender of victims' bodies, in addition to whatever other factors rendered them vulnerable to trafficking crimes. An implication is that when people of color, and especially women of color, are underrepresented in anti-trafficking efforts, the anti-trafficking movement misses opportunities to benefit from their experiences and their insights into ways to counter various forms of trafficking crimes. The Washington Anti-Trafficking Response Network (WARN) is one multi-NGO partnership in which male and female Caucasians and people of color (with various national origins) collaborate to provide a range of culturally competent, multilingual, trauma-informed expert services for victims of every form of trafficking.[12] Led by the staff at the International Rescue Committee of Seattle, WARN's partner organizations include the Refugee Women's Alliance, API Chaya, the Northwest Justice Project Farm Workers Unit, YouthCare, and Lutheran Community Services Northwest. WARN affiliates take a client-empowerment approach, seeking to support clients in whatever way they themselves determine they need to rebuild their lives after having been trafficked. From finding affordable housing and job training to connecting clients with healthcare services and providing support during legal proceedings, WARN member organizations coordinate closely with each other regarding each client's needs, often for months and sometimes for years.

Some people of color who want to participate in anti-trafficking efforts told me that they feel excluded by the mere fact that they are often a distinct, visible minority. The first time I spoke publicly on my observations about race and gender patterns among trafficking victims and anti-trafficking actors was at a weekend event designed to help foster multisector collaboration against trafficking. We were meeting in a racially diverse city, with leaders from several sectors including MANGOs, schools, civic groups, and law enforcement. I invited the crowd of about 200 to scan the faces around the room with me. I noted that although this group was diverse in terms of sector, there were many more women than men in the room, and very few people of color—fewer than a dozen, according to my quick count. After stating that I had noticed similar patterns at anti-trafficking meetings in every city where I had attended them, I acknowledged that as a white, middle-aged woman, I'm part of the "majority" in anti-trafficking efforts, prone to assuming that the way things are is just fine. I posed some questions about possible reasons and implications, in the form of "I wonder why . . . ?" and "I wonder whether . . . ?" I encouraged attendees to discuss such questions with their collaborators and invited them to share their reflections with me as well.

When the session in which I spoke ended, a dozen attendees queued up to talk with me, including several people of color. Their feedback was emotionally charged, yet strongly positive. I was quite moved by the comments of an African American man—the only one in the room that day. Choked up and with halting words, he told me that he owns his own business, which gives him the flexibility to do some volunteering. He lives in a wealthy, largely white, suburb, and regularly attends anti-trafficking MANGO meetings there and in the city. "At many meetings, I am the only black man in the room, like I am today. I feel like I'm a neon sign and invisible at the same time. People don't know what to make of me. I think some wonder if I'm a recovering pimp. I'm a dad with four kids who wants to help stop human trafficking. I know that lots of domestic victims are black, and lots of black boys think being a pimp is cool. I want to help reach black kids, but nobody I know talks about that." We chatted for a few minutes, and I urged him to start the conversations he wants to be part of. His parting words to me were, "Please keep talking about race."

That interaction illustrates how a pressing issue that brings people together—in this case, the desire to stop trafficking—can hide in its skirts substantive issues that influence the outcomes of the very process designed to forward joint efforts. Unrepresentative race and gender distribution among the actors in anti-trafficking collaborations has subtle, but important, effects. Let's go on to explore them further.

HOW RACE AND GENDER AFFECT ANTI-TRAFFICKING EFFORTS

The following incident is not one I witnessed. Rather, it is an account, authored by a well-known and respected nonsurvivor anti-trafficking leader and published with the approval of the survivor she describes, of an awareness-raising event intended for elected officials.[13]

Here is the story. Having been invited to speak to an audience of elected officials (a group who, according to US government statistics, are overwhelmingly white and male), the nonsurvivor anti-trafficking activist decided to asked the National Survivor Network (NSN) whether there was a locally based survivor willing to share the speaking podium with her, believing that "a survivor of human trafficking would be her or his own best advocate." This was an instance of the best kind of platforming, introduced in chapter 3. There was, indeed, a local survivor-activist willing to collaborate in this way. Later on, when the nonsurvivor wrote about the event, she praised the survivor's courage and insights. She also recalled the following:

> [The survivor] walked on stage, a lovely, professional-looking blonde woman, looking every bit the part of a conservative politician's daughter. She then further disarmed the audience by projecting a picture of her 14-year-old self hanging out with her young friends. Any preconception that underage sex trafficking could only happen to *other people's children* flew right out the window.[14] (Emphasis in the original)

In analyzing this account through the lenses of race and gender, I am not criticizing either the survivor or the nonsurvivor. I do not know how this particular survivor came to be the one who shared the stage with the nonsurvivor. It is possible the nonsurvivor's invitation was directed specifically to that survivor by someone in the NSN for some reason, or perhaps that survivor was the only person who responded to the general request the nonsurvivor made via the NSN. The nonsurvivor, a white, professional woman herself, described the scene as she perceived it, affirming the survivor.

Her description, though, articulates a dynamic that many survivors of color rail against. In their words, whites only start to care about trafficking when they realize that it happens to people who look like them or their children. The nonsurvivor's account of how this dynamic functioned in a gathering of politically powerful, white men does not make her a perpetuator of the dynamic—rather, it validates the double-edged response nonwhite survivors experience when they witness whites identify with images and testimonies of white survivors. I imagine the nonsurvivor's words ring true for many survivors of color—they agree with her about what happened in that event—but raises more ire than appreciation for any support whites offer in response to it. When all is said and done, no matter what survivors of color do, no matter how hard they strive, they will not end up "looking every bit the part of a conservative politician's daughter." They know that no matter what they have suffered, their stories will not evoke the same kinds of response as did the white survivor's.

This account illustrates a critical tension about vulnerability to crime that is not unique to human trafficking crimes. The tension is between two points. The first point is that no one is fully safe from "Crime X," even more privileged populations. Articulating this validates the experiences of people in populations who are not thought to be among the victims. The second point is that some, often less privileged, populations are disproportionately victimized by Crime X. When the first point about Crime X is stressed publicly, and especially to political elites, there may be a better chance at garnering more resources to combat the crime. At the same time, in emphasizing the first point publicly, it is easy for the audience to miss the second point, which can worsen the situation for the populations who are already disproportionately impacted. In other words, if the fact that African American females are the population most likely to be victimized by sex trafficking is glossed over by anti-trafficking activists, it will be ignored by elected officials and other power brokers as well.

My intent in highlighting this story here is to invite my fellow white readers to think hard about whether and how our responses to human trafficking vary based on the hues we perceive, or imagine we perceive, in the skin of victims and survivors. Setting aside for the moment the characterization of the survivor as "professional-looking," if white survivors indeed trigger a different response from white audiences than a survivor of color would, what are the implications? When our concern about human trafficking increases because we see victims who resemble ourselves or our children, is this simply a function of basic human self-interest, or is it a form of racism? And if we recognize racism within ourselves, what do we do about it?

Keeping in mind the discussions of status and profession from chapters 2 and 3, I turn now to the nonsurvivor's description of the survivor as "professional-looking." Although the phrase is ambiguous, we can agree that it means something other than phrases describing a woman as looking slovenly or provocative. In high-status work contexts in the United States (such as the gathering of elected officials to whom the survivor spoke), the dress code calls for business attire. For women, business attire typically consists of tailored, coordinated suits with pants or knee- or calf-length skirts, blouses with conservative necklines, and closed-toe, low-heeled dress shoes, along with hosiery, minimal jewelry, and neatly styled hair.[15] Social scientists have found that women in business attire are perceived as more intelligent and capable than women in "sexy" attire such as low-cut blouses and short skirts.[16] This means a woman who can afford to dress professionally is able to position herself publicly as having status as well as intelligence and competency. These are all good things to have. But achieving and maintaining a professional appearance can be difficult for survivors of any race who struggle financially or have not been coached in this area of social mores. So the "professional appearance" of the survivor who spoke at the event described above was, on the one hand, likely to have helped her audience be receptive to her words, and on the other hand, points up the gap between her and other survivors who lack the resources or coaching to develop such an appearance.

The account I have analyzed demonstrates that ideas about race and other aspects of appearance—one's own and others'—shape attitudes. So do ideas about gender. And since everyone has both a particular skin tone and a gender (whether particular or ambiguous) that shape their interactions with society in myriad ways, race and gender affect our experiences in collaborations and elsewhere.[17] Everyone experiences race, gender, and class dynamics in organizational settings through countless interactions with the individuals and groups that comprise an organization. Each interaction shapes norms and expectations for future interactions—that is, the social order of the organization. Correspondingly, when people from different organizations interact, norms and expectations about race, gender, and class are negotiated implicitly, if not explicitly, and another form of social order is co-constructed.

Consider the reflections of a nonwhite survivor-activist on an interaction she had with a white male NGO leader:

> I want to point out how far we've come. [Five years ago] I spoke at a conference, and talked with a nationally known [white] leader whose organization is based there. I asked him "why do you think we're ignoring the kids of the street here [in the conference city]?" He replied "There aren't any on the street here." I said "Yes, there are, and I think the reason they are being ignored is that they are black kids." He gasped and excused himself quickly. But now, that organization is dealing with that. There *has* been progress. (Fieldnote; emphasis in original)

It took a lot of courage for that survivor to articulate, to a white man, her suspicion that street kids were being ignored because they are black. Her forthrightness must have shocked him. But she used three excellent rhetorical moves. First, she preceded her statement with a thought-provoking question. Second, she framed the question in the first person plural, inviting the leader to think with her. Third, she prefaced her statement with the phrase "I think," thereby positioning it subjectively, rather than making a bald declarative statement such as, "The reason they are being ignored is . . . ." It is easy to dismiss any declaration by saying "No, it's not." It is harder to disagree with or dismiss a statement that begins with "I think. . . ." Remarks like these can open up an organization to change its focus. It is possible that her comments persuaded him to think, to perceive his city and his organization's actions differently than before, and to begin the process of imagining a different form of organizational action in the future.

The internal sense that each of us has about what our gender and race means *to* us, and what others' genders and races mean *for* us, is culturally shaped and deeply rooted in our individual and (semi-)collective psyches. This shapes our perceptions of various facets of the problem of human trafficking in several ways. At a profound level, painful experiences with people—even with just one person— can imprint in us a wariness toward others of the same gender and race. In the words of one middle-aged, black, female survivor-activist who had been trafficked into commercial sexual exploitation as a child:

> Because I worked the Magnificent Mile in Chicago, most of my clients were white men. It's taken me a long time to come to trust that there are white men who are good and trustworthy, who won't nod their heads agreeing with me [professionally] during the day, and later that night [proposition me]. (Fieldnote)

There are countless white men who have interacted with this woman in anti-trafficking efforts over the years, having no idea what fear their gender-race compositions, their very beings, evoked in her. If they noticed her wariness, some may have made critical attributions about her, accusing her—in their thoughts, if not their words—of having a bad attitude, and perhaps, as a result, withdrawing from her. Such interactions most likely confirmed and deepened this survivor's wariness. But by her own account, there were other white men who (whether or not they knew she was a survivor) demonstrated respect and earned her trust, and thereby helped her heal.

The accounts I have related in this section have served to help illustrate the ways that race and gender intersect, and how larger historical patterns and societal dynamics around race and gender show up in—and influence—anti-trafficking efforts. Although race is not extricable from gender in anyone's body, within the realm of anti-trafficking efforts the dynamics of gender are more pronounced—and more frequently referenced—than race. For these reasons, the next section focuses on gender.

A Closer Look at Gender in Anti-Trafficking Efforts

When we hear accounts of people who share our gender experiencing particular types of exploitation, it is human to identify with them and imagine ourselves in their shoes, even without any explicit invitation to do so. When it comes to people who are taking certain types of action against trafficking, the same is true. In the realm of anti-trafficking efforts, though, we are often explicitly and differentially addressed based on our gender, particularly in regard to exploitation in commercial sex industries. For instance, part of the National Association of Attorneys General (NAAG) 2011–2012 "Pillars of Hope" campaign was for elected officials to "take a pledge of zero tolerance for sex trafficking." All of the state Attorneys General were urged by Indiana's Greg Zoeller to sign it. A part of Zoeller's explanation of the pledge was directed specifically to men:

> Although not all Attorneys General have jurisdiction to actually prosecute traffickers under their state laws, all Attorneys General can use their convening authority to draw attention to the issue, help to strengthen state laws by increasing penalties for both the traffickers and the customers of trafficking, and encourage collaborative models in victim protection and prosecution of the criminals involved. Finally . . . men must step up and take a leadership role in promoting zero tolerance.[18]

By tagging on a direct appeal to men to "step up" and "take a leadership role" in ending trafficking, Attorney General Zoeller was not simply implying that men drive the demand for sex trafficking by buying sex (something he could have stated directly).[19] He was also appealing to an American cultural ideal of active male leadership, a conception of masculinity implying that it is not enough for men to just be. Instead, they must be active; they must "step up" and do.

Several men who help lead anti-trafficking efforts talked with me about a sense of collective guilt they carry for the ways that many men degrade women via sexual assaults and domestic violence as well as enslavement. These men choose to focus their efforts on empowering female victims as a way of trying to redeem the harm done by other men. For instance, when I asked one male leader of a MANGO in an interview how he got involved in anti-trafficking work, he explained that his previous job had been with a refugee resettlement agency. Another nonprofit had conducted a workshop on human trafficking for the staff in his organization, and "by the end of that workshop, I felt embarrassed to be male. I felt the men of integrity have been silent too long. That's when I became passionate about human trafficking." Another man with years of experience in advocacy against domestic violence whom I interviewed said he came to see patriarchal patterns of objectifying women and of male dominance as a common root to both domestic violence and the commercial sexual exploitation of women. He sought a way to leverage what he called his "white male privilege" on behalf of female trafficking survivors. Eventually he co-founded a nonprofit with a female survivor-activist. One of his roles in their organization is to lead "encounter" and "accountability" groups for men who want to learn more egalitarian ways to relate to women. These men illustrate some of the many ways that gender hierarchies can be rectified when men and women work together as equals to counter trafficking. Unfortunately, that is often not what happens.

In the news media, men are usually characterized in action roles, either as traffickers or interveners. In contrast, messages about trafficking from the news media almost always characterize victims as females, casting women and girls in a passive role, powerless to extricate themselves. The implied message about femininity in general is that it requires rescue. Starting around 2005, countless public awareness-raising campaigns initiated by MANGOs have echoed those traditional gender role tropes. Rather than helping female victims, they increase the psychological and cultural barriers that female trafficking victims must breach in order to make informed decisions about their own safety and well-being. In addition, the binary of females as victims and males as rescuers ignores the fact that not all people who are trafficked are female and that not all are heterosexual. Such framings perpetuate the pattern of rendering male and transgender victims of every form of trafficking invisible.[20]

Awareness-raising campaigns initiated by federal agencies have been more balanced, depicting both women and men as either potential victims or interveners in assisting victims. The public service announcement video titled "Faces of Human Trafficking," released by the DOJ's Office for Victims of Crime in January 2014, goes even further in portraying that anyone can be a victim. It presents a montage of brief statements from four men and six women, each with different ethnicities. The most potent aspects of that announcement are the role statements: "I am a son," "I am a mother," "I'm an author," and "I'm an advocate," each followed by the refrain, "I am a survivor." It is repeated ten times in rapid succession, each time by a different person—not actors, but actual survivors.[21] The message to those currently being victimized has to do with loss or gain of agency: anyone can be trafficked *and* anyone can become a survivor. This includes men in the effort in a way that helps meaningfully, that avoids setting them into dominating roles, and that acknowledges the variations among victims of trafficking.

The understandings we each have about what our gender means to us, and what others' genders mean for us, can also shape people's approaches to trafficking victims and survivors by evoking maternal or paternal instinct. Such instincts have biological foundations: adult humans are wired to respond to the needs of children in general and to their own offspring in particular. But they are not just biological; such instincts are expressed in culturally shaped ways.[22] The accounts told about or by trafficking victims, especially those who were trafficked as children or youths, often elicit a parental-type of response from caring adults. This is evident in the verbs that are used commonly to describe how people want to help victims: rescue, restore, shelter, protect, and nurture. Parentally styled responses are encouraged by the fact that the most frequently discussed type of trafficking victim in the United States is "girls." Note that these parental responses are not androgynous. They are gendered; that is, they are culturally patterned paternal or maternal approaches toward a girl child.

According to nearly every victim service provider (VSP) I interviewed, the primary problem with a parental approach is that it can feel infantilizing rather than empowering to victims. Subtly or blatantly, it can undermine the ability to assume control over one's own decisions, an essential step for someone whose agency has been wrested away. Secondly, whatever form of trafficking a victim has experienced, it has damaged his or her ability to trust, and likely changed his or her understanding of "normal" gender roles. Thirdly, when a victim of any age who has been coerced, abused, and exploited (whether by men or women) is approached by well-meaning adults offering a parental form of engagement, things can backfire—especially if parental figures he or she had trusted as a child were exploitative. On one hand, a victim's unmet needs can feel so intense that no matter what's offered, it feels good for a time but is never enough. On the other hand, grief and resentment over the care, safety, and opportunities a victim has missed out on can make it difficult for her or him to accept anything that is offered. The only way for victims to move through, and past, these losses is for them to be supported in figuring out what she or he needs now, to ask for that, and to receive it with no strings attached. So what can caring adults offer?

In many cases, what is needed are long-term, consistent, victim-defined "coaching" relationships. The coaching approach is resonant with a feminist approach to therapy, in which the therapist seeks to establish a "power with" relationship vis-à-vis the client versus a "power over" relationship. Egalitarian-focused coaching roles can leave behind a gendered, pseudo-parental stance in favor of one that is more gender-flexible. Further, this approach addresses one of the cross-sector "intersections" where breakdowns in collaboration occur—that is, between professional victim service providers and others who lack professional training but want to help victims directly. When would-be interveners reflect on the differences between an empowering, coaching approach versus an infantilizing, parental approach, they may be better able to perceive the value of the expertise that victim services specialists have to offer.

Another issue arises with gender dynamics in the collaboration process itself—that is, in how different gender roles tend to play out when men and women try to work together to form and enact plans for anti-trafficking activity. A 2014 international survey conducted by the Danish firm Innovisor polled over 5,000 professionals from sixty publicly owned companies in thirty countries about work-related topics. It found that across all thirty national-cultural contexts, "women are keener than men to collaborate and express a clear desire to collaborate even more than they already do today—a desire that men don't appear to share."[23] This may help explain the experiences several female interviewees related about occasions when men with whom they were required to collaborate on anti-trafficking work seemed uninterested in thinking jointly. Of course, this is a population-style study, one where differences are tested across large numbers for statistical significance; individual results, as they say, will vary. Nonetheless, keeping in mind that there may be different predispositions toward or away from the act of collaboration may help participants identify problems in the process and bring those problems forward for productive discussion.

Consciously and subconsciously, we carry culturally and historically shaped ideas, norms, and expectations of race and gender into interorganizational communication—that is, into our interactions as organizational representatives with representatives from other organizations. For example, there are differences between individuals' ideas about what it means to be men or women, and about what is "normal" or "appropriate" or "good" behavior for men and women in various contexts. When such differences surface during collaboration attempts, they can cause short-term or long-lasting breakdowns in a partnership. Nowhere is this more apparent than when the professional roles themselves are traditionally gendered. In my fieldwork, I observed consistent patterns in how female and male law enforcement communicated with each other within and across levels of law enforcement agencies. I also noticed ways that the female officers or agents adopted some of their male colleagues' mannerisms, gestures, postures, and ways of speech when interacting with them—and then shed those when interacting with other women. In light of the almost identical percentages of female sworn officers and federal agents in law enforcement and male social service providers (around 20 percent in both cases), law enforcement can be best understood as a male "gendered profession," and social services can be best understood as a female "gendered profession." The term "gendered organization" was coined by Joan Acker in a 1990 article to refer to the underlying logic and dynamics of organizations that have historically been populated primarily by one gender.[24] The concept of gendered organizations has been extended by other scholars to be applied to networks and professions as well.[25]

Several of the female victim service providers I interviewed described feeling subordinated by the law enforcement representatives with whom they are expected to collaborate—and not solely because of the authority held by the law enforcement sector. The law enforcement sector as a whole operates within a paramilitary structure with a hierarchy of ranks and protocols. The structure of the sector has been widely critiqued as patriarchal—that is, as a system where men hold greater power and where male-oriented norms are considered the most acceptable. That does not mean that everyone who works in law enforcement personally supports patriarchy. But it is not surprising that some victim service providers express a sense of chagrin about the gendered assumptions they think some male law enforcement representatives hold. As one service provider put it:

> I don't know who made the push to get law enforcement and victim service providers to work together so much, but this marriage has given the male law enforcement officers a lot of power. I can't imagine victim service providers wanted this. It's like the victim service providers are now the mommies putting the Band-Aids on [trafficking victims] and staying home, out of the way of the law enforcement daddies. (Interview)

Comments like this demonstrated that when female victim specialists work with male law enforcement, patriarchal gender role norms, as well as the kinds of structural power differences between the sectors discussed in chapter 2, can make it difficult for them to collaborate well. A foundation of mutual respect must be cultivated, as I will explain further in chapter 6.

To sum up this section, there are a myriad of ways our concepts of masculinity and femininity and of maternalism and paternalism are shaped by our respective cultures. It is better to reflect on those understandings consciously than to have them unconsciously shape anti-trafficking efforts. In the above examples, we have seen both the damaging effects and some sterling efforts to work around the difficulties associated with the issue of gender in anti-trafficking efforts. Understanding the unintended results of the way gender is cast and enacted can lead to more effective ways of effecting anti-trafficking goals.

Race, Gender, and Professional Norms

Just as there are particular patterns of interaction within and between gendered organizations and professions, there are also patterns of race-based interaction in and between organizations and professions in which a large majority of members share a common ethnicity or race. Scholars have documented an array of challenges for people from the minority race or ethnicity as well as for the minority gender. One of them is the practice of promoting oneself or one's organization. As we saw in chapter 3, this is a necessary activity; on the one hand, it positions a person within an organization, and on the other hand, it positions one's organization within its industry or sector and with others. However, researchers have found that self-promotion has different meanings for racial minorities and women than it does for Caucasians and men in North America.[26] For members of racial minorities in a majority Caucasian team, and for women working on a majority male team, self-promotion is difficult and fraught with risks. Self-promotion is also viewed quite differently across cultures and classes.

According to a summary of research on workplace culture by Adia Harvey Wingfield, a sociologist who studies black professionals, in US workplaces the corporate culture is generally structured around white, middle-class norms. These norms extend to what she and other sociologists of emotion and work call "the feeling rules" that characterize these environments. In US corporate culture, such rules define emotions like calmness, amiability, and congeniality as appropriate for the workplace. Only under certain, specific conditions are emotions like anger and frustration considered tolerable. She cites another researcher's study of the legal profession, which found the following:

> Litigators are expected to assert "strategic friendliness" where they are only as polite, congenial, and amiable as is necessary to achieve a particular goal. They also are able to display feelings of aggression, anger, and belligerence towards other attorneys outside the firm and to any subordinates, but not to superiors. Paralegals, in contrast, are expected to conform to emotional norms of being nurturing, caretaking, and deferential to attorneys, and are not supposed to display their feelings of anger and irritation to attorneys.[27]

That study of the legal profession also showed that feeling rules are stratified by status and gender; that is, male and female employees, in different positions, must follow different rules:

> Litigators, who are mostly men, are permitted and even expected to show anger and frustration openly, but women attorneys and (mostly female) paralegals are not, as it is viewed as "unfeminine" and therefore unseemly. Paralegals, who are usually women, are expected to be deferential and nurturing, and displays of aggression and curtness are discouraged—unless the paralegals in question are men. In this particular field, then, appropriate emotional displays vary by occupation and gender, but they generally include strategic friendliness, anger, and assertiveness for men, coupled with caretaking and deference for women.[28]

Two caveats regarding the concept of "feeling rules" are that, first, no one follows them all the time, and second, there are always individual exceptions, such as a male social worker who joined an all-female victim services team and came to be treated as "one of the gals" after he had earned their trust. I saw a parallel exception when a female investigator won the acceptance of her male teammates and engaged with them as a buddy. That said, I recognize the validity of gender- and profession-stratified "feeling rules" described in the study of the legal profession because I witnessed similar rules enacted in interactions between some male law enforcement officers and some female victim service providers. These became particularly apparent on several occasions as I moved between task force meetings and private interviews with representatives from one sector or the other. In some task force meetings, the men from law enforcement expressed annoyance or frustration with service providers, but I never heard a female service provider reciprocate by expressing her frustrations during a meeting. Instead, on a few occasions, I observed female service providers in tense meetings stiffen, or inhale and hold their breath, then vent after they had left the meeting room. When I asked one in an interview whether she had told the men what frustrated her, she responded with an analogy about elephants and mice, saying that "when a mouse dances with an elephant, the goal of the mouse is to survive the dance."

The quote about the mouse-elephant dance expresses the kind of collaborative nominalism that can arise among those who perceive themselves as disempowered by race, gender, or other power-laden differences in interorganizational relations. When people feel they must focus on ways to "survive the dance," they do not see themselves as partners building or sharing a mutual identity. They do what they must, but they are neither willing nor able to invest in the collaboration beyond what is required; instead, they look for ways to minimize interacting with those from the other organization or sector who evoke fears for them. The partnership may continue, particularly if it is mandated by funders or other external requirements, but it will not become robust or generative.

Such dynamics, when unaddressed, can make a leaky vessel of a promising collaboration. Collaborations that avoid the kinds of gender- and race-based power imbalances we have been discussing in this chapter are likely to be more generative, for reasons I explain in the next section.

WHY AND HOW TO DIVERSIFY COLLABORATIONS

You may be asking yourself at this point whether collaboration, with its built-in and hard-to-solve problems arising from race and gender conceptions, is really worth the effort. This seems like a good spot to restate a key point from chapter 1. The primary reason why organizational representatives must collaborate across sectors against human trafficking is that it is simply not possible to effect the kinds of political, cultural, and economic changes necessary to stop trafficking without large-scale and intensive multisector collaboration. There are times when those who work against trafficking in every sector feel trapped in collaborations to which they are obligated to participate. I encourage you to believe that viewing a partnership as an unchangeable stalemate is ineffectual at best and counterproductive at worst. Moments of paralysis or breakdown are excellent diagnosticians: They indicate that a time has come to change the dynamic of the collaboration by adding in a new partner. Notice that I did not advise changing partners, because chances are good that any so-called change of partners will result in a similar state of paralysis. Wherever you go, there you are.

The international survey-based study by Innovisor that I cited above found that both men and women are 40 percent more likely to collaborate with people of their own gender. An Innovisor researcher suggested that based solely on anecdotal evidence, similar biases may also exist when it comes to ethnicity and religion.[29] What if the survey had included questions about respondents' general preferences regarding collaboration partners' cultural norms (which often, but not always, correspond with race), educational/training background, status, values, and beliefs? I predict the findings would have indicated preferences leaning toward similarities on each of those as well. But collaborating only with those with like characteristics has two flaws: First, in many instances it simply doesn't fit the bill for solving the problem at hand. And second, we gain much by working with people who offer different perspectives than we do. Many studies over several decades have found that to the extent we are mindful of our own blindnesses and weaknesses, we value the benefits of gaining other perspectives, especially when addressing challenging problems. Without a realistic awareness of our own limitations, we persistently opt to work with people like us when given a choice. It is, quite simply, less taxing. So in addition to the overarching reality that human trafficking will not end without large-scale, systemic changes that require everyone's best efforts, the more immediate reason to strive to diversify collaborations against trafficking is this: without the perspectives that are currently underrepresented in your corner of the movement, you risk settling for limited ideas and predictable solutions.[30]

Allow me to relate some encouraging instances of collaborations that work to counteract gender and culture norms by finding space for those voices that might otherwise be inaudible. One place where men and women are working together across tribal, racial, cultural, and state lines is in the area around the Bakken Shale Formation that straddles Montana and North Dakota and stretches into part of South Dakota. The boom in natural gas and oil extraction there since 2008 has corresponded with the mushrooming of "man camps" (temporary housing compounds for transient, mostly male, workers). These compounds are situated in rural areas populated primarily by relatively isolated Native American tribes. Large numbers of Native youths and women have been exploited sexually and in other ways by residents of the man camps, and other crimes have increased as well. In 2014, several North Dakota NGOs, which serve a range of vulnerable populations and have complementary expertise, built a coalition to develop a coordinated response and to engage more support from state and federal law enforcement and social service agencies. The founding partners of the Force to End Human Sexual Exploitation (FUSE) include the First Nation Women's Alliance, Prevent Child Abuse North Dakota, North Dakota Women's Network, the National Association of Social Workers-North Dakota, and the Council on Abused Women's Services North Dakota. Near the end of 2014, FUSE organized a two-day, multisector conference for leaders from across the Bakken Shale region, at which Native and non-Native speakers shared "concerns about the environmental, social, sexual, tribal, and social justice effects of extractive industries such as fracking and pipelines."[31] This was an excellent way to begin collaborative efforts on a base of understanding the various viewpoints of those who were affected by the changed circumstances fostering a rise in human trafficking.

Once a decision has been made to build a diverse collaboration such as FUSE, or to diversify an existing one, it is vital that existing partners think broadly together about their collective strengths and limitations and about the kinds of perspectives, ideas, and expertise that would enrich the collaboration. There must be some kind of value offered to the invitee(s) to motivate them to accept. Further, any invitee considering joining an existing collaboration in which the prior partners have a lot in common, or even just one or two very important things in common, will want to hear what is expected and assess the extent to which leadership (and responsibilities) will be shared. Few people are willing to be a "token," platformed but not empowered, as, say, the only survivor-activist on a conference planning committee, the one woman on a law enforcement task force, or the sole person of color on an all-white leadership council.

One of the few US-based, anti-trafficking NGOs that makes an explicit, public statement about the value it places on multiculturalism is Polaris, which engages in both mobilization and advocacy efforts and service provision to victims. This organization affirms, "We both embody and celebrate multiculturalism among our clients, staff, and supporters, and cultivate an environment of respect and openness to the diversity within our organization."[32] Polaris collaborates with an extensive array of other organizations from multiple sectors. Demonstrating respect for a potential collaborator begins with offering an appropriate level of shared leadership and finding out what would make the collaboration appealing to them. As this chapter shows, this must include factoring in effects of race and gender that might disadvantage one participant or sector over another. In chapter 5 we will continue exploring how respect can be demonstrated across differences, moving on from race and gender to consider differences in beliefs and values.

Why Beliefs, Values, and Priorities Are Hard to Align

GOING WHERE FAITH-BASED ORGANIZATIONS ARE SCARCE

After checking in at a two-day conference on countering labor trafficking, organized by a self-formed group of academics, fair labor advocates, and elected officials, I was handed the conference program. I did a quick "sector scan" of all the panelists to see which sectors were represented and which were not. This conference program had a particularly diverse set of panelists. In addition to the sectors represented in the organizing group, panelists included a county detective, a federal investigator, a physician, survivor-activists, mobilization and advocacy nongovernmental organization (MANGO) leaders, victim service providers, leaders from immigrant community groups, and business leaders. I noted the absence of any representatives from faith-based organizations (FBOs) among the panelists and determined to keep an eye out for FBO representatives among the attendees.

Puzzling for a moment over the absence of FBOs at a relatively large anti-trafficking conference in this particular city (where there are at least five or six such organizations that are fairly prominent), I chose a chair with a good view at the edge of the room. There were about 200 people milling around. I settled back to watch other attendees arrive, noting who greeted whom, who remained silent, and how people introduced themselves, their organizations, and their anti-trafficking work. Through prior observation sessions and interviews, I had noticed that the way people who work on human trafficking describe their work signals some things about the values that inform their work.

The organizers of this conference had flown in some of the speakers from other parts of the country, and provided accommodation for them for a couple nights. The room in which the event took place was large; the venue, though not posh, was in a central location and cost a sizable amount to rent.

Meals were included in the conference registration fee. To cover all these expenses, the organizers charged well over $100 for advance registrants, a bit less for students, and more for walk-ins. One of the co-organizers told me that they were holding their breath hoping enough people would register that they would break even.

A young woman claimed the seat next to mine, and I noticed her nametag did not include an organizational affiliation. As we chatted, I asked what she did, and was surprised when she told me she worked for a Christian FBO with two paid staff and a handful of volunteers. I mentioned that I had not noticed her organization on the attendee list. She chuckled and said, "That's because we have a shoestring budget, the organization cannot afford to send anyone to conferences, and none of us earn enough to afford this ourselves. My uncle saw an announcement about this conference, and offered to pay my registration fee. That's what made it possible for me to be here today."

On my way back from the lunch buffet, I happened to pass by a cluster of people, two men and a woman, whose nametags all referenced an FBO. I introduced myself, and said I was curious to learn about their organization and what it did to counter trafficking. The older of the two men was very genial, and happily explained how their organization does awareness raising on human trafficking as part of the services it provides to recent immigrants. I asked casually if any of the three of them happened to know any other FBO representatives in attendance. They shook their heads, and the older man said, in a sad tone, "I noticed there aren't any FBOs on the panels. Perhaps they did not feel welcome." Just then, one of the elected officials from the conference organizing group approached the three FBO representatives and greeted them enthusiastically: "Are you the folks from [Organization X]? I'm so glad you're here! We had invited several faith-based groups to participate in this conference, but they all declined." The FBO man replied, "We noticed and were surprised by the lack of faith-based groups on any panel, much less the lack of a panel representing a range of faith-based perspectives." The elected official shrugged and said, "We could not find any who were willing and able to participate. I'm not sure why. But I'm really glad you came."

As she departed, the older man shook his head in amazement. "What a surprise! I was guessing that other faith-based organizations are not here because they felt excluded. But from what she just said, they excluded themselves!" Sensing he was churned up and had a lot to say, I suggested we move outside the lunchroom to a quieter spot. He continued: "I think we Christians need to broaden our perspectives and our knowledge. There are speakers I've heard here today that I want to learn a lot more from and I wish other FBOs would, too. I believe it defeats our [FBO] purpose to not partici-pate in [multisector] meetings like this." I pointed out that many nonprofits,

including FBOs, do not have funds to cover non-essentials such as conference registration fees. He nodded, but said, "Determining what is essential
is also a matter of priorities."

Later on, a law enforcement officer (who had been at the event and with
whom I discussed the scant presence of FBOs) observed the following:
"From my experience, especially among many evangelical, faith-based organizations, there is not much more than lip-service given to labor trafficking.
So, I think one reason the organizers didn't see much interest from the faith-
based organizations was based on the aspect that the discussion revolved
around labor [trafficking], not sex trafficking." (Fieldnotes)

VALUES, BELIEFS, AND PRIORITIES

An entire book could be written about three factors—values, beliefs, and
priorities—and their importance in anti-trafficking efforts in general and
collaboration in particular. In the fieldnote excerpt above, we see glimpses of
how each of the three factors is related to the trafficking and trafficking collaboration, and how all three affect interorganizational relations within and
across sectors. For the purpose of this book, let's define "values" as motivating
ideals about what matters, and "beliefs" as ideas about what is real and true
and how the world works. (In regard to the latter terms, note that some organizations use the term "principles" rather than "beliefs" as a label for these
kinds of ideas.) It is useful to consider the reciprocity of "value" and "beliefs":
Our conceptions of the world (beliefs) underpin our ideas of what matters
(values), and our values, in turn, affect our views of what the world is like and
how it works (beliefs). Using these admittedly simple definitions, I hope we
can agree that everyone has beliefs whether they include spiritual dimensions
or not, just as everyone has values. I think we can also agree that the priorities
of an individual or an organization are shaped by both values and beliefs. In
this chapter I focus on the interpersonal and interorganizational processes—
which, as we have seen in previous chapters, often happen simultaneously—
of ascertaining values and beliefs and attempting to negotiate alignment on
them with current or potential collaborators.

As I stated in chapter 1, every anti-trafficking actor attempting to collaborate with another actor has hopes and fears while attempting the project of
working together. Obviously every actor hopes for success and fears failure in
their anti-trafficking efforts, whether those efforts are pursued collaboratively
across sectors or not, but collaboration brings its own potential dangers to

the endeavor. Each of the aspects of interorganizational relations discussed in chapters 2, 3, and 4—that is, power, reputation and status, and gender and race relations—also gives rise to hopes and fears for anti-trafficking actors across all sectors. So, too, are hopes and fears spawned in the realm of values and beliefs for actors in every sector. Every organization, like every person, holds some ideas about what is real and true and how the world works—that is, has particular beliefs. And the very definition of "values" as motivating ideals about what matters implies how dearly values are held, even when they go unnamed. The prospect of having one's values and beliefs validated, much less shared, by a collaborator is a common hope that motivates many initiatives toward collaboration. Conversely, the possibility that one's values or beliefs will be criticized, or used as the basis for exclusion, is a common source of fear. This kind of fear precipitates defensive moves that in themselves may be perceived as offensive by other parties.

A central theme of this chapter is that both the foundational beliefs and guiding values of organizational leaders shape the aims, priorities, and cultures of organizations and therefore that they also shape how organizational representatives interact with each other. It could be said that the more bureaucratic the organization, the less influence wielded by individual leaders' beliefs and values. Nonetheless, when leaders in any organization establish focal priorities for a team, or shape a group's approach, their personal values and beliefs are inextricably intertwined with organizational and broader professional or sector-based values and beliefs.

Collaboration scholars Chris Huxham and Siv Vangen observe the following:

> [Interorganizational] collaborations are, of course, enacted by individuals . . . who are generally linked to the various organizations that form the collaboration. Commonly, they are acting in a representative function. In the course of collaborative activities, such individuals tend implicitly (and often unwittingly) to converse about their aims, and those of their partners, at three levels: the level of collaboration, the level of participating organization, and the level of the participating individuals.[1]

I contend that in multisector collaboration against human trafficking, those three levels of "conversation"—the interorganizational collaborative level, the intraorganizational level, and the interpersonal level—occur regarding beliefs and values as well as aims. Indeed, since beliefs and values underlie aims, conversations about one are intertwined with conversations about the others. Based on my fieldwork, I concur with Huxham and Vangen that such conversations are sometimes explicit and sometimes implicit and unwitting.

Huxham and Vangen go on to explain that three corresponding sets of aims play into and are produced through these multilevel conversations: collaborative aims (shared between partnering organizations), organizational aims, and individual aims. Collaborating aims pertain to what organizations aspire to achieve together, and how they will work together. In the context of interorganizational collaboration, organizational aims are what each partnering organization hopes to gain for itself from participating in the collaboration. Huxham and Vangen note that sometimes organizational representatives "try to incorporate into the collaboration's agenda aspects of their organization's aims that relate to the formal collaborative purpose, but differ from it."[2] Individual aims reflect the aspirations of the participating individuals and typically relate to career progression or what Huxham and Vangen call "personal causes," which I suggest are likely to stem from personal beliefs and values.

Although most organizations generate explicit statements about their aims or mission, relatively few anti-trafficking organizations from any sector make their organizational values and beliefs or principles explicit and public. More often, they are conveyed informally, orally, and implicitly through an organization's priorities and modes of action. The Laboratory to Combat Human Trafficking (LCHT) provides an excellent explanation of the benefits of identifying organizational values and stating them publicly:

> LCHT has chosen the following values . . . to guide our work with careful intention and purpose. They are the foundation from which we operate and the core of who we are as an organization. We choose to be forthcoming about our values so that we can both distinguish our collective values as an organization from our personal values as individuals and so that those who are unfamiliar with our organization can easily and quickly get an understanding of how we choose to approach the anti-trafficking field.[3]

I agree with the Lab's rationale that making organizational values and beliefs explicit can be helpful to individuals working within the organization (or who are considering joining it). Doing so can also be useful in interorganizational relations. Below are statements of organizational values from three different types of NGOs, paraphrased lightly for the sake of space:

A. Our organization is grounded in a set of values and organizational beliefs that provide a foundation for all our programmatic activities. We strive to embody and model these values within our organization and within the anti-trafficking movement: service, reality- and impact-centered programs, empowerment, non-violence and respect, transformative innovation, and a holistic approach. (US-based NGO with multiple domestic and international programs that include victim services and mobilization and advocacy efforts)[4]
B. Our coalition values: a commitment to leading the way as brokers of change in the anti–human trafficking movement; the pioneering spirit, by developing groundbreaking, innovative means of tackling the issue of human trafficking; human dignity and basic human rights for all individuals; collaboration with a diverse group of organizations in order to be more effective and build community capacity. (US metro-area MANGO coalition with nineteen member organizations from multiple sectors)[5]
C. This alliance supports the sharing of knowledge, working experiences and working methodologies amongst its members, in order to enhance the effectivity of collective anti-trafficking activities. It welcomes cooperation with all organizations, agencies or persons who share its principles. The alliance is organizationally independent and will refrain from any party political, governmental, commercial, or religious affiliations. However, members are autonomous and free to enter into affiliations of their choice, as long as these are not contradictory to the alliance's Basic Principles. (International network with over 100 member NGOs from all regions of the world)[6]

There is a noteworthy contrast between organization B's value on "collaborating with *a diverse group of organizations* in order to be more effective and build community capacity," and organization C's statement that it "welcomes cooperation with all organizations, agencies or persons *who share its principles*" (emphases added). We will consider the differences between these value statements later in this chapter. For now, my intent is not to analyze closely the values of any specific organizations, but rather to make clear that all organizations have particular values and beliefs that have some relationship to the individual values of an organization's leaders, and that they also relate to the type of organization. In the three examples above, the first is a singular centralized organization; the second, a coalition of proximate organizations from multiple sectors; and the third, a network of distributed organizations from the same sector. Because organizational values and beliefs, along with aims, come into play in interorganizational relations, it is important to consider them when reflecting on interorganizational and multisector collaboration.

We have seen that patterns in credentialing norms, gender and racial dynamics, and aspects of organizational cultures (such as the "feeling rules" I discussed in chapter 4) become ingrained over time in organizations, professions, and sectors. So also do values, beliefs, and priorities. An individual's personal values, beliefs, and priorities may well influence their choice to work within a particular organization, profession, and sector. It is also the case that as individuals are schooled, trained, and socialized into an organization, profession, and sector, the historically patterned values, beliefs, and priorities of the collective entities influence the individuals within them. (This is true whether individuals internalize or resist incorporation; either way, they are affected.) With so many different individual and collective ideas about what is real and true and so many ideals about what matters coursing through each interaction between representatives of anti-trafficking organizations and agencies, the conflicting cross-currents can be very uncomfortable. While alignment among organizations and sectors is appealing to many, all these complexities make already-existing alignments of values and beliefs difficult to find. Such alignments are also often hard to build, and even harder to sustain, as organizations evolve due to changes in leadership, funding, and priorities.

Tensions stemming from differing values, beliefs, and priorities exist within and between every sector. In what follows, I will provide several examples of how values surface and get negotiated, referring to alliances between different law enforcement agencies; between victim service providers and law enforcement officers; and between FBOs and areligious NGOs, whether MANGOs or victim service provider organizations. Following these illustrative examples, I will highlight some of the common themes that are apparent in them, including the hopes and fears they reveal.

TENSIONS BETWEEN LAW ENFORCEMENT AGENCIES

When I asked police officers and federal investigators about the collaboration challenges they experience, nearly all mentioned difficulties related to differences in values in working with other types of law enforcement, both within and beyond their home agencies. For instance, within police departments and federal agencies, there are patrol units whose staff must respond to many kinds of emergencies on a routine basis. People from patrol units stressed the value of immediate action as they described the impatience they sometimes felt with the slow pace and lack of a clear action plan on the part of detective or investigation units. Conversely, the value of methodical, systemic analyses to uncover trafficking networks and to locate and freeze traffickers' assets before they can be transferred out of the United States was what mattered to investigators, who were patently frustrated with colleagues who disrupt or compromise a long-running federal investigation by launching a hasty takedown operation or by rushing through a witness interview.

Here is an example gleaned from one of my interviews: A female federal investigator had been developing a labor trafficking case over several weeks in a city in which she had not previously worked. When she had collected the background data she needed, she initiated a raid on the business in coordination with local police. Knowing in advance that a particular female victim could be a key witness, she arranged a quiet place where she and a police detective could try to calm the victim and get her to talk.

From the federal investigator's perspective, things were going well. She had established some rapport with the woman, who was beginning to talk openly. Then suddenly the door to the room was flung open and a second police officer bolted in. He interrupted the federal agent, saying to the woman, "I have a couple questions," and then, according to the investigator, proceeded to berate and accuse the woman of being an accomplice. The woman began to cry, and she shut down. After that officer left the room, the federal investigator did all she could to calm the woman. The woman stopped crying and opened up a bit again, but did not speak as freely as before. In relating this incident to me, the federal investigator commented, "I wish I had addressed that cop when he first entered the room. Perhaps if I'd said, 'How can I help you?' he would have realized he was interrupting." It is possible that the interrupting officer would have responded to an indirect question from the investigator as a verbal cue to back out of the room. But it is also possible that the local officer was part of a patrol unit and therefore strongly committed to the value of immediate action so that he would not have noticed or responded to a verbal cue. In either case, the kind of conversation cue the agent floated in retrospect during our conversation might not have been effective. As we talked further, the agent concluded that before she initiated any more interventions in co-ordination with law enforcement personnel from other agencies, she would draft a protocol for the whole operation and try to get advance agreement from everyone about who would be involved in which steps and how questioning would be handled.

A second federal investigator, with whom I discussed the disrupted interview situation, responded that although the tensions between patrol and investigative unit values are strong and prevalent, and often play out in the kind of situation I described, they happen within, as well as between, law enforcement agencies at every level. He stressed that he thinks police detectives are typically better trained and more experienced than most federal investigators in interviewing victims of crime, and that he has seen federal agents disrupt interviews and investigations more often than police. He suggested that a different reason for the officer's disruptive behavior could have been that the officer lacked understanding—or the desire to understand—the dynamics of human trafficking crimes or victim-centric investigations in general. Elaborating, he continued:

> I think all agencies have these people who "have to put their two cents in." In essence, these officers or agents have to insert themselves and make sure they "get their questions in" or make their statement (verbal or operationally) to the perpetrator or victim in order to feel good or important. Usually these questions or their statement (usually an opinion) does nothing more [than] instill anger in the victim or suspect and make things worse. (Correspondence)

This investigator was suggesting that some individuals bring their ego values into work settings and perform in ways that are more self-promoting than collaborative. That phenomenon is certainly not limited to the law enforcement sector, and it underscores the importance of cultivating individuals' buy-in on organizational values. However, instances such as a disrupted investigatory interview also make obvious the need for more robust coordination within and between patrol and investigatory units, as well as between law enforcement agencies. There is great societal benefit both in what might be considered the chief value of patrol units (that is, fast response) and in an investigation unit's value of systematic analysis. The necessity of both values becomes apparent when we imagine living in a society in which law enforcement has only one or the other. The solution is not the subordination of one value to another, but rather a negotiation of the productive tension that arises between the two.

Some other collaboration challenges mentioned by law enforcement officers and prosecutors in relation to human trafficking work centered on differences between agencies' structures and protocols, such as those discussed in chapter 2. However, in comparing their accounts, it became clear that underlying some collaboration difficulties are systemic, sector-based values that work against collaboration. For example, in a semipublic discussion involving several investigators and prosecutors and digital technology developers, it was agreed that just as prosecutors are resistant to sharing data about cases they are developing, so are many law enforcement investigators, at every level and in every agency. It was also agreed that more data sharing, especially across agencies, could enable better, faster investigations. The technologists went on to start brainstorming tools they could build to make data-sharing easier for investigators, both within and across agencies. Interestingly, the investigators and prosecutors involved in the discussion were skeptical about whether their colleagues would be open to using any of the technologies being suggested, for the following reasons:

From the perspectives of the investigators and prosecutors who participated in that discussion (and others with whom I spoke), neither investigators nor prosecutors are incentivized to share case data. To the contrary, there was wide agreement that they are disincentivized from doing so. Among the reasons cited were that salary raises (which more than one investigator noted are modest in comparison to the private sector), promotions, and professional reputations are linked to the number and type of cases investigated and prosecuted successfully by individuals. Given the difficulty of investigating human trafficking cases, and the length of time required for such investigations, human trafficking case work could actually impede an investigator's or prosecutor's career advancement, whether they collaborate or not. Some investigators stated that there is often no "reward" for helping other investigators solve their cases. Rather, collaboration-minded investigators perceive suspicions from other investigators (especially from other agencies) if they ask too many questions. They described having the sense that other investigators fear that a colleague who wants to collaborate may mess up "their" investigations by gaining too much information about them. Others in the LE sector perceive the perennial competition for agency or division status and funding (discussed in chapter 2) and protectionist managers as the primary hindrances to collaboration. One federal investigator explained the following in an e-mail to me:

> All federal agencies have to seek funding from Congress, and [for LE agencies] the "stats" that come from arrests/convictions/seizures come into play. The "gaps" in collaboration are often not at the agent level, but at management levels, both externally between agencies and internally between offices/groups. Agents many times want to work together, but managers get concerned about stats and how it may come into play with funding for personnel, equipment, or even keeping offices open. A shift in this system, for us, could be as simple as making our case management database accept more than one "arresting" stat. In essence, only one office can "claim" a stat such as a seizure, arrest, indictment, or conviction without doubling the stat—for example, making it appear that there were two arrests instead of one. (Correspondence)

Several other law enforcement officials from various agencies talked with me about their own strong desires to collaborate more robustly with others in law enforcement—and their consequent frustrations with higher-ups instructing them not to or transferring them to other divisions if they got too involved in collaborative work.

The discussions I had with a variety of people from the law enforcement sector about barriers to collaboration made clear the strong presence of sector-wide values of individual (and agency) autonomy and achievement and the absence of value accorded to collaboration and support roles. In the terms of a framework for practical research called "cultural-historical activity theory,"[7] there is a fundamental, systemic contradiction between the autonomy and achievement values of the law enforcement sector and the value of collaboration. No matter what data-sharing tools are developed, no change in data-sharing practice is likely unless there is a cultural shift within the law enforcement sector that increases the worth of collaboration in investigations in the sector's value system. Such a shift, to be effective, will need to be manifested in the systems that provide incentives for various actions—that is, in the realm of professional recognition and advancement. The benefits, in the form of more sensitive and successful collaboration, are obvious.

TENSIONS BETWEEN VICTIM SERVICE PROVIDERS AND LAW ENFORCEMENT

Having considered several values-based aspects of tensions within the law enforcement sector, we will now explore ways that differences in values and beliefs create tensions in collaborations between victim service providers and law enforcement agencies. To begin unpacking these tensions, we will start by considering the differences between these sectors in their concepts of a "victim-centered approach" to human trafficking.

Since at least the mid-2000s, the U.S. Departments of Justice, State, Health and Human Services, and Homeland Security have used the term "victim-centered" to characterize their ideal approach to human trafficking. State and local governments have adopted the term, as have many NGOs. According to the federal Strategic Action Plan on trafficking:

> The victim centered approach seeks to minimize retraumatization associated with the criminal justice process by providing the support of victim advocates and service providers, empowering survivors as engaged participants in the process, and providing survivors an opportunity to play a role in seeing their traffickers brought to justice. In this manner, the victim centered approach plays a critical role in supporting a victim's rights, dignity, autonomy, and self-determination, while simultaneously advancing the government's and society's interest in prosecuting traffickers to condemn and deter this reprehensible crime. An understanding of a victim centered approach in the United States developed over time to respond to the needs of crime victims and continues to evolve as we learn new lessons and establish promising practices.[8]

Hundreds of webpages, pamphlets, and personnel-training media produced by law enforcement and victim service providers employ the "victim-centered" phrase. But a close reading evidences differences between these two sectors in how that tends to be conceptualized. The Department of Homeland Security (DHS) explains victim-centeredness this way:

> DHS utilizes a victim-centered approach to combat human trafficking, which places equal value on identifying and stabilizing victims and on investigating and

prosecuting traffickers. Victims are crucial to investigations and prosecutions; each case and every conviction changes lives. DHS understands how difficult it can be for victims to come forward and work with law enforcement due to their trauma. DHS is committed to helping victims feel stable, safe, and secure.[9]

The DHS conceptualizes victim-centeredness as an approach that values "identifying and stabilizing victims" and "investigating and prosecuting traffickers" equally. But attempting to equally balance the priority of these two aims is a difficult challenge, as demonstrated in the account from the federal investigator above about a police officer barging in and berating a woman the investigator was trying to calm and interview. Several investigators who are strongly committed to a victim-centered approach, and well trained in it, representing every level of law enforcement, admitted to me that it is sometimes quite difficult to discern how best to accomplish both of their aims. "Victim specialists" who are employed by several kinds of law enforcement agencies face a dilemma in this regard as well.[10] It seemed to me that they experience more angst about this dilemma than do investigators, since their job descriptions require them to simultaneously support and advocate for victims—and to "back the badge" of their investigative counterparts.[11] Several confided that in some moments it is impossible to do both well.

Unsurprisingly, the nuts and bolts of implementing a victim-centered approach create tensions between law enforcement investigators and victim service providers. NGO victim service providers, in addition to using the term "victim-centered," also typically describe their work as "client-directed" or "client-driven." Through such terms, victim service providers convey that they value the choices of a victim/client above all else. NGO victim service providers tend to not experience the dilemma described above between supporting victims and bringing traffickers to justice; because they prioritize victims' wishes, that dilemma largely dissipates.

Interestingly, the description in chapter 1 of the victim-centered approach from the 2014 version of the "Human Trafficking Task Force e-Guide" (which was produced by a multisector committee comprised of NGO victim service providers, law-enforcement-based victim specialists, several kinds of investigators, and prosecutors) reflects the perspective of NGO victim service providers. The section devoted to defining and explaining their victim-centered approach adopted language from texts produced by NGO victim service providers:

> *In a victim-centered approach, the victim's wishes, safety, and well-being take priority in all matters and procedures.* . . . Service provider and law enforcement partnerships are crucial to the provision of a comprehensive and victim-centered response to human trafficking. . . . A comprehensive effort should include organizations with expertise in reaching targeted populations in culturally sensitive and linguistically correct ways, as well as those with expertise in trauma, emotional bonding, climate of fear, and other circumstances. The victim-centered approach plays a critical role in supporting victims' rights, dignity, autonomy, and self-determination, regardless of whether they chose to report or cooperate with law enforcement. For victims who do choose to work with law enforcement, employing a victim-centered approach to criminal investigations is fundamental to a successful criminal case.[12] (Emphasis in original)

In sum, even though both sectors use the term "victim-centered," because of differences in some of each sector's core values, they conceptualize it differently and emphasize different aspects of it. Based on my fieldwork, the core values of the law enforcement sector center on truth and justice, manifested in both the safety of the victims and the successful prosecution of the trafficker.

In contrast, the core values of the victim service provider sector center on confidentiality and victim empowerment. The following explanation of "client-driven services," written for law enforcement by a victim service provider, illustrates how these values are implemented:

> Our services are meant to be long-term and exist within and beyond the timeline of investigation and prosecution. Our goal is to help clients become independent and self-sufficient and build lives for themselves free from exploitation, abuse and vulnerability. Our services are informed by clients' short and long-term goals.[13]

Collaboration between law enforcement and victim service providers is essential to countering human trafficking. However, the values-based differences between these sectors give rise to significant tensions. There have been many instances in which attempts at collaboration between these sectors have failed—and task forces have been paralyzed or dissolved—as a result of these tensions and the conflicts that ensue from them. For those reasons, the 2014 update of the "Human Trafficking Task Force e-Guide" includes additional sections on ways to improve collaboration and manage conflict between these two sectors in particular as well as others. A section addressing the roles of task force members from the victim services sector includes pointed instructions on the need for "trusted brokers" between the two sectors:

> *Foster communication between law enforcement and other service providers in the region.* Victim service provider task force members should work to broker relationships and channel communication among law enforcement and the larger group of organizations and victim advocates doing human trafficking work within the region. By serving as designated points of contact for questions, disputes, and requests, the task force members can become the trusted brokers who prevent much of the confusion, misunderstandings, and negative experiences that often arise from untrained, multi-lateral interaction between individuals on both sides of the victim service provider–law enforcement divide.[14] (Emphasis in the original)

Beyond being a remarkably forthright statement on the history of "confusion, misunderstandings, and negative experiences" that have plagued attempts at collaboration between law enforcement and victim service providers, this passage and others like it in the e-Guide point to the kinds of communication and mediation skills that are essential for negotiating functional partnerships despite unchanging differences in the core values by which each sector operates. Fundamentally, the tension between the tendency toward mutual suspicion and the need to build trust—known to be a systemic paradox in many interorganizational collaborations—is very evident between the LE and VSP sectors. That sector-based tension shapes interactions between individuals, even those who have never met before.

Take, for example, the story I heard from a police detective whom I will call "Tim." At a time and in a state where prostituted youth were arrested and held in detention, Tim led a multiagency task force dedicated to countering the commercial sexual exploitation of minors. Although as a member of the law enforcement sector he was not allowed to advocate publicly for changes to his state's law, in private conversations it was evident that he was frustrated by some of them, and in particular he hoped to see "safe harbor" laws passed so that prostituted youth could be cared for as victims rather than detained as criminals. (This is an example of how sector-based constraints or norms can create tensions for the individuals who work within them, but disagree personally. Such tensions are compounded for those government employees and grantees who are prohibited from advocating for legal reform.)

After several attempts to visit teenage victims in detention, Tim told me he gave up because of the undermining response he got from victim service providers who also were trying to intervene on behalf of prostituted youth who were being detained. As he talked about the suspicions he encountered from the VSPs, his face bore an expression of pain and sadness. "Sometimes when I tried to visit girls in detention, the social work people would be really suspicious and ask me skeptical questions about my motives in front of the girls, like 'what are you doing here?' and 'why do you want to talk with them?' They could have introduced me to the girls, as 'here is a detective who is concerned about you and wants to help you get what you need.'" He paused and looked down, and I realized he was looking at photos of his family on his desk. Then he continued, "Why could they not see me as a father of teenage girls myself, who cares and wants to help?"

What we have seen are the ways differing values and beliefs between individuals, organizations, and sectors create tensions that challenge collaboration. Although such tensions are likely to exist in any interorganizational or cross-sector interaction, for the sake of brevity we will examine just one more set of multisector relations through the lens of values and beliefs. Having already demonstrated the perennial tensions between nonprofit nongovernmental organizations that stem from having to compete for donor dollars, I explain in the following sections how differences in the beliefs and values between such organizations also create tensions that affect collaboration.

FAITH-BASED ORGANIZATIONS AND COUNTER-TRAFFICKING EFFORTS

In 2014, in a groundbreaking demonstration of interfaith collaboration, world religious leaders representing Buddhism, Islam, and Hinduism joined Christian leaders of the Catholic, Orthodox, and Protestant traditions in signing a Joint Declaration of Religious Leaders against Modern Slavery. At the same time, many agreed to collaborate in the Global Freedom Network, pledging, "We will work together to make ours the last generation that has to fight the trade in human lives."[15] In the United States, religious leaders and faith-based organizations have been very involved in anti-trafficking efforts since the late 1990s.[16] There are many Jewish congregations and faith-based organizations that engage in countering various forms of modern slavery.[17]

However, anti-trafficking faith-based organizations in the United States are predominantly Christian, though within that, a broad theological spectrum of Orthodox, Catholic, and Protestant traditions is represented.[18]

A large and still-growing number of evangelical Protestant organizations have been quite vocal and visible in anti-trafficking efforts since the mid-1990s. Most of these focus their efforts primarily, if not exclusively, on countering sex trafficking,[19] though there are notable exceptions of evangelical organizations (in some cases, large coalitions of them) that have a demonstrated track record in countering forced labor in many industries. One of these is the Wesleyan Holiness Consortium, composed of sixteen Christian denominations, which issued a Declaration of Freedom in 2013 that included a pledge of sustained action against every form of slavery and oppression: "We commit ourselves and our ecclesial resources to working for the abolition of all forms of slavery, trafficking, and oppression and to participate in intentional networks, conversations, and actions that provide hopeful alternatives."[20]

A second exception is the Faith Alliance against Slavery and Trafficking (FAAST):

[FAAST was established to] help equip Christians to holistically respond to human trafficking. One of the avenues FAAST uses to do this is through encouraging public policies that may reduce the prevalence of human trafficking and other contemporary versions of slavery, both in the United States and internationally.[21]

FAAST functions as an umbrella organization to conduct policy advocacy on behalf of its member organizations, advise members of best practices in counter-trafficking efforts, and help strengthen collaboration between faith-based organizations. In contrast to many evangelical organizations that largely overlook labor trafficking and rarely mention the victimization of immigrants in the United States, FAAST is active in seeking to reform U.S. immigration policies to reduce human trafficking crimes against immigrants.

Given that immigrants represent a disproportionate share of the victims of both sex trafficking and labor trafficking within the United States, FAAST has assembled this new brief to examine the reasons that foreign-born individuals are uniquely vulnerable to situations of human trafficking. It provides a number of immigration reform policy recommendations that would significantly reduce the incidence of human trafficking.[22]

Given the large number of evangelical faith-based organizations involved in counter-trafficking efforts, they are a significant force in the anti-trafficking movement. I suggest that if even one-third follow the examples of FAAST and the Wesleyan consortium and broaden their focus to address the spectrum of forced labor beyond commercial sexual exploitation, significant breakthroughs could happen in terms of victim identification, policy reform, and cultural and economic shifts. Further, some of the tensions between faith-based organizations and areligious NGOs would be reduced, for reasons I explain in the next section.

TENSIONS BETWEEN FAITH-BASED AND ARELIGIOUS NGOS

Some anti-trafficking faith-based organizations are victim service providers (VSPs), others focus on mobilization and advocacy efforts (MANGOs). I use the term "faith-based organization" (FBO) to refer to NGOs that define themselves as ministries, religious groups, or faith-motivated organizations. I use the term "areligious NGOs" to refer to any nonprofit that makes no claim about faith or religion as part of its organizational identity. Figure 5.1 depicts these two dimensions in relation to each other to represent the four primary types

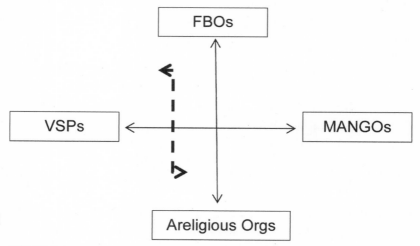

FIGURE 5.1
Types of Anti-Trafficking NGOs

of trafficking-centered NGOs I observed: faith-based MANGOs, areligious MANGOs, faith-based VSPs, and areligious VSPs.[23] In every city in which I conducted fieldwork and interviews, there were deep tensions between some of the anti-trafficking NGOs that identify themselves as faith-based and some that do not. In each city, the most numerous and intense tensions among NGOs were between faith-based and areligious VSPs, as depicted by the dashed double arrow between those quadrants. I suggest some possible reasons below.

I must note here that while there are distinct differences between types of NGOs, differences among the types of individuals who affiliated themselves with them (either as paid staff or volunteers) were not as clear cut. I met many people who affiliated themselves with more than one type of NGO—for example, a staff member of an areligious VSP who also volunteers for a FBO MANGO, or someone who volunteers for both an areligious MANGO and a FBO VSP. Unsurprisingly, all the FBO representatives I talked with mentioned having a personal religious faith that corresponded with that FBO. However, I also met many people of faith, from various religious traditions, employed by or volunteering for areligious NGOs dedicated to countering human trafficking. I observed some FBOs that made no attempt to engage participants in collective spiritual practices, such as prayer during meetings, and some areligious organizations that did.

Through interviews with paid staff and unpaid volunteers affiliated with all four types of nonprofit/NGOs, I learned that they perceive several reasons for tensions between FBOs and areligious NGOs. All these reasons stem from differences in beliefs (that is, ideas about what is good and real and how the world works) or values (motivating ideals about what matters). Although FBOs are by no means homogeneous in their beliefs or in the values that shape their efforts, they tend to articulate organizational values, priorities, and sometimes specific activities and programs in relation to their religious beliefs, thereby demonstrating that those beliefs hold strong value for them. In contrast, areligious NGOs tend to characterize their organizational values, priorities, and sometimes even their activities and programs, in relation to beliefs or principles regarding human rights (specifically, that human rights are good and real and how the world works, or at least how it should work). For many areligious NGOs, beliefs about human rights hold strong value. Although religious beliefs and human rights beliefs are by no means mutually exclusive, they do provide two different points of orientation. Such differences in belief and values shape collaboration dynamics. One such pattern I observed was where each type of nonprofit was more likely to collaborate with others of its same type; areligious VSPs created referral networks comprised of other areligious VSPs, and FBO VSPs created referral networks comprised of other FBO VSPs. Among the FBOs, evangelical Protestant FBOs were most likely to collaborate only with each other. Non-evangelical FBOs were just as likely to collaborate with areligious NGOs as with other FBOs; in fact, they seemed to be more accepted by areligious NGOs than they were by evangelical FBOs.

From observations and interviews, I identified five reasons for the tight-knit clustering of evangelical FBOs into their own intra-sector coalitions, and (not unrelatedly) their absence from many multisector coalitions and events (such as the conference described at the beginning of this chapter). The first reason is theological: they believe human trafficking stems from evil, and that human efforts to counter trafficking must be grounded in prayer—that God will overcome evil and redeem all that has been ruined by it. The following quote from an e-mail invitation to a "Freedom Prayer Gathering" illustrates a type of theology that is common among evangelical FBOs:

> Let's call all Christians (ecumenical) to pray for our region, nation & world around victims-survivors of slavery & human trafficking. As you know, it is a spiritual warfare and there is a great darkness in our cause. But we have a greater God who loves justice, hears the oppressed and is moving within His people to help with freedom, restoration and abolishment of slavery & human trafficking. Please join me and others to call the Church to pray and join in this fight.[24]

As I explained above, evangelical FBOs not only have specific religious beliefs, *they also place a strong value on those beliefs*. This is foundational to their identity, and it is also a reason why neither areligious NGOs (which have different beliefs), nor non-evangelical FBOs (which may have similar religious beliefs, but value other things, such as collaboration, more highly) are comfortable collaborating closely with evangelical FBOs. It must also be noted that some areligious NGOs, namely ones that will only collaborate with organizations that agree with their principles (beliefs), also place a strong value on their principles and consider fidelity to their principles to be a higher value than collaboration with differently principled others. The alliance that produced value statement C cited earlier in this chapter exemplifies this type of areligious NGO.

A second motivation for intra-sector coalitions among evangelical FBOs is that they seek to integrate their beliefs explicitly in their efforts against human trafficking by using such methods as prayer and Bible teaching, and to describe their efforts in terms of their beliefs, often using quotations from the Bible or theological terms. NGOs that don't share those beliefs are uncomfortable with those practices. A third motivation is that although most leaders of evangelical FBOs think that collaboration with other FBOs is both good and necessary,[25] they perceive collaboration with other types of NGOs and other sectors as of questionable goodness and unnecessary.

Many (although not all) the leaders of evangelical FBOs with whom I spoke seemed to think collaborating with other types of NGOs, or entities from other sectors, is at best an unnecessary waste of time. This leads to the fourth reason for intra-sector, rather than intersector, coalitions: evangelical FBOs fear that the "price" of collaboration with other types of NGOs could be the compromising of their beliefs and values and relinquishment of the power to act in accordance with their beliefs. However, that view is not shared across all evangelical FBOs. For instance, when I told the older man featured in the fieldnote excerpt at the beginning of this chapter that some Christian FBO leaders had told me they do not want to collaborate with non-FBOs, he was chagrined. He responded as follows:

> Christian FBO leaders who don't want to invest time and energy in collaborating with non-FBOs are going against the example of Jesus. FBOs should follow the example of Jesus and go to whoever is willing to engage with them. It is self-righteous of FBOs to think that they don't need non-FBOs to combat human trafficking. This problem is so large, we need everyone to address it. We need to learn from each other. We [FBOs] have to keep trying to build bridges.

The fifth and final reason I found for why some evangelical FBOs are reluctant to collaborate with other types of NGOs and entities from other sectors is that their leaders fear their organization might lose its position within the evangelical realm if it becomes too closely linked with "outside" entities. The leader of an FBO explained this dynamic in the following way:

Every organization has its own protection mechanism. They have to make sure that what they are doing is in line with what their own constituencies want. So if they are asked by an umbrella organization [such as a coalition] to go beyond that, and some organizations lack experience in that kind of broad coalition, that might prohibit them from venturing out [into the broader interorganizational realm of the umbrella organization]. Churches and faith-based organizations have a hard enough time trying to align among themselves within the evangelical world. For example, when I'm talking with pastors, they talk about developing a forum for networking, but it's still very limited. They mean their youth pastors from a few churches will organize two events a year together. That's it. So it is risky for leaders of faith-based organizations to work too much with other types of organizations. (Interview)

The five reasons FBOs avoid cross-sector collaboration that I have presented in this section came from different sources, but each was confirmed by more than one source. Any of them, or all of them, could be concerns for any particular FBO. On the other hand, some FBO leaders were unconcerned about any of these issues. Unsurprisingly, their FBOs were among those most actively collaborating across sectors. Moreover, those leaders are attempting to persuade their counterparts in other FBOs to engage more broadly. As one FBO leader put it, "I wish that more Christians would figure out a way to translate their faith motivation into a language that connects better with a pluralistic context."

Some areligious NGOs, both MANGOs and VSPs, have their own reasons to avoid collaborating with FBOs in general and evangelical FBOs in particular. First, some areligious NGOs fear that collaboration with FBOs could compromise some of their core values, such as being tolerant of many beliefs, and cause them to lose the trust of other partners. Second, areligious VSPs are often particularly concerned about the prospect of evangelical FBOs "proselytizing" victims when they are traumatized or emotionally fragile, or making spiritual practices such as Bible reading and prayer a condition for receiving services. Third, established areligious NGOs are skeptical about some recently formed FBOs' lack of knowledge about the breadth and complexity of human trafficking, their lack of experience, and their lack of professional credentials. Fourth, areligious VSPs with significant training and experience doubt less-trained and less-experienced FBO VSPs' abilities to keep survivors safe and obtain appropriate and comprehensive services for them. Fifth, areligious NGOs express skepticism about the longevity of FBOs' commitment to anti-trafficking efforts and wonder how many FBOs will disintegrate as quickly as they formed. A sixth reason areligious NGOs articulated for distrusting FBOs is that they perceive FBOs as significantly diluting citywide or regional anti-trafficking efforts by forming their own exclusively FBO coalitions and thereby siphoning resources (attention and leadership, as well as funds) away from established efforts and organizations.

Finally, areligious NGOs that are involved in efforts to counter forms of forced labor beyond commercial sexual exploitation are distressed that most evangelical FBOs focus narrowly on the latter. In other words, they are concerned about what remains out of the FBO spotlight. Another layer in that tension is that NGOs that attempt to address forms of trafficking that disproportionately affect immigrants in the United States suspect that the Republican Party's opposition to efforts at immigration policy reform is a key reason that most evangelical FBOs do not address the exploitation and trafficking crimes to which immigrants are subjected. The leader of an areligious VSP seemed to be articulating this concern in a comment she made publicly regarding a news article someone else shared about the systemic practices of rape, degradation, and forced labor many female immigrant agricultural workers endure. The VSP leader's response to the group was, "If you say you are working against human trafficking you must also be addressing oppression, poverty, and injustice."

The consequence of the tensions that stem from differences in beliefs and values may be that mutual distrust is growing right when and where it needs to recede in order to foster the larger-scale, longer-term structural changes necessary to eradicate slavery. Any or all of the reasons I identified could explain why I observed only three evangelical FBO VSPs collaborating robustly (that is, sharing referrals and swapping services) with areligious VSPs, and one of those collaborations fell apart during the course of my fieldwork. In the two collaborations that succeeded, the evangelical FBO leaders (who were less experienced than their areligious VSP counterparts) went to great lengths to earn professional credentials similar to their counterparts, and to earn their trust by demonstrating, consistently over a year or more, respect and a strong desire to learn. Fieldnotes from a multisector coalition meeting and an interview excerpt tell how one of those collaboration successes happened:

I noticed as the meeting got started that Liz, the director of an evangelical FBO VSP [about which I know little] had been allotted significant time on the agenda to provide an overview of what her organization is and does. She was introduced by the leader of a prominent areligious VSP, whose introductory comments included, "[Organization X] is a valuable partner." In her overview of the organization, the leader of the evangelical FBO VSP was explicit about it being faith based, but she also noted that the services it offers are available to anyone, with no questions asked about clients' beliefs. When the FBO leader concluded, both the areligious VSP leader who had introduced her and a prosecutor expressed their appreciation of her as a leader and of her organization. The leader of the areligious VSP affirmed her attitude of learning and collaboration. The prosecutor thanked her for providing effective, reliable services to victims, even on short notice. I have not heard those kinds of affirmations before in a coalition meeting. (Fieldnote)

Later I had an opportunity to interview Liz. I noted the affirmations I had heard about her work. When I asked how she and her colleagues had developed the organization and earned the trust of those who affirmed her in the coalition meeting, Liz responded as follows:

We knew when we started our organization that most VSPs in our area are not faith-based and are suspicious of FBOs, thinking FBOs lack the necessary knowledge and qualifications to work in this realm, and fearing we will spiritualize clients' problems, and suspecting us of proselytizing—basically they are afraid FBOs cause more harm than good. I knew I had a lot to learn from them, and that I had to gain their trust by demonstrating my respect for them and eagerness to learn from them and build an organization that would cooperate with them. For the first year or two that I attended coalition meetings, I said very little, and I watched and listened closely. I observed which people and organizations were respected well, and who had influence, and I listened to learn what those people are concerned about. Then I started initiating conversations with those people, one on one. I would summarize my understanding of their goals and concerns, and something I had learned from them, explain how I was applying those insights in our organization, and then ask them to teach me more. Little by little that built their trust that I really did respect them and would complement, not compete with, their work.

Liz's approach disarmed her skeptical counterparts in areligious organizations, relieved their fears, and demonstrated her commitment to collaboration as well as her competency. To their credit, Liz's counterparts were willing to be persuaded rather than prejudging her for her religious beliefs or holding her inexperience against her.

In contrast, leaders of other evangelical FBOs I talked with described unsuccessful attempts to collaborate with areligious NGOs and the forms of painful exclusion they experienced. One such leader, Ann, explained in an interview that she had created the NGO she leads "to provide an avenue for Christians to get involved in anti–human trafficking work. At that time HT was relatively new for most people. I started [Organization X] as a way for people in congregations to help, since the existing organizations back then required professional expertise like victim service provision, or law enforcement."

Ann's city has a strong, diverse, citywide coalition of nonprofits (Coalition A). When I noticed that Ann had made no reference to Coalition A, I asked her if she was familiar with it. She responded:

> My [FBO] has a really weird relationship with Coalition A, in part because I had been going to the meetings of both Coalition A and Coalition B [a county-level coalition] but I stopped after I saw leaders from A and B talking together after a Coalition A meeting one time, in a way that led me to perceive they were talking about the organization I'm with, and the next day, even though I'd had a good relationship with the leader of Coalition B, and had had a couple productive talks with someone else there about our organization providing volunteer mentors for victims they work with, the leader of Coalition B told me on a phone call that they did not want to work with us because we are a Christian organization. I'm pretty sure the Coalition A leader poisoned Coalition B leader's view of our organization. After that I attended two more Coalition A meetings, but then my e-mail address was removed from their listserv, and I stopped getting info about their meetings more than a year ago.

Following that rejection, the leader told me she had decided to stop attempting to collaborate with any "secular" NGOs. I asked her, "What do you think the trade-offs have been of not collaborating with secular NGOs?" Here is her response:

> Trying to work with them was very unpleasant and stressful, always having to defend our beliefs and what we're doing; it was very difficult working with the secular groups. After separating from them, it has been a lot easier; it is sad, but sometimes I guess it is easier to not be encumbered by negative things,

dynamics. With so much to do, it's better for me and the organization I lead to just focus on the work that needs to be done that we can do, without spending energy on trying to work with groups that don't want to work with us.

It is easier to focus on building my org than to build collaborations—at least than to build collaborations with other NGOs that are secular. We have good collaborations with other FBOs, and with some government agencies. [She laughed saying that.] You'd think it would be harder for us to work with government agencies, but actually it's harder to work with secular NGOs. I'm not attending any more secular meetings, other than Coalition B meetings, because there is so little benefit, and they are time wasters.

The final question I asked her was: "What kinds of impacts would be possible if FBOs and secular groups could work together well? Would the impacts be any greater?" Her response conveyed more resignation than conviction:

Probably, but the majority of our speaking engagements are with churches; we connect well with Christians. It's harder for Coalition A to do that. We all have our own niche, e.g., Coalition A can talk with Rotary Clubs, but if we were to collaborate, I don't know . . . I think it's all worked out as well as possible now, and we're each doing our own thing, and that's fine. In an ideal world, we'd all work together, of course.

It is important to remember that exclusionary acts between FBOs and areligious NGOs happen in both directions, for multiple and complex reasons. To balance the preceding pain-filled account of an evangelical FBO leader who was rejected and excluded by her areligious NGO counterparts, the following is an equally pain-filled account of a non-Christian who was turned down for a volunteer opportunity by an evangelical FBO.

IRRECONCILABLE DIFFERENCES

For some organizations, whether faith based or areligious, a shared commitment to particular beliefs by anyone who wants to volunteer with the organization, much less be employed, is viewed as foundational. There are areligious NGOs and FBOs that welcome anyone who wants to work with them, either as volunteers or paid staff, or as partner organizations within and beyond the nonprofit sector, and this stance is reflected in value statement B from earlier in this chapter: "We value collaborating with a diverse group of organizations in order to be more effective and build community capacity." But some organizations in both categories will only accept workers (paid or unpaid) who share their beliefs, exemplified by value statement C by the alliance, stating that it "welcomes cooperation with all organizations, agencies or persons who share its principles." The latter stance can cause tensions between anti-trafficking actors, whether individual or organizational, particularly those who share values with such an organization but do not subscribe to its beliefs. The following interactions illustrate this dynamic.

One evening I attended a meeting of a regional coalition made up of several small anti-trafficking groups, several of which were based in local churches, others consisting of geographically based community groups. There were also a smattering of college students in attendance. Jean, a recently retired woman who had founded the regional coalition and who was also a lay leader in her church, had received permission from that church for the coalition to meet in one of its rooms.

That night Barb, a young Buddhist I had met previously, attended the coalition meeting for the first time. Jean started the meeting by standing and stating, "I don't know about any of you, but this issue of human trafficking overwhelms me. I know I can't change anything on my own, so I start these coalition meetings by praying for God's help. Please pray with me if you'd like." She proceeded to pray aloud with her eyes closed, briefly and conversationally, asking for God's guidance and intervention to stop human trafficking, ending her prayer in the name of Jesus. Most around the room closed their eyes and bowed their heads, and some mouthed words silently as Jean prayed; most were simply still. I noticed Barb bow her head as well. At the end of the meeting Jean asked for a moment to pray aloud again to ask God's help in carrying out the plans that had been made. Again, Barb bowed her head.

After the meeting ended, I asked Barb if she'd like to go to a nearby café to chat for a few minutes. Over steaming mugs, I asked her what she'd thought of the coalition meeting, and specifically, how she had felt about the Christian prayers at the beginning and end of it. Barb smiled wanly, and said, "At least she explained why she was doing that and made it clear that anyone was welcome to be there whether or not they prayed." When I asked whether she sometimes felt excluded by Christians in anti-trafficking efforts, her expression turned sad, and she told me that just that week she had offered to volunteer for an explicitly Christian faith-based organization (FBO) that had an innovative approach that impressed her—and had been turned down because she is not a Christian. She opened her laptop and shared with me the e-mail exchange she had with a staff member at the FBO regarding the faith commitment it required of all volunteers and paid staff. Barb had written the following:

> Hello, I am interested in volunteering with your organization in the . . . program. I feel that I meet or exceed all of the qualifications for the program except for one element: the fact that I am not a Christian. I am writing to simply ask why my faith has to come into question to become an intern. I would be more than happy to write a statement of faith and have someone at my temple fill out a spiritual reference form for my Buddhist faith. I do not see why being or not being a Christian would have any impact on someone's ability to be a good [volunteer], and their ability to help the exploited and abused. I am very passionate about the anti–human-trafficking movement and I was excited to discover your [volunteer] program in my research. I was very disappointed to find, however, that your organization discriminates based on faith and I would like to know why. I am very interested to hear back from you.

Within twenty minutes she received this response:

> Thanks for your support for [Organization X] and interest in our [volunteer] program. Glad to hear that you're planning on applying! Your question about our Christian identity as an organization is a good one. [Organization X]'s staff members are Christians from a variety of traditions who want to be authentically engaged in the battle for justice; not as an abstraction, but as a struggle on behalf of real people who are victims of horrific abuse and violence. [Organization X]'s work is founded on the Christian call to justice articulated in the Bible—for example, Isaiah 1:17 commands us to "Seek justice, protect the oppressed, defend the orphan, and plead for the widow."
>
> Several supporters have asked why [Organization X] is a faith-based organization and what our policy is on hiring those who do not share our faith. . . . [Organization X] provides a conduit for people motivated by their faith to confront injustice in a shared atmosphere of faith and prayer. Our first witness of Christ is through the initial actions we take on behalf of our clients—literally bringing rescue—which allows us to demonstrate God's heart for justice. While [Organization X] does not directly proselytize as a part of our mission mandate, we do answer questions openly and honestly about our faith if/when asked. In our work, we partner with and engage non-Christian organizations and individuals; though our shared spiritual disciplines lead us to hire Christians. Our

staff intentionally draws strength and unity from their common commitment to the teachings of Jesus Christ and communion of daily prayer, and this can prove to be uncomfortable for non-Christians.

So, to answer your question directly, we would not be able to consider your application without a statement of faith. I do hope that the information above helps explain our reasons for doing so. If you don't think [Organization X] would be a good fit for you, I'd encourage you to learn about other partnership organizations leading the fight against human trafficking [names four prominent organizations, with URL for each]. Please do let me know if you have any further questions or concerns about this.

I noticed several dimensions to the chasm between Barb and the FBO staff member. Barb wrote vulnerably, as an individual, asking for acceptance of her faith by the Christian FBO. The FBO staff member responded kindly but firmly and impersonally as a representative of the FBO, as required by her position. Both Barb's query and the Christian FBO staff member's response were authentic, respectful expressions of deeply held beliefs and values that were, in the end, fundamentally irreconcilable. Barb stated not only that she holds a particular set of spiritual beliefs ("my Buddhist faith") but also that she is part of a religious community ("my temple"); these are foundational to her individual identity. The Christian FBO staff member explained that particular Christian spiritual practices (Bible-reading and corporate prayer) as well as adherence to the teachings of Jesus are foundational to the FBO's identity and work, noting that "this can prove to be uncomfortable for non-Christians." The other nonprofit organizations that the FBO staff member suggested as options for Barb were prominent, areligious organizations with which that FBO had long-standing partnerships. However, Barb had been motivated to apply to volunteer with the Christian FBO because she greatly respected its distinctive approach to anti-trafficking work. The response from the FBO staff member about the reasons for the organization's faith-based boundaries/discrimination puzzled her theologically and pragmatically, and she wrestled aloud in our conversation with how to reconcile her respect for the FBO's work and the sense of rejection she felt from this exclusion.

This was a difficult situation, and I invite you to extend empathy to all three parties: Barb, the FBO staff member whose job it was to respond to Barb's inquiry, and the FBO itself. The FBO's policy is stated on the organization's website, and it is legal under the US Civil Rights Act of 1964, which permits a religious organization to hire only those who share its religion.[26] Moreover, this FBO is the opposite of isolationist: it collaborates intensively with multiple partners in every sector, including many areligious ones, and it is well respected across sectors. It is an example of an FBO whose leaders so value its beliefs and the spiritual practices of Bible reading and prayer that they prioritize a common commitment to those beliefs and practices by all members of the organization.[27]

SUMMARY

This chapter has explored the way beliefs, values, and priorities shape organizations and sectors and interactions between them. By looking closely at tensions between law enforcement agencies, between victim service providers and law enforcement, and between different kinds of nonprofit/NGOs, we have seen the foundational importance of beliefs and values to the identities of organizations and sectors. Given this, it would be neither honest nor responsible of me to simply call for tolerance of differences in values and beliefs. Some values are incommensurate with each other, and some beliefs are contradictory. Not all differences in beliefs and values can be reconciled—and not only in anti-trafficking efforts. Studies from the realm of interprofessional healthcare have led to similar conclusions, finding that "conflicts between values and interests underlying different agencies and professions" can stymie attempts at collaboration, and fracture partnerships.[28]

As the correspondence between Barb, a Buddhist woman, and a Christian FBO demonstrated, irreconcilable differences exist in the realm of values and beliefs, and they influence collaborations in many ways. Sometimes such differences preclude it entirely. In that latter circumstance, as long as organizations are functioning legally without corruption, I think the tenets of a democratic society imply that conceding to nondestructive non-collaboration is better than striving to annihilate an opposing actor. This is one reason the NGO Polaris expressly values the practice of non-violence:

> We encourage the practice of non-violence among our staff and volunteers, not only because we believe it is right, but also because we believe it is most effective. The practice of non-violence requires us to first ask how we can be better or help others be better, rather than destructively criticize or support the disempowerment of others or other organizations. It is the ethic that helps protect movements from destructive internal politics and in-fighting, while

encouraging self-improvement as organizations, and mutual constructive support and collaboration.[29]

My overarching argument in this chapter is that it is best to negotiate mutually constructive forms of collaboration when possible and nondestructive non-collaboration when necessary. The latter is achieved by first acknowledging the universal presence and importance of widely ranging beliefs and values. The second strategy is to strive to ascertain one's own individual, organizational, and sector-based beliefs and values as well as those held by others. The final is to grant the right to exist without harassment even to organizations with fundamentally opposing values and beliefs.

That said, I witnessed many occasions when anti-trafficking actors with differing values or beliefs were able to find ways to work together. In an interview, a Christian philanthropist who routinely engages in multisector work on several complex problems including human trafficking articulated a similar observation: "It seems by being aware of our differing underlying values/beliefs we can honor our differences in a way that affirms that these differences exist within the broader population and also within trafficking victims themselves." Research on multisector work in other realms has shown that the processes of identifying, articulating, and acknowledging each partner's beliefs and values can dissipate tensions:

> Since values are internalized and largely unspoken, they can create important obstacles that may actually be invisible to different team members struggling with a problem. For a solution to be reached, the professional values must be made apparent to all professionals involved.[30]

Sometimes, making beliefs and values explicit and acknowledging the tensions among them is all it takes to make collaboration across such differences possible.

Throughout this book, we have explored the influences of many types of differences on interorganizational collaboration. By now it is clear that many of the challenges in collaborating against human trafficking are systemic in nature—that is, they are rooted in societal forces and sector characteristics that shape relations between anti-trafficking organizations. In the final chapter, I discuss three overarching practices—attitudes manifested in actions—that are evident in every successful anti-trafficking collaboration.

6

The Perfect Storm and Paths through It

[As a survivor-activist,] I know so little about freedom that my experiences are limited. How can I expect to know the true boundaries of what is possible? Nonsurvivors similarly have a limit to what they can know about the experience of slavery. By working in partnership, however, we can utilize our individual strengths and account for the gaps in our partners.

—*Minh Dang, 2014*[1]

All those who work against trafficking are searching for ways to do so more effectively. From the halls of government to the streets, shops, fields, and offices where police, social workers, business owners, community leaders, and attorneys work against trafficking, people in every sector affirm both the necessity of collaborating to counter human trafficking and the capacities and limitations of our respective perspectives and positions. In the words of collaboration expert David Straus, "Collaboration itself rests on the fundamental values of respect for human dignity and the right of stakeholder involvement."[2] For the same reasons that we insist on the dignity of all persons, enslaved or not, we must extend respect to all who strive to end slavery and do all we can to ensure integrity in those efforts.

Agreement on the value of integrity is essential across sectors, because the potential for deceit and fraud exists in every sector. Those who understand the dynamics of greed and opportunistic exploitation that drive human trafficking will not be surprised that fraud has occurred within and among anti-trafficking organizations. People have created fictitious accounts of trafficking victimization (see, for example, Somaly Mam), raised funds for non-existent anti-trafficking programs (for instance, Katerine Nastopka, also known as Lady Catarina Pietra Toumei, founder of the "Rescue Children from Trafficking Foundation"), and have faked expertise on trafficking to enrich themselves (for example, William Hillar, who received numerous teaching and training contracts from the FBI between 2000 and 2010 on the basis of false credentials). Each of these forms of fraud damages the anti-trafficking movement as a whole, both directly and indirectly. Fraud diminishes trust on multiple levels and thus increases the difficulty of collaborating. On the other hand, a realistic view of the possibility of fraud can lead to the development of expectations and protocols for transparency and accountability that strengthen integrity and reward those who exercise it.

Even well-intentioned collaboration has its hazards, and in the same way, understanding the difficulties associated with it equips us to better navigate its hazards—of which there are many. It is no wonder that people who work against human trafficking are prone to "collaboration fatigue," a condition I will discuss further below. There is no guarantee that collaborating will generate what we hope for, much less anything good. Things can go wrong, very wrong, people and organizations can get hurt, and enslavement might continue unabated despite our best efforts at collaborating against it. Throughout this book, I have noted cautions that leading experts on cross-sector collaboration offer about the hazards of building, much less sustaining, multilateral, robust collaborations. We have seen that prior studies on multisector collaboration, from the realms of healthcare, social service provision, business, and education, have found that collaboration requires painstaking and sometimes painful work to overcome countless disagreements, misunderstandings, and competitions. In this book I have presented many examples from the anti-trafficking realm that evidence similar challenges. While some of those experts address power relations, few consider gender and racial dynamics in interorganizational interactions, and even fewer discuss the fundamental role of beliefs and values in shaping organizational priorities and approaches. This book has examined all three, and has demonstrated how we reproduce challenges to collaboration just by being ourselves and doing our jobs. That trifold mirror in which we have examined our organizations and sectors evokes our inner urge to run for the closest rock we can hide under until the storm passes—until we realize we carry the storm with us.

I have invited readers to consider that every organization brings a set of collective hopes and fears to interorganizational interactions. These include hopes for validation and fears of marginalization. They also include hopes for an end to exploitation and fears about the changes that will be required to accomplish what we all say we want—as well as fears about the implications of maintaining the status quo on human trafficking. What can a willing but overwhelmed anti-trafficking leader, in any sector, do in the face of this "perfect storm" of collaboration challenges?

In view of all these complexities, there can be no single protocol. The path forward will be unique for each organization, depending on all sorts of factors. In the Collaboration Resources section at the end of the book, I suggest some group exercises designed to foster reflective and constructive communication about each of the challenges discussed in this book, places to find useful tools and resources on interorganizational and multisector collaboration, and a list of some practical books on building and managing collaborations. But tools and resources do little good without certain foundational practices—that is, attitudes expressed in actions. As I reflect on the instances of constructive and robust collaborations I have seen in counter-trafficking efforts, I see three such foundational practices that are evident in all of them. So in this chapter, I offer these recommendations: respect, trust, and persevere.

RESPECT

The foundation and essential precondition for any collaboration is respect. Respect involves acknowledging both the strengths and vulnerabilities of other organizations and sectors. Respect the contributions one's collaborators make, but also respect partner organizations' distinctive aims, beliefs, and values, along with the simple fact that they are willing to consider collaborating. Dr. AnnJanette Alejano-Steele, codirector of the Laboratory to Combat Human Trafficking since 2005, described the basis of her respect for other anti-trafficking organizations this way:

> Having had the privilege of having access to so many collaborative opportunities both in academia and in the nonprofit sector, I believe that humans do the best they can to work with one another with whatever tools they have available. Some simply have fewer tools than others, and some have the privilege of holding seats in more spaces compared to others. Some are able to devote particular

time to developing partnerships, and as importantly, to maintaining and cultivating partnerships in the face of change and fiscal uncertainty for the counter
trafficking movement. Furthermore, definitions and responses to human trafficking are rife with political, ideological and cultural meanings. All of these
factors are a lot to manage, and humans can collaborate to do extraordinary
things . . . or fail miserably under the most ideal of conditions.[3]

In this passage, Dr. Alejano-Steele conveyed her recognition of the disparate
capacities, opportunities, and limitations with which anti-trafficking organizations function. By choosing to believe that others do the best they can with
what they have, she enacts respect.

There are always costs to collaborating, so approaching each interaction
with a genuine appreciation for one's own and one's collaborators' investment
of time, energy, and resources is essential. Observations in the federal government's e-Guide about the costs of collaborating to law enforcement and victim
service providers hold true (in adapted ways) for other sectors as well:

> Many victim service provider and law enforcement organizations are chal-
> lenged by their capacity to release personnel to participate in operations that
> remove them from their core responsibilities. Victim service providers often
> have personnel fulfilling multiple responsibilities, with large caseloads, in
> addition to being organizational experts on human trafficking. Likewise, law
> enforcement officers carry large caseloads and, in some instances, operate as
> generalist investigators across multiple crime categories, including human
> trafficking. Time is a large constraint on task force members, due to the length
> of time needed for a successful trafficking investigation and the constraints of
> non-task force work obligations.[4]

In order to build mutual respect among task force members, Seattle's
DOJ-funded task force, the Washington Advisory Committee on Trafficking (WashACT), developed the following "WashACT Norms: Rules of
Engagement for Collaboration in WashACT" for interaction among task
force members:

1. Honor our in-person time together through active engagement during
   WashACT meetings.

2. Respect the diverse professions of WashACT members, as well as distinct roles and perspectives, and differences in capacity & experience/expertise levels.

3. Accurately and proactively acknowledge the accomplishments of other groups.

4. Call on each other when someone's experience is relevant regardless of past history.

5. When you have asked for someone's guidance and input, report back when possible.

6. Provide constructive feedback when asked and receive feedback as a gift.

7. When criticism seems necessary, confine it to the specific action/campaign/idea rather than undermining a group or member organization, or WashACT as a whole.

8. Confront challenges and provide constructive criticism face-to-face or on the phone.

These "rules" were distilled from suggestions elicited through an anonymous web-based survey. The initial suggestions reflected a mix of the suggesters' positive and negative experiences in prior interactions. These rules reference many aspects of interactions in which a demonstration of respect strengthens interorganizational relations. Conversely, transgressing norms such as these conveys disrespect or lack of regard toward collaborators.

In addition to respecting others, it is also vitally important to respect one's own organization by recognizing its capacities, limits, forms of power, and aspirations. Collaboration experts Huxham and Vangen address this insightfully:

> If you are feeling vulnerable, it is worth remembering that the apparently powerful organizations would probably not be wanting to collaborate with you if you did not have something to offer over and above what they can provide themselves. If you can identify what this is, it can put you in a good negotiating position. On the other hand, if you are collaborating with organizations which are smaller than yours, it is worth remembering that they may be feeling much more vulnerable than you at first imagine. If you wish the partnership to be on roughly equal terms, you may need to find ways to demonstrate this to them. Paying attention to communication and especially to careful use of language is essential.[5]

Every organization and sector has vulnerabilities. The people who work within them may be more or less aware of them at various times. Sometimes the perceptions of people from other sectors or organizations about the vulnerabilities of one's own sector or organizations can be helpful to hear when they are offered with respect and empathy. In the following section, we will explore some of the particular vulnerabilities of survivor-activists in collaborations, as seen through their own eyes and as perceived by others.

Respecting the Effects of Trauma Experienced by Survivor-Activists

Every human wants to be respected, but for survivors of trafficking, respect is particularly significant and sensitive. A key element in cultivating respect for survivor-activists is developing empathy for the challenges some face in maintaining their sense of agency. One described the process she uses to check in with herself each day:

> I have to ask myself before any event, including this morning, "Do I really want to speak today?" Because slavery is about not having a choice, I give myself a choice. Every time I enter a hotel room, I am frightened, and I have to talk to myself, saying, "This is not the same, I'm safe here." Those are the effects of slavery. (Conference panelist's comment)

The ambivalence that sometimes afflicts survivor-activists has consequences for those who seek to collaborate with them. Five nonsurvivor interviewees from sectors including victim service providers, law enforcement officers, and mental health experts independently initiated discussions with me about what they consider to be one of the most sensitive aspects of multisector collaboration involving survivors. This is the way that the effects of trauma compromise some survivor-activists' ability to participate constructively and consistently in collaborations. One mental health expert who has participated in multisector collaborations with survivor-activists explained:

> This is something of a taboo subject, but an ongoing challenge for survivors is maintaining their own stability while participating in the [anti-trafficking] movement. Having worked in multilateral partnerships with several survivors, I have noticed that survivors' need for absolute flexibility in accountability, particularly when their trauma is triggered, is not addressed. It is sobering, and maddening, and at times frustrating—particularly when there are deadlines to

be met. Of course, we also see this in other movements involving trauma, such as the movements against domestic violence and sexual assault. (Interview)

All five nonsurvivor interviewees related accounts of survivor-activists' outbursts of anger that seemed disproportionate to the situation, repeated instances of last-minute cancellations of hard-to-schedule meetings, and on-again, off-again patterns of engagement in collaborations. All of these are common manifestations of post-traumatic stress disorder. And all had strained relations between survivor-activists and those from other sectors.

The nonsurvivors were unanimous in recommending that everyone who interacts with survivor-activists learn about the lasting effects of trauma in order to better understand and respect what survivors contend with. Each of these interviewees strongly affirmed their desire for, and valuing of, coleadership with survivor-activists. Several spoke of their hope that all survivors have support for working through their experiences as they participate in multisector collaborations. Several also spoke of the necessity for survivors, in order to avoid further trauma to themselves, to have access to training in developing and maintaining healthy boundaries for themselves when they are reaching out to and serving those who have been more recently victimized. This is fostering respect to oneself, something that is a baseline for having respect for others.

To summarize this section, the demonstration of respect for others is foundational to collaboration. Survivor-activists bring essential knowledge and talents to the collaborative mix, and at that same time, by definition, have trauma in their backgrounds. So an understanding of the effects of trauma is essential for everyone who seeks to collaborate with survivors, in order to better respect their needs. That said, all individuals and organizations have their own particularized vulnerabilities and limitations that also need to be understood and respected. Collaborations have more chance of success when respect takes the forefront.

TRUST

Trust follows respect, because trust building begins with demonstrating respect and support for collaborators. In contrast to respect, which can be enacted between strangers, trust is earned over time. Research has shown that participants in all kinds of interorganizational collaborations wrestle with trust. Chris Huxham and Siv Vangen, experts in interorganizational collaboration, point out that although conventional wisdom considers trust a necessary precondition for successful collaboration, in practice the start point for many organizations entering a partnership is suspicion rather than trust.[6] Therefore, it is important to be mindful of the process of trust building. Huxham and Vangen suggest thinking of trust building in any collaboration as a looping process, beginning with these two factors: One is the development of shared expectations about the future of the collaboration, whether based on reputation or past behavior or on contracts and agreements. The other factor is willingness to take the risk of trusting each other enough to initiate the collaboration. Huxham and Vangen argue that if both of these factors are enabled, then trust can be built up gradually by establishing some modest aims initially. Successful outcomes from modest aims strengthen trusting attitudes, which then underpin more ambitious collaboration.[7]

The federal e-Guide provides an apt description of the process of trust building:

> All great relationships are built on trust. It is not readily given nor should it be presumed to exist until it has been earned. . . . Building trust is . . . a necessary part of effective collaboration that takes time. Task force meetings, joint trainings, open discussions, challenges to existing practices, productive debriefings of encountered experiences, and other interactions among task force members all provide opportunities for effective teambuilding.

> Trust is established over time through the shared experience of working together on one trafficking case at a time, and by communicating or debriefing about the experiences of that case, regardless of whether there was a successful outcome.[8]

Sometimes distrust between organizations and sectors has developed due to historical patterns of disrespect, repeated over time until trust becomes hard to imagine anymore. A survivor-activist victim services provider, who had experienced repeated rejections from potential collaborators, said the following:

> I'm going to be really honest, I don't have a lot of partners in my city. I try to partner, but I get responses like "We already do that; we don't need to work with

you," and "We're afraid you'll steal our clients." There are plenty of survivors who need help. How can that be right? What does that say about their hearts? Those kinds of things hit my trust issues, which I admit I still have. It makes me wonder, "Do you know I'm a survivor? And if you do, and you treat me this way, this must be how you treat the survivors who are your clients. What do you do when you've made 500 lunch and dinner requests and someone cancels every time?" I still play nice and stay in the sandbox, because otherwise I wouldn't be practicing what I preach. But it tests my trust issues. (Fieldnote)

Most unfortunately, one of the hard lessons survivor-activists can teach is that deep-seated distrust can become self-predicting and self-fulfilling, so that when one expects to be disrespected, one invites disrespect, and distrust deepens. The survivor-activist quoted above makes a vital move by resolving to "still play nice and stay in the sandbox." Not only is she practicing what she preaches, but she is also continuing to convey a willingness to trust. Cultivating trust and demonstrating a willingness to trust are both essential to overcoming the challenges of collaboration.

Initiating Cross-Sector Conversations

Another way that trust can, and must, be built is through people in every sector initiating respectful interactions, beginning with simple conversations, with people in other sectors. Dr. Alejano-Steele writes:

In order to cultivate partnership, one requires space in which to dialogue, discuss, and parse out challenges in a safe setting. Clearly articulated project values helped to provide the foundation of the settings for dialogue. Note that I stated "safe," not "comfortable"; this is the learning edge of collaborative learning— getting to places of agreeing to disagree while aiming for a shared goal.[9]

Based on the positive results I have observed and experienced in my own personal experiments with cross-sector interactions during the course of researching and writing this book, I am confident that Dr. Alejano-Steele's suggestion is relevant to everyone. But it is especially important that nonsurvivors in each sector initiate this trust toward survivor-activists, who belong to the sector in the anti-trafficking movement that feels most marginalized and for whom there are the most obstacles to overcome on the path toward multisector collaboration.

When survivors speak publicly, their talks are often well attended and receive strong applause from attendees. However, outside those panel sessions, I noticed a curious pattern of (non)interaction between survivors and nonsurvivors. In my observations, survivor-activist participants often sat or stood together during meals and coffee breaks at such events and rarely engaged in conversation with other event attendees. This seemed like a classic chicken-and-egg social cycle whereby insecurity or prior experiences with marginalization motivate people to stay in physical proximity to and conversation with those with whom they feel secure (or similarly marginalized) rather than moving toward and initiating conversation with others. The "closeness" of their group inhibits people who are not part of it from moving toward and initiating with those in it, thus increasing the sense of marginalization by those in the "close" group. That all-too-common and unfortunate social dynamic between survivors and nonsurvivors is exacerbated further by the vulnerability experienced by those who have publicly disclosed their experiences of being trafficked, and is augmented by the awkward and uncomfortable feelings experienced by those who have witnessed such disclosures and are not confident in their ability to respond appropriately and constructively. Despite whatever awkwardness nonsurvivors feel, it is essential that we initiate the trust process with survivors. To initiate conversations with survivors or anyone else you have heard speak, simply say thank you, or ask someone what they are working on. These moves express appreciation, respect, and interest—all door-openers. In addition to trust building through one-on-one interactions, there are ways that trust building occurs between organizations through public communication, as we will consider next.

Evaluations as Trust-Builders

The practices of conducting evaluations of anti-trafficking initiatives—and making those evaluations available publicly—do more than assess the success of particular programs. They also serve to build trust across the anti-trafficking movement by enacting transparency among organizations outside of the common relationships in which transparency and accountability are expected, such as between partners in a collaborative project or between a funder and a grantee. The International Justice Mission (IJM) is one of the few anti-trafficking NGOs that has an in-house "program design and evaluation unit." It conducts multi-method assessments of IJM programs, and posts many of its assessments online.[10] It is possible even for small organizations to have evaluations conducted at a relatively low cost by collaborating with academic researchers when the program is of substantive interest to them or the evaluation process is instructive to students. To illustrate, Businesses Ending Slavery and Trafficking (BEST) leveraged a modest grant and a partnership with social work researchers to generate a high-quality evaluation of its training program for hoteliers.[11] Externally conducted evaluations of collaborations are rare, but they can be immensely valuable to the larger anti-trafficking movement as well as to the collaboration partners. In 2012, Chab Dai, an anti-trafficking coalition comprised primarily of NGOs, had an in-depth evaluation conducted on its coalition model and on the impact of the coalition on anti-trafficking efforts in Cambodia (its primary base).[12] The insightful evaluation report, although obviously focused on Chab Dai, is a terrific resource for any NGO involved in interorganizational collaboration and a model for how evaluations of collaborations can be conducted.

Lessons from a Sentencing Hearing

Relationships of mutual trust and respect among anti-trafficking actors generate many positive outcomes for counter-trafficking efforts. Sometimes all that is needed is a one-time display of multisector support. On one instance I received a brief e-mail from a mobilization and advocacy nongovernmental organization (MANGO) leader, asking if I was available to attend a particular sentencing hearing at a local county courthouse the following week. I already trusted that leader, and I was able to trust, from my past experience of the frequency (limited) and the types (specific) of requests he makes of me, that he would respect my time. Based on these, I agreed to attend even though I did not know much about the hearing nor why my presence could be helpful. When we had a chance to talk, he explained that the sentencing hearing was for a man with the last name of Willhell, who had been arrested for attempted commercial sexual abuse of a minor. Willhell had posted an ad online seeking sex with a teen. An undercover detective responded, pretending to be a fifteen-year-old girl. They agreed to meet at a fast-food restaurant. When Willhell showed up, he had $100 in cash—the amount they had negotiated as payment for sex—and condoms. He was arrested, a jury had found him guilty as charged, and the prosecuting attorney had requested a sentence within the state's legally stipulated range for this crime, which is fifteen to twenty months in prison along with a fine and the requirement to register as a sex offender. However, Willhell claimed this was his first time soliciting sex from a minor, and after the conviction the county judge questioned the prosecutor's reasons for seeking a prison sentence for him. According to people who attended the verdict hearing, when the jury returned a guilty verdict, the judge told the prosecutor he was surprised by the sentence that "a first-time offender like Mr. Willhell" faced. The judge questioned whether it was possible for Willhell to avoid prison time, saying, "Of course, we don't have a victim at all in this case—it is a fictitious child with a police officer sitting at the keyboard, playing that role." The prosecutor's response was, "Mr. Willhell is no less guilty because a police detective showed up to meet him instead of a fifteen-year-old child. It is very tempting to look at the problem of demand on a case-by-case basis and say, 'Oh, this guy doesn't seem so bad or that guy doesn't seem so bad; he just made a mistake.' But the problem is that there isn't just one guy here or there who does this—there are literally thousands." In these public comments the prosecutor conveyed confidence that sentencing guidelines would be followed.

But after the verdict hearing, the prosecutor called the MANGO leader—one with whom he had built trust over several years—privately, and asked for help. He admitted that he was not confident the judge would follow the sentencing guidelines. The prosecutor had a hunch that the presence of a few concerned citizens at the sentencing hearing might help persuade the judge, but feared that having too many people there might cause the judge to feel bullied and become defensive. So he asked the MANGO leader to find a handful of people to show up for a sentencing hearing that would take place a few days later. He knew the MANGO had the capacity to mobilize a lot of volunteers on short notice, and he trusted that the MANGO leader would abide by his strategy of having just a few in the courtroom. I happened to be one of the people the MANGO leader contacted, and after I learned what was needed, I offered to bring a companion with me. The MANGO leader lined up another volunteer, and the four of us met outside the courtroom at the appointed time.

We had a few minutes to talk with the prosecutor before the hearing, and he thanked us heartily for coming. None of us had attended a sentencing hearing previously, and so we wanted to know what to expect. The prosecutor answered our questions patiently, without any condescension. He described correspondence he had had with the judge following the verdict hearing, the challenging questions the judge had asked, and the responses he had provided. He confided that he doubted the judge would follow the sentencing guidelines. He intended to object if the guidelines were not followed and to appeal the sentence if necessary. He was visibly weary, discouraged that the judge did not seem to be concerned that if a detective had not happened to succeed in catching Willhell, an actual teenager would have been victimized. But he also was clearly very grateful for and encouraged by our presence. His words and his demeanor in that conversation conveyed, on the one hand, his strong commitment to persevering on behalf of trafficking victims, and on the other, the uphill battle that that felt like to him.

Except for a reporter and a woman (presumably someone related to the offender), the courtroom was empty when the four of us entered. The attorneys, their staff, and the offender entered, then the judge. When the prosecutor spoke to the judge, he did so with a calm confidence that masked his fears. He motioned to the four of us, introducing us by name and by profession, elaborating a bit about the MANGO leader as "the executive director of a city-wide coalition of citizens who are concerned about human trafficking" and describing me as "a professor who studies human trafficking." He explained briefly that we had come to the hearing because we cared about victims of human trafficking and wanted to see justice carried out. He stated the sentence he was requesting for Willhell, noting that it was consistent with state sentencing guidelines. The judge listened to the defense attorney's argument for a lower sentence, then moved to a decision without much discussion with either attorney. He issued the sentence requested by the prosecutor. There was no way to find out whether or to what degree our demonstration of multisector (MANGO and academic) support for justice against trafficking crimes influenced the judge; someone in his position is unlikely to disclose that kind of information. What was abundantly clear was that we had encouraged the prosecutor, convincing him of the wisdom of his decision to risk reaching across sectors to request support from a MANGO.

The situation I just described holds several lessons regarding collaboration. First, it demonstrates that mutual respect and trust are possible between prosecutors and MANGOs, sectors that do not interact directly very often in the counter-trafficking realm. A second lesson is that a prompt, effective response to a cross-sector request builds trust and respect. The

MANGO leader in this situation recruited a small number of volunteers requested by the prosecutor, and he selected ones who could commit to showing up at the courthouse on a weekday afternoon. In delivering what had been requested, the MANGO leader undoubtedly deepened the prosecutor's trust in him personally and in the MANGO itself. A third lesson is that transparency among collaborators about the challenges of working against trafficking in each sector increases mutual understanding and paves the way for more robust collaboration in the future. The prosecutor's lack of condescension, and his openness with the MANGO volunteers about his doubts before the sentencing hearing, deepened the volunteers' understanding of the challenges of prosecuting trafficking crimes and increased our motivation to be supportive in future cases. It was the kind of collaboration experience that motivates people to continue collaborating. This is critical for reasons I unpack in the next section.

PERSEVERE

Two-thirds of the 186 respondents to the 2012 national survey on partnership conducted by the Laboratory to Combat Human Trafficking reported that their organizations participate in at least two to four interorganizational partnerships.[13] The phenomenon of "collaboration fatigue" has been discussed in research on collaboration for at least a decade. William Haskin, an expert on collaboration within the private sector, defines it as "a condition of exhaustion brought on by an onslaught of information, forced interaction, and general low-value collaboration."[14] In view of risks of collaboration fatigue, the final suggestion I offer is to consider carefully when, how, and with whom your organization will collaborate, invest in those partnerships, and then persevere. Everyone who contends against human trafficking realizes that it is a monumental task and does not expect immediate or easily attained results. We need to bring the same resolve to our collaboration efforts. To use the imagery of the survivor-activist quoted in the previous section, we need to decide—before beginning to collaborate—that we are going to do all we can to stay in the sandbox.

Whatever one's beliefs and values, the example set by the evangelical faith-based victim service provider who earned the trust of areligious counterparts (described in chapter 5), is useful to all. Her strategy was to start humbly, earn trust, ask what is needed, and develop aims and approaches in dialogue with same-sector counterparts and partners in other sectors. Doing these things requires significant perseverance, especially when contending with historically patterned distrust or discrimination. But cultivating robust collaborations is like climbing a virtually untrod mountain, not sprinting through a street race. Preparation, survival skills and tools, and resolve to persevere are essential.

From Gas Stations to State Rest Areas and Back Again

At the beginning of chapter 2, I related the first part of the story about how a handful of concerned citizens in Washington State launched a campaign to persuade gas station managers all along I-5 to put up anti-trafficking posters prior to the 2010 Winter Olympics in Vancouver, British Columbia. Their next step was to get permission from the Department of Transportation to put posters in state rest areas, and that required permission from the state legislature. Early in 2010, more than two hundred e-mails were exchanged over the course of a few weeks as several MANGO leaders negotiated with the office of the state's leading legislator on human trafficking initiatives and the DOT capital facilities director about the design, placement, and display timeframe for the "temporary" posters (and what type of adhesive could be used). To recap, the lead victim service provider had concerns about the poster approved by the lead legislator (and therefore by the DOT), but the VSP's concerns were sidelined by the MANGOs for the sake of getting something— anything—with the national hotline number on it posted in rest areas prior to the start of the Olympics. Where the story left off, dozens of volunteers had downloaded and printed copies of the legislator-DOT-approved poster, and in the weeks before the Olympics, they posted these, plus a few unapproved posters, in rest areas along both I-5 and I-90 using (most of the time) DOT-approved, double-sided tape. But there is more to this story, both in term of constructive outcomes and in terms of lessons for multisector collaboration. These chiefly have to do with perseverance.

While MANGOs were coordinating to mobilize volunteers to put up the temporary posters in the restrooms of state rest areas during February 2010, the legislature amended the legal code, granting the DOT permission to work with MANGOs to develop policies regarding anti-trafficking posters in state rest areas. This was landmark legislation, since the state DOT had not previously had permission to interface directly with anti-trafficking advocates.

Furthermore, the legislation granted the DOT the latitude to develop policies about poster content and placement in bathroom stalls, as shown in the following, entitled "Human trafficking informational posters at rest areas":

> The department may work with human trafficking victim advocates in developing informational posters for placement in rest areas. *The department may adopt policies* for the placement of these posters in rest areas and *these policies must address, at a minimum, placement of the posters in bathroom stalls.* The posters may be in a variety of languages and include toll-free telephone numbers a person may call for assistance, including the number for the national human trafficking resource center at (888) 373-7888 and the number for the Washington state office of crime victims advocacy. (RCW 47.38.080, emphasis added)

By the time this legislation passed in the spring of 2010, the leaders of the four MANGOs who had participated in postering the gas stations and temporary rest areas were in agreement that a better poster was needed, and furthermore, that input from VSPs and survivors was essential to developing it. Robert Beiser, who was at that time a volunteer with the MANGO Seattle Against Slavery took the lead in negotiating the process of developing a new multilingual, victim-addressed poster, with tacit, if not explicit, support from other local MANGOs. Robert worked doggedly with several local VSPs to broker agreement on the content of the poster. The only element everyone agreed upon from the start was that the national human trafficking hotline number should be presented prominently. As for the rest, there were multiple, conflicting opinions on whether images would be used, and if so, which ones; in which languages the information should be presented; what the English-language text would say; who would decide what should be said in the other languages (that is, whether the English words would be translated or whether an equivalent but culturally specific message would be used); and who would compose the non-English texts.

Negotiating those questions with VSPs and trafficking experts from multiple language communities, and then working with a graphic artist to incorporate their input, required an iterative process of drafting, vetting, and revising the poster over several months. Robert later reflected that it did not occur to him to update the DOT during that period—an oversight he would come to regret. The outcome of the negotiations was a visually striking poster with a simple message. In English, it read, "No one should force you into work or prostitution. You have rights in the United States, regardless of immigration status. If you or someone you know is being forced to work, please call for help." The same message was presented (in culturally appropriate but not literal translation) in Spanish, Russian, Tagalog, Korean, Chinese, and Vietnamese. Logos from endorsing organizations—including VSPs and law enforcement agencies as well as Seattle Against Slavery, the MANGO that led the poster development effort—lined the bottom row.

From the beginning of the MANGO leaders' contact with the lead legislator and DOT officials in early 2010, the MANGOs had assured their government contacts that there would be no cost to the state in permitting anti-trafficking posters at rest areas. So having accomplished the production of a poster that bore endorsements from key VSPs, law enforcement, and the state Attorney General's office, Seattle Against Slavery launched a fund-raising campaign in November 2010 to cover the costs of printing and installing the posters in rest area kiosks and bathrooms. In mid-February 2011, Robert e-mailed Sam, the DOT official he had e-mailed a year previously. It was that 2010 e-mail from Robert to Sam that sparked the request from Virginia in the legislator's office for me to be a "sole contact" for the DOT, but Robert did not mention any of that. Rather, he politely (re)introduced himself, and asked how the DOT would like to instruct MANGO volunteers regarding putting up the "no one should be forced" poster in rest areas. He also acknowledged, "During the last round of posting, there were some errors by volunteers regarding size and posting method, so in reviewing the e-mails you sent last time, I wanted to check in regarding the details and make sure we give advance notice to the regional staff of the SRAs." Robert attached the widely vetted poster, and asked if it would be permissible for volunteers to start posting it in ten days.

The response he received was courteous but discouraging. The responding DOT official, a colleague of Sam's, stated that only the "approved" poster from 2010 could be posted in rest areas. Furthermore, she explained, "the placement of posters by volunteers during the Olympics last year created some difficulties; so WSDOT will no longer allow individuals to post information at safety rest areas" without a permit, which must be renewed annually, and posters would have to be installed by the DOT's "current traveler information vendor." The latter clause increased the cost of the project for Seattle Against Slavery exponentially, but it ensured that the posters would be installed behind Plexiglas shields to prevent theft and minimize damage by vandals. Other stipulations of the permitting process were listed in the e-mail, and the DOT's brand-new permit application form was attached.

Among other requirements, the permit application stated that applicants must have a Federal Tax ID number or 501(c)(3) status and must agree to designate one individual as the point of contact (this latter clause was undoubtedly a reaction to the DOT's pre-Olympic frustration over what must have felt like an e-mail onslaught from multiple MANGO leaders—and my refusal to be the "sole contact" for the DOT). Determined to succeed, Robert and his coleaders at Seattle Against Slavery pressed on, and within four months they had succeeded in persuading the DOT to approve the poster that had been endorsed by VSPs and law enforcement agencies, and in raising the additional amount of funds required to pay the DOT's vendor for installation. Multiple versions of the poster were produced, and made available for download on Seattle Against Slavery's website.[15] One version used four photos borrowed from materials produced by the U.S. Health and Human Services agency (this version is displayed in figure 6.1); a second version was text-only. Seattle Against Slavery's permit application was submitted and approved by the DOT in June 2011—much to the relief of everyone involved.

Any triumph in anti-trafficking efforts is a reason to rejoice, and a multi-sector collaboration that publicizes a phone number for potential victims to reach help is no small victory. Posters were installed in the kiosks and restrooms of every rest area in the state by the end of 2011, and the permit has been renewed by the DOT each year since, thanks largely to the remarkable perseverance of Seattle Against Slavery leaders. Calls from Washington to the national hotline increased dramatically in 2012, and continued to climb in 2013 and 2014. Although there are several possible factors in that increase, the presence of hotline-promoting posters in rest areas, private businesses, and other locations is almost certainly one of those factors.

But the story is not over yet. The results of the collaboration in Washington proved to be infectious. As news spread about the victim-addressed poster created in Seattle, MANGOs from other states contacted Seattle Against Slavery to request the poster files, which were freely shared. By 2015, the languages employed and the endorsement logos at the bottom of the poster had been customized for use in seven other states: Alabama, Florida, Georgia, Idaho, Oregon, South Carolina, and Texas. The payoffs of perseverance con-

FIGURE 6.1
Victim-Addressed Poster. Courtesy of Seattle Against Slavery

tinued as MANGOs in Idaho lobbied their legislature to follow Washington's example. In March 2015, Idaho amended its state code to permit its DOT to "allow posters and signs to be placed by non-profit, anti–human trafficking organizations in or around" rest areas.[16] Later that month, with explicit reference to the successful implementation of the 2010 legislation permitting anti-trafficking posters at DOT rest areas, Washington's legislature again broke new ground in counter-trafficking efforts by passing legislation requiring all public restrooms to post human trafficking hotline notices.[17] The reason I titled this part of the story "from gas stations to state rest areas and back again" is that when this law is implemented, Washington's businesses with public restrooms, such as gas stations, restaurants, and grocery stores will all display the national human trafficking hotline number.

The gas station and rest area poster story (begun in chapter 2 and continued in this chapter) depicts ways that MANGOs, VSPs, state legislators, and agency officials can, and should, work together. The more obvious positive outcomes from these collaborations were many: the production of a victim-addressed, multilingual poster; new legislation permitting the postering process; a DOT anti-trafficking-poster permitting process; and the successful raising of funds to print and install posters in every rest area in the state each year. Additional positive outcomes, though less obvious, were also many. They included the strengthening of Seattle Against Slavery's relationships with local VSPs and legislators, the successful negotiation of a mutually respectful partnership between Seattle Against Slavery and the DOT, and greater knowledge on the part of many within Seattle-based MANGOs of what it takes to collaborate with government agencies. Clearly, respect, trust, and perseverance build on each other.

FINAL REFLECTIONS

The need for multisector collaboration against human trafficking is great, and the challenges are many, deep-rooted, large-scale, and systemic. It is these challenges (not any particular individual, agency, organization, or sector) that make such collaboration difficult and costly. Collaboration requires painstaking and sometimes painful work to overcome countless disagreements, misunderstandings, and competitions.

I hope this book has proved encouraging to everyone who has struggled with attempts at collaboration around human trafficking, everyone who has wondered whether robust collaboration is possible or worth the effort, and everyone who is considering giving up on multisector collaboration. Not every cross-sector partnership will gel, and not all collaborations will accomplish their collective aims. But perseverance will pay off in vital ways.

Respondents to the 2012 national survey on partnership among anti-trafficking organizations conducted by the Laboratory to Combat Human Trafficking reported that the interorganizational efforts in which they participate generate many significant outcomes. Some of the types of counter-trafficking outcomes they attributed to persevering in partnerships included the following:

- Increased awareness of human trafficking
- A community-coordinated response to trafficking
- The development of protocols and tools
- The identification of survivors and development of protection services
- Greater success in prosecuting traffickers

It can take years of multisector work to accomplish these kinds of outcomes, but each one both builds on previous work and provides a foundation for that which follows. During the period of this study, three of the cities where I conducted fieldwork had particularly strong, multisector ecologies of anti-trafficking efforts that gave rise to multiple instances of each of these types of outcomes.

One key to persevering is recognizing that most people who work on countering human trafficking, whether as an assigned part of their job or via their own initiative, whether paid or as a volunteer, engage with the issue on multiple levels. All are touched by the cruelty of the crime and by the resilience some survivors demonstrate. They each rue their—our—complicity in exploitative political-economic systems. For all of them, personal concerns, values, and beliefs influence how they take up or resist the values of the organization with which they work, while the values of their sector affect them as individuals whether they embrace those values or strive to change them. Police officers serve their communities in other ways when they are off-duty—for instance, as volunteers in youth mentoring programs or at food banks. Some leaders of areligious anti-trafficking NGOs are themselves people whose personal faith is foundational to their lives and work. Some social service providers have earned law degrees, and many hold the values of bringing perpetrators to justice alongside the overarching aim of their sector to care for and empower victims and survivors. Many citizens who volunteer in anti-trafficking efforts also hold jobs in the private sector—they bring various kinds of professional expertise to their volunteer efforts, and catalyze anti-slavery initiatives in their industry. They all wish their work was unnecessary, and yet they keep going.

I, too, am engaged with the problem of human trafficking on multiple levels, both professionally and personally. As a university-based researcher, I am part of a sector that carries some general status and ideology markers that only partially overlap with my personal beliefs and values. In addition to being a professor and researcher, I am also—as a white, female, middle-aged American citizen—a consumer, the mother of a child of a different race (adopted transnationally before I knew anything about the risk of child trafficking via adoption), and a practicing Christian. Because of all these factors, I, like other workers in anti-trafficking, hold multiple and sometimes conflicting values—and it is precisely these multiple values that allow me to empathize with each of those I interviewed for this book. My hope is that the book helps everyone who reads it understand differing perspectives better—their own as well as those of people who differ from them.

To conclude, I have demonstrated in this book that collaboration is shaped by complex interactions between embodied individuals, organizations, sectors, and the intersecting social, political, and economic contexts in which it takes place.[18] Over the course of this book, we have seen the necessity of recognizing perceived power differentials, whether due to the sector or status of an organization or to differences in the demographics of the people who represent a sector in a particular setting. We have considered how such differences influence efforts at collaboration and discovered potential ways to overcome some of the obstacles any or all of these create in collaborative work. We have examined examples of ways that leadership structures and communication processes can be democratized in multisector coalitions. We have reflected on the variety of beliefs and values that bring actors into counter-trafficking efforts, shape their aims, and influence how they work. We have explored how identifying common values and developing shared norms can support multisector interactions.

These practices require investments of time and resources to plan and to implement consistently throughout the life of a multisector coalition. Such practices become more costly when attempts at collaboration break down. This is because it is easier to sustain carefully designed and well-led collaborations than to overcome disillusionment over failed collaborations. However, sometimes it is necessary—though costly—to reshape counter-productive patterns, such as organizations retreating into intra-sector interactions. Sometimes it is useful to consider whether alliances that were built around originally like-minded organizations within or even across sectors have become exclusionary forces that need to be disintegrated to make space for new collaborations.

I have now done what I set out to do in this book. That is, I have done my best to make a persuasive case that multisector collaboration against human trafficking is essential, it is possible, and it is worth the investment. I hope this book has challenged and inspired you (even though it may have provoked you on occasion). Most of all, I hope it strengthened your resolve to collaborate well. The rest of the story remains to be written—together.

Collaboration Resources

Throughout this book I have addressed common problems in anti-trafficking collaborations. I have also suggested approaches for mitigating common challenges experienced in such multisector partnerships. Finally, I promised that I would provide some resources that could be helpful in building better collaborations to counter human trafficking. I hope that you will find the following exercises, tools, case studies, and examples of organizations' mission and values statements useful. I provide clickable links for these and additional resources at http://CollaboratingAgainstTrafficking.info.

SECTION I: EXERCISES FOR MULTISECTOR GROUPS

Role playing has several benefits. It helps expand participants' understanding of the challenges and constraints faced by others, and it can result in greater empathy. Role play scenarios can also help generate innovative strategies and solutions to complex problems. Lastly, for the purposes of surfacing and addressing sensitive or contentious subjects, role play scenarios can sometimes be more constructive than direct discussion. The other suggested exercises involve direct discussions; it may work best to try a role play scenario first. While no single exercise can save the life of a doomed collaboration, these types of tools can help partnering organizations create a good foundation for working together, or navigate through a rough patch.

ROLE PLAY SCENARIOS

Role Play Scenario #1. Aim: Foster understanding of each sector. Participants: 3 or more people

Preparation: Assign each participant a sector to represent the following:

- **Law enforcement and government agencies** (various levels and branches)
- **Nonprofits** (various types), including general and specialized victim service providers, a mobilization and advocacy NGO, an immigrant community organization, a community policing organization, a faith-based organization, and a foundation/donor organization
- **Private sector entities** including small, medium, and large companies, and an industry association
- **Youth and education leaders**, including those in K–12 and higher education, and youth services
- **Survivor-activists**

Tasks: Assign the group one of the following tasks, or make up your own, and have the group figure out who can (or must) do what to accomplish the task:

- Get anti-trafficking signage posted in all the state rest areas.
- Persuade city council to adopt and enforce a slavery-free procurement system for city purchases.
- Train all hotel and transportation company employees in the city about how to identify trafficking victims.
- Eliminate forced labor from nail salons in the city.

Role Play Scenario #2. Aim: Foster understanding of trafficking investigations and prosecution. Participants: 3 or more people.

Preparation: Assign individuals to roles from the following list:

- City police detective
- County sheriff
- FBI agent
- County prosecutor

- Assistant U.S. Attorney
- NGO-based victim advocate or service provider

Tasks: Assign the group one or more cases from the following list:

- An ad appears online requesting sex from a "hot young teen."
- A boy is arrested by street cop for possessing cocaine. When questioned about how he has the money to buy coke, he says he has been pimped out in three states.
- The National HT Hotline forwards a credible tip that some kitchen staff at a Thai restaurant in the city had their passports confiscated by the restaurant owner.
- Someone from a nearby suburb calls 911 reporting that a non-English-speaking female is confined indoors in the house next door.

The group will then discuss the following questions:

- What are the challenges of investigating trafficking cases for local (municipal/county-level) law enforcement agencies?
- What are the challenges for federal law enforcement agencies?
- What makes collaboration between local and federal LE difficult?
- How should investigators and prosecutors work together, and what makes that challenging?

Role Play Scenario #3. Aim: Foster understanding of victim services provision. Participants: 3 or more people.

Preparation: Assign people roles from the following list:

- Victim specialist employed by law enforcement
- General victim services staff member
- Specialized victim service provider
- Youth advocacy organization staff member
- Domestic violence shelter staff member
- Immigration advocacy group member
- County mental health agency staff member

Tasks: Choose one or more tasks from the following list. For the task given, discuss (1) how different roles would play a role in that task, and (2) how they might productively interact with each other.

- Double the capacity for wraparound victim services including housing in the city, to prepare for a large influx of victims expected in a month.
- Create a multilingual translation network that is competent to help with trafficking victims.
- Create a mental health provider network that is competent to help with trafficking victims.

DISCUSSION EXERCISES

Values Exercise. Brainstorm a jointly viewable list of at least ten values that are relevant to anti-trafficking efforts. Have each person rank their top three or four values, after which each individual will present their ranked list to the group with a brief explanation of the ranking. If time and resources permit, use an online tag cloud tool to create the ranked lists, and enter demographic data such as sector, profession, gender, race/ethnicity, and religion. Create and display multiple views of the digital tag cloud using ranked values crossed with any of the demographic data.

Develop a Process for Collective Decision-Making. Use the "Stages of Discussion Model" (from page 221 in David Straus's [2002] book *How to Make Collaboration Work*) as a basis for jointly planning how you will move from ideas to action.

Going Deeper. Select a moderator to facilitate a semistructured conversation about how partners' personal attributes, background, values, and beliefs, as well as the aims, resources, and constraints of his or her organization or sector affect how they engage in collaborating against human trafficking.

Develop a Set of Communication Standards. Using the "rules for engagement" example from a multisector task force presented in chapter 6, jointly craft an agreement on how communication within and between meetings will take place, what will be the norms for interaction and information sharing, and what processes to use for simple and complex conflict resolution. Include when and how these elements will be reevaluated. Refer to the Books on Multisector Collaboration section below for help.

SECTION II: ONLINE TOOLKITS

There are a growing number of manuals, guides, and toolkits for collaboration available online. Here are some I recommend:

- The DOJ has a "Human Trafficking Task Force e-Guide" available at https://www.ovcttac.gov/taskforceguide/eguide/3-operating-a-task-force/resources-34-addressing-common-operational-challenges/.
- The University of Kansas Work Group for Community Health and Development provides a Community Tool Box online. It includes a section on multisector collaboration that has excellent material and resources. This is available at http://ctb.ku.edu/en/table-of-contents/implement/improving -services/multisector-collaboration/main.
- The InterSector Project's Toolkit can be found at http://intersector.com/toolkit/.
- The resource section of the Collective Impact Forum can be found at http://collectiveimpactforum.org/resources.

SECTION III: CASE STUDIES OF MULTISECTOR COLLABORATION

Reading analyses of multisector collaborations in other issue realms can spark helpful insights about collaboration dynamics around human trafficking. Each of these links is to an open access library of online case studies:

- The InterSector Project: http://intersector.com/cases/
- FSG Collective Impact in Action: http://www.fsg.org/OurApproach/CollectiveImpact.aspx
- FSG Collective Impact Knowledge Exchange: http://fsg.org/KnowledgeExchange/FSGApproach/CollectiveImpact.aspx
- The Collective Impact Forum: http://collectiveimpactforum.org

SECTION IV: HELPFUL SUGGESTIONS DEVELOPING FINANCIAL SUPPORT FOR COLLABORATION

The following section of the OVCTTAC's "Human Trafficking Task Force e-Guide" provides some information on funding for collaboration: https://www.ovcttac.gov/taskforceguide/eguide/3-operating-a-task-force/34-addressing-common-operational-challenges/sustainability/financial-support/.

SECTION V: EXAMPLES OF ANTI-TRAFFICKING ORGANIZATIONS' MISSION AND VALUES STATEMENTS

These organizations' statements of mission and values are well developed, and interestingly different from each other:

- Free the Slaves: http://www.freetheslaves.net/about-us/mission-vision -history/
- Freedom Fund: http://www.freedomfund.org/about-us/#Mission
- Laboratory to Combat Human Trafficking: http://www.combathumantraf ficking.org/who-we-are/mission-vision
- Polaris: http://www.polarisproject.org/about-us/overview/mission-and -values
- Shared Hope International: http://sharedhope.org/about-us/our-mission -and-values/

SECTION VI: SURVIVORS' EXPERIENCES WITH CROSS-SECTOR COLLABORATION (OR LACK THEREOF)

Each of the following books centers on survivors' accounts of trafficking crimes they endured. Survivors' interactions with representatives from social services, law enforcement, or healthcare providers while they were under the control of a trafficker or in the aftermath are part of each book. The interactions they describe point to the need for better cross-sector collaboration in every aspect of counter-trafficking efforts.

Austin Smith, Holly. *Walking Prey: How America's Youth Are Vulnerable to Sex Slavery*. New York: Palgrave Macmillan, 2014.

Brennan, Denise. *Life Interrupted: Trafficking into Forced Labor in the United States*. Durham, NC: Duke University Press, 2014.

Bales, Kevin, and Zoe Trodd, eds. *To Plead Our Own Cause: Personal Stories by Today's Slaves*. Ithaca, NY: Cornell University Press, 2008.

Murphy, Laura T., ed. *Survivors of Slavery: Modern-Day Slave Narratives*. New York: Columbia University Press, 2014.

Oriola, Bukola. *Imprisoned: The Travails of a Trafficked Victim*. Spring Lake Park, MN: Bukola Publishing, 2012.

BOOKS ON MULTISECTOR COLLABORATION

The books below are insightful and useful guides to creating and managing various kinds of interorganizational and multisector collaborations to address complex social problems. As the titles indicate, they are written for leaders in various types of organizations.

Austin, James E., and M. May Seitanidi. *Creating Value in Nonprofit-Business Collaborations: New Thinking and Practice.* San Francisco: Jossey-Bass, 2014.

Butler, Phillip. *Well Connected: Releasing Power, Restoring Hope through Kingdom Partnerships.* Colorado Springs, CO: Authentic Publishing, 2006.

Crawford, Karin. *Interprofessional Collaboration in Social Work Practice.* Thousand Oaks, CA: Sage Publications, 2012.

Hardy, Brian, Bob Hudson, and Eileen Waddington. *What Makes a Good Partnership?: A Partnership Assessment Tool.* Edited by Strategic Partnering Task Force. Leeds, UK: Nuffield Institute for Health, Community Care Division, 2000. https://www.conservationgateway.org/ConservationPlanning/partnering/cpc/Documents/AssessingStrategicPartnership.pdf.

Kamensky, John M., and Thomas J. Burlin, eds. *Collaboration: Using Networks and Partnerships.* Edited by Mark A. Abramson and Paul R. Lawrence, IBM Center for the Business of Government Book Series. Lanham, MD: Rowman & Littlefield Publishers, 2004.

Leathard, Audrey, ed. *Interprofessional Collaboration: From Policy to Practice in Health and Social Care.* New York: Brunner-Routledge, 2003.

Mattesich, Paul W., Marta Murray-Close, and Barbara R. Monsey. *Collaboration: What Makes It Work: A Review of Research Literature on Factors Influencing Successful Collaboration.* 2nd ed. St. Paul, MN: Amherst H. Wilder Foundation, 2001.

Office for Victims of Crime Training and Technical Assistance Center. "Human Trafficking Task Force e-Guide: Strengthening Collaborative Responses." Department of Justice: Office of Justice Programs: Office for Victims of Crime. https://www.ovcttac.gov/taskforceguide/eguide/.

Straus, David. *How to Make Collaboration Work: Powerful Ways to Build Consensus, Solve Problems, and Make Decisions.* San Francisco: Berrett-Koehler Publishers, 2002.

Notes

CHAPTER 1: THE COLLABORATION DILEMMA

1. George W. Bush, "Address to the United Nations General Assembly," United Nations, September 23, 2003, http://www.un.org/webcast/ga/58/statements/usaeng030923.htm.

2. Barack Obama, "Fact Sheet: the Obama Administration Announces Efforts to Combat Human Trafficking at Home and Abroad," White House Office of the Press Secretary, September 25, 2012, http://www.whitehouse.gov/the-press-office/2012/09/25/fact-sheet-obama-administration-announces-efforts-combat-human-trafficki.

3. This brief summary is drawn from the Research Network on the Legal Parameters of Slavery, "Bellagio-Harvard Guidelines on the Legal Parameters of Slavery," Queen's University Belfast School of Law, 2012. These guidelines are available online in multiple languages at http://www.law.qub.ac.uk/schools/SchoolofLaw/Research/HumanRightsCentre/Resources/Bellagio-HarvardGuidelinesontheLegalParametersofSlavery.

4. I use the terms "victim" and "survivor" in this book, in keeping with the US government's rationale for its use of both terms: "The term 'victim' has legal implications within the criminal justice process and generally means an individual who suffered harm as a result of criminal conduct. 'Victims' also have particular rights within the criminal justice process. Federal law enforcement agencies often use the term 'victim' as part of their official duties. 'Survivor' is a term used by many in the services field to recognize the strength it takes to continue on a journey toward healing in the aftermath of a traumatic experience. . . . [B]oth terms are intended to honor those who have suffered, or are suffering, the effects of being trafficked." Quoted from p. 8 of U.S. Government, "Coordination, Collaboration, Capacity: Federal Strategic Action

Plan on Services for Victims of Human Trafficking in the United States, 2013–2017," Office for Victims of Crimes. January 2014. http://www.ovc.gov/pubs/FederalHu manTraffickingStrategicPlan.pdf.

5. The information on industries in which cases of trafficking have been identified was compiled from fieldnotes as well as these sources: National Crime Justice Reference Service, "Statistical Overviews: Human Trafficking" (Washington, DC: Office of Justice Programs, U.S. Department of Justice, 2013), https://www.ncjrs.gov/ ovc_archives/ncvrw/2013/pdf/StatisticalOverviews.pdf; and National Crime Justice Reference Service, "Crime and Victimization in the United States: Statistical Overviews" (Washington, DC: Office of Justice Programs, U.S. Department of Justice, 2014), 30–31, https://www.ncjrs.gov/ovc_archives/ncvrw/2014/pdf/StatisticalOver views.pdf. It must be noted that the types of victims identified by law enforcement and victim service providers reflect both chance and the particular strategies employed to identify those victims (and perhaps not others). For example, when law enforcement agencies prioritize investigations of trafficking in one industry (e.g., the commercial sex industry) over investigations of trafficking in other industries (e.g., agriculture, construction, or garment manufacturing), the number of victims identified in the first industry is likely to be higher than in the others. Moreover, when law enforcement proactively searches for domestic, minor females who are victims of commercial sexual exploitation, that is the type of victim they are likely to find, as opposed to male, transgender, adult, and foreign national victims. In addition, some types of victim may have more access to victim service providers than other types, or be more likely to seek help.

6. See http://www.unodc.org/unodc/en/treaties/CTOC/.

7. Quotation from Office for Victims of Crime Training and Technical Assistance Center, "Human Trafficking Task Force e-Guide: Strengthening Collaborative Responses," Department of Justice: Office of Justice Programs: Office for Victims of Crime, https://www.ovcttac.gov/taskforceguide/eguide/.

8. Laboratory to Combat Human Trafficking, *The Colorado Project: National Survey Report* (Denver, CO: Laboratory to Combat Human Trafficking, 2013).

9. For an early example of the use of these terms by the US government, see U.S. Department of Justice, "Bush Administration Hosts First National Training Conference to Combat Human Trafficking: President George W. Bush and Attorney General John Ashcroft Address Conference," Department of Justice, July 16, 2004, http:// www.justice.gov/archive/opa/pr/2004/July/04_ag_489.htm.

10. Reference to Hillary Rodham Clinton's 2009 addition of *partnership* to the 3Ps and quotation from U.S. Department of State, Office to Monitor and Combat Trafficking in Persons, "The 3Ps: Prevention, Protection, and Prosecution," *Democ-*

racy and Global Affairs, 2011. Yvonne Zimmerman contends that the addition of the term *partnership* "into core elements that structure and guide the United States' anti-trafficking policy . . . confirms the more collaborative diplomatic posture of the United States' anti-trafficking stance" during the Obama administration. She also argues that the range of entities and sectors named as important partners in anti-trafficking efforts expanded under Obama. See Yvonne C. Zimmerman, *Other Dreams of Freedom: Religion, Sex, and Human Trafficking* (New York: Oxford University Press, 2013), 167–68.

11. U.S. Department of State, *Trafficking in Persons Report*, 10th ed., June 2010, http://www.state.gov/documents/organization/142979.pdf. The overview of partnership from this report can also be found at http://www.state.gov/j/tip/rls/tiprpt/2010/142748.htm.

12. For more information about the PITF, its members, and its reports, see http://www.state.gov/j/tip/rls/reports/pitf.

13. U.S. Department of Justice, "Bush Administration Hosts First National Training Conference to Combat Human Trafficking: President George W. Bush and Attorney General John Ashcroft Address Conference."

14. Duren Banks and Tracey Kyckelhahn, "Characteristics of Suspected Human Trafficking Incidents, 2008–2010" (Washington, DC: Bureau of Justice Statistics, Office of Justice Programs, U.S. Department of Justice, 2011), http://www.bjs.gov/content/pub/pdf/cshti0810.pdf.

15. Office for Victims of Crime, "OVC Initiatives to Expand Services to Human Trafficking Victims," Office of Justice Programs, U.S. Department of Justice, http://www.ovc.gov/news/human_trafficking.html.

16. Proposal requirement quotations are from the 2013 call for proposals posted online at https://www.bja.gov/funding/13humantraffickingsol.pdf. Proposal requirements evolved somewhat in the period from 2004 to 2014.

17. Grantees as of 2014 are listed at http://ovc.ncjrs.gov/humantrafficking/traffickingmatrix.html. For an excellent analysis of how defunded task forces are adapting, see John Vanek, "Human Trafficking: Building an Agency's Social Capital through a Social Justice Response," *Police Chief* 81(July 2014): 48–54, http://www.policechiefmagazine.org/magazine/index.cfm?fuseaction=display&article_id=3414&issue_id=72014.

18. U.S. Government, "Coordination, Collaboration, Capacity: Federal Strategic Action Plan on Services for Victims of Human Trafficking in the United States, 2013–2017." The impetus for this unprecedented plan was presented by President Obama on September 25, 2012, in Barack Obama, "Fact Sheet: the Obama Administration Announces Efforts to Combat Human Trafficking at Home and Abroad."

19. Excerpt of public statement by US president Barack Obama on March 15, 2015, quoted from Barack Obama, "Statement by the President on the Meeting of the Interagency Task Force to Monitor and Combat Trafficking in Persons," White House Office of the Press Secretary, March 15, 2012, http://www.whitehouse.gov/the-press-office/2012/03/15/statement-president-meeting-interagency-task-force-monitor-and-combat-tr.

20. Obama, "Fact Sheet: The Obama Administration Announces Efforts to Combat Human Trafficking at Home and Abroad."

21. John Vanek and I coined the term "mobilization and advocacy NGO" (with the acronym MANGO) in an article we wrote on relations between such organizations and law enforcement agencies. See Kirsten A. Foot and John Vanek, "Toward Constructive Engagement between Local Law Enforcement and Mobilization and Advocacy Nongovernmental Organizations about Human Trafficking: Recommendations for Law Enforcement Executives," *Law Enforcement Executive Forum* 12, no. 1 (March 2012): 1–11.

22. Office for Victims of Crime Training and Technical Assistance Center, "Human Trafficking Task Force e-Guide: Strengthening Collaborative Responses." Source URL for quote: https://www.ovcttac.gov/taskforce-Guide/e-Guide.

23. Ibid. Source URL for quote: https://www.ovcttac.gov/taskforce-Guide/e-Guide/3-operating-a-task-force/33-other-task-force-activities/outreach-awareness.

24. Ibid. See https://www.ovcttac.gov/taskforce-Guide/e-Guide/3-operating-a-task-force/31-task-force-membership-and-management/members.

25. Ibid. Source URL for quote: https://www.ovcttac.gov/taskforce-Guide/e-Guide/3-operating-a-task-force/33-other-task-force-activities/outreach-awareness.

26. Ibid. Source URL for quote: https://www.ovcttac.gov/taskforce-Guide/e-Guide/3-operating-a-task-force/34-addressing-common-operational-challenges.

27. Ibid. Source URL for quote: https://www.ovcttac.gov/taskforce-Guide/e-Guide/3-operating-a-task-force/34-addressing-common-operational-challenges/managing-conflict.

28. Adapted from a description of community organizing in R. Fisher and E. Shragge, "Challenging Community Organizing: Facing the 21st Century," *Journal of Community Practice* 8, no. 3 (2000): 1. See also Katherine R. Cooper, "Exploring Stakeholder Participation in Nonprofit Collaboration" (PhD dissertation, University of Illinois Urbana-Champaign, 2014).

29. Office for Victims of Crime Training and Technical Assistance Center, "Human Trafficking Task Force e-Guide: Strengthening Collaborative Responses." Source URL for quote: https://www.ovcttac.gov/taskforce-Guide/e-Guide/3-operating-a-task-force/34-addressing-common-operational-challenges/managing-conflict/.

30. Ibid. Source URL for quote: https://www.ovcttac.gov/taskforce-Guide/e-Guide/3-operating-a-task-force/34-addressing-common-operational-challenges/managing-conflict/.

31. My fieldwork-based findings are corroborated by a 2012 national survey of representatives from 122 US organizations across sectors that participate in anti-trafficking collaborations. See Laboratory to Combat Human Trafficking, *The Colorado Project: National Survey Report.*

32. A growing array of organizations dedicated to fostering multisector collaboration on complex societal problems are gaining audiences among leaders in business, government, and civil society. Examples include the InterSector Project (http://intersector.com), FSG Consulting (http://fsg.org), and the Collective Impact Forum (http://collectiveimpactforum.org).

33. Michael J. Papa, Arvind Singhal, and Wendy H. Papa, *Organizing for Social Change: A Dialectic Journey of Theory and Praxis* (New Delhi: Sage Publications, 2006), 62.

34. If you are an organization leader looking for a straightforward, practical guidebook, I recommend David Straus, *How to Make Collaboration Work: Powerful Ways to Build Consensus, Solve Problems, and Make Decisions* (San Francisco: Berrett-Koehler Publishers, 2002). If you have already read a basic guidebook and are puzzling over some complications in collaborations, I recommend Chris Huxham and Siv Vangen, *Managing to Collaborate: The Theory and Practice of Collaborative Advantage* (New York: Routledge, 2005).

35. See the history of the "new abolitionist movement" on pp. 314–47 in Allen D. Hertzke, *Freeing God's Children: The Unlikely Alliance for Global Human Rights* (Lanham, MD: Rowman & Littlefield Publishers, 2004).

36. Joann Keyton, Debra J. Ford, and Faye I. Smith, "A Mesolevel Communicative Model of Collaboration," *Communication Theory* 18, no. 3 (2008): 381.

37. Ibid., 382.

38. Findings based on those data have been published in Kirsten A. Foot, "Actors and Activities in the Anti-Human Trafficking Movement," in *The Dark Side of Globalization*, ed. R. Thakur and J. Heine (New York: United Nations University Press, 2011), 249–65; and Kirsten A. Foot, Amoshaun Toft, and Nina Cesare, "Developments in Anti-Trafficking Efforts: 2008–2011," *Journal of Human Trafficking* 1, no. 2 (July 2015).

39. By "actor" I mean any individual or collective entity that does something.

40. For European perspectives on counter-trafficking collaboration challenges, see Barbara Limanowska and Helga Konrad, "Problems of Anti-Trafficking Cooperation," in *Strategies against Human Trafficking: The Role of the Security Sector,*

ed. Cornelius Friesendorf (Vienna and Geneva: National Defence Academy and Austrian Ministry of Defence and Sports, 2009), 427–58; and Helga Konrad, "The Fight against Trafficking in Human Beings from the European Perspective," in *Trafficking in Human$: Social, Cultural and Political Dimensions*, ed. Sally Cameron and Edward Newman (New York: United Nations University Press, 2008), 161–80. The 2012 impact evaluation report on the Chab Dai Coalition provides keen insights into the challenges of collaborating against trafficking in Cambodia. See Giorgio Algeri, *Impact Evaluation of Chab Dai Coalition and Its Role Within the Anti-Human Trafficking Sector in Cambodia* (Phnom Penh: Chab Dai Coalition, 2012).

41. Keyton, Ford, and Smith, "A Mesolevel Communicative Model of Collaboration."

42. These two risks were initially articulated by Minh Dang in her review of an earlier version of this chapter.

43. Throughout the book I provide full citations for all published material, including organizational texts from publicly available websites and publicly available statements by individual anti-trafficking experts. However, in order to minimize the chance of harming any collaboration, in conducting this research I committed to protect the anonymity of everyone I interviewed, so when the use of names was necessary for the sake of a smooth narrative, I used pseudonyms. Moreover, because I conducted the research through informal conversations in which I was a participant, interactions I witnessed, as well as interviews I conducted, I do not provide specific citations for most quotes. Since I was able to interview some people multiple times over several years, some passages contain multiple quotes by the same person from different times. When relevant, I provide a brief description of the context in which the quoted statement was made.

44. Thomas Nagel, *The View from Nowhere* (New York: Oxford University Press, 1989).

45. For an overview of how the validity of participatory action research is established, see Robin McTaggartt, "Is Validity Really an Issue for Participatory Action Research?," *Studies in Cultures, Organizations, and Societies* 4, no. 2 (1998): 211–36.

46. See http://www.inittoendit.org/ for example.

47. See http://enditmovement.com/#together_we_can and https://www.facebook.com/ENDITMovement.

48. I differentiate "interorganizational," "cross-sector," and "multisector" as follows: The first refers to events between two or more organizations within the same sector. The second refers to interactions between organizations from two different sectors, while the third refers to interactions among organizations from more than two sectors. As examples, see the 2013 call for proposals issued by the U.S. DOJ/Bureau of

Justice for law enforcement and service providers to submit jointly for Enhanced Collaborative Model grants at https://www.bja.gov/funding/13humantraffickingsol.pdf. Also see the mission statement of the Hunt Alternatives Fund at http://www.huntal ternatives.org/about/mission-and-history, and the description of the Alliance to End Slavery and Trafficking, led by the Humanity United foundation and comprised of Humanity United grantees, at http://www.endslaveryandtrafficking.org/about-atest.

49. Laurie K. Lewis, Matthew G. Isbell, and Matt Koschmann, "Collaborative Tensions: Practitioners' Experiences of Interorganizational Relationships," *Communication Monographs* 77, no. 4 (2010): 460–79.

50. See Foot and Vanek, "Toward Constructive Engagement Between Local Law Enforcement and Mobilization and Advocacy Nongovernmental Organizations About Human Trafficking: Recommendations for Law Enforcement Executives."

51. The approach I take in this book is consistent with the theme-based theory of collaborative advantage developed by British collaboration experts Chris Huxham and Siv Vangen (2005). Similarly to them, I seek to "understand and capture the complexity of the practice of collaboration and convey it in a way that will seem real to those who experience it in their working lives" and provide a "basis for thoughtful action" by articulating tensions inherent to interorganizational collaboration. See Huxham and Vangen, *Managing to Collaborate: The Theory and Practice of Collaborative Advantage*, 38–39.

52. For this conceptualization, I draw on Ivy Ken, *Digesting Race, Class, and Gender: Sugar as a Metaphor* (New York: Palgrave Macmillan, 2010).

53. Pippa Hall, "Interprofessional Teamwork: Professional Cultures as Barriers," *Journal of Interprofessional Care* 19, no. S1 (May 2005): 188–96.

CHAPTER 2: POWER IN COLLABORATION

1. For a good overview of ways to think about power dynamics in interorganizational collaboration, see Nuzhat Lotia and Cynthia Hardy, "Critical Perspectives on Collaboration," in *The Oxford Handbook on Inter-Organizational Relations*, ed. Steve Cropper et al. (New York: Oxford University Press, 2008), 366–89.

2. Lewis, Isbell, and Koschmann, "Collaborative Tensions: Practitioners' Experiences of Interorganizational Relationships," 471.

3. Ibid.

4. Three excellent sources on power dynamics in interorganizational collaboration are Cynthia Hardy and Nelson Phillips, "Strategies of Engagement: Lessons from the Critical Examination of Collaboration and Conflict in an Interorganizational Domain," *Organization Science* 9, no. 2 (1998): 217–30; Chris Huxham and Siv Vangen, "Leadership in the Shaping and Implementation of Collaboration Agendas: How Things Hap-

pen in a (Not Quite) Joined-Up World," *Academy of Management Journal* 43, no. 6 (2000): 1159–75; and Jill M. Purdy, "A Framework for Assessing Power in Collaborative Governance Processes," *Public Administration Review* 72, no. 3 (2012): 409–17.

5. For an illuminating explanation about how disadvantaged stakeholders experience collaboration and a proposal for how to level the playing field in collaborative decision-making, see E. Watson and P. G. Foster-Fishman, "Exchange Boundary Framework: Understanding the Evolution of Power within Collaborative Decision-Making Settings," *American Journal of Community Psychology* (2012): 1–13.

6. For insights on the foundational tensions in collaboration between government agencies and nongovernmental organizations (both for-profit and nonprofit), see John M. Kamensky and Thomas J. Burlin, eds., *Collaboration: Using Networks and Partnerships*, eds. Mark A. Abramson and Paul R. Lawrence, IBM Center for the Business of Government Book Series (Lanham, MD: Rowman & Littlefield Publishers, 2004); and Elizabeth T. Boris and C. Eugene Steuerle, eds., *Nonprofits and Government: Collaboration and Conflict* (Washington, DC: Urban Institute Press, 1998). For insights on the dynamics of collaboration between for-profit and nonprofit organizations, see James E. Austin, *The Collaboration Challenge: How Nonprofits and Businesses Succeed Through Strategic Alliances* (San Francisco: Jossey-Bass, 2000); and James E. Austin and M. May Seitanidi, *Creating Value in Nonprofit-Business Collaborations: New Thinking and Practice* (San Francisco: Jossey-Bass, 2014). Phillip Butler has translated collaboration principles from the business world for leaders of faith-based organizations and analyzed some of the tensions such organizations experience when attempting to collaborate within their sector; see Phillip Butler, *Well Connected: Releasing Power, Restoring Hope through Kingdom Partnerships* (Colorado Springs, CO: Authentic Publishing, 2006). However, according to interorganizational communication scholar Dr. Matt Koschmann, there is a paucity of research that unpacks the role of religious partners' faith in collaborations with areligious partners. His exploratory study of an anti-trafficking collaboration in Mexico between faith-based and areligious partners is an excellent starting point; see Matt Koschmann, "Integrating Religious Faith in Human Rights Collaborations," *Journal of Communication and Religion* 36, no. 2 (2013): 1–17.

7. Colorado Legislature, *Concerning Human Trafficking*, 69th General Assembly, Second Regular Session, HB 14-1273, July 1, 2014, http://www.leg.state.co.us/clics/clics2014a/csl.nsf/fsbillcont2/0E5766A9A4ACD1F387257C300005Fa09/$FILE/1273_01.pdf.

8. Ibid., 6–7.

9. Washington Legislature, *Concerning the Trafficking of Persons*, 64th Legislature, SB 5884, March 2015, http://apps.leg.wa.gov/billinfo/summary.aspx?bill=5884&year=2015#documents.

10. Ibid., 3–4.

11. *Seattle Times* Staff, "Help Vulnerable Girls and Women Leave Prostitution," *Seattle Times*, December 20, 2009, http://www.seattletimes.com/opinion/help-vulner able-girls-and-women-leave-prostitution.

12. YouthCare, "The Bridge Continuum of Services for Sexually Exploited Youth," http://www.youthcare.org/our-programs/services-sexually-exploited-youth#.VQ9P dOESNuo.

13. Laboratory to Combat Human Trafficking, "About the Colorado Project to Comprehensively Combat Human Trafficking," http://lcht.hotpressplatform.com/ about/theproject.

14. Embrey Family Foundation, "Mission without Borders Guidelines," http:// www.embreyfdn.org/embrey/index.php?option=com_content&view=category&id= 37&layout=blog&Itemid=37.

15. Partnership for Freedom, "About Us," http://www.partnershipforfreedom.org/ about/.

16. Partnership for Freedom, "FAQ: What Is the Partnership for Freedom?," http://www.partnershipforfreedom.org/details-faq.

17. Partnership for Freedom, "About Us."

18. Partnership for Freedom, "Winners," http://www.partnershipforfreedom.org/ winners.

19. Justice and Mercy Philanthropy Forum, "About Us," http://justicemercyforum .homestead.com/about.html.

20. The Freedom Fund, "About Us," http://www.freedomfund.org/about-us/.

21. http://www.freedomfund.org/wp-content/uploads/2015/03/Senior-Research -and-Evaluation-Officer-JD-FINAL-17Mar15.pdf.

22. Imago Dei Fund, "Grant Application Form," http://www.imagodeifund.org/ application.html.

23. Alliance to End Slavery and Trafficking, "About ATEST," http://www.endslav eryandtrafficking.org.

24. For a fascinating and troubling analysis of the effects of chronic underfunding on organizations and employees in the social services sector, see Sandra L. Bloom and Brian Farragher, *Destroying Sanctuary: The Crisis in Human Service Delivery Systems* (New York: Oxford University Press, 2010).

25. International Association of Chiefs of Police, *Backing the Badge: Working Effectively with Law Enforcement: Police-Based Victim Services* (Alexandria, VA: International Association of Chiefs of Police, n.d.), http://www.theiacp.org/Portals/ 0/pdfs/responsetovictims/RESOURCES_DOCUMENTS/TS_Links/9_Backingthe Badge.pdf. 13.

26. Quoted from Washington Anti-Trafficking Response Network, "Collaborating with WARN" (Seattle, WA: n.d.), document downloadable from https://www.ovct tac.gov/taskforceguide/eguide/3-operating-a-task-force/resources-34-addressing -common-operational-challenges.

27. See http://www.justice.gov/crt/about/spl/documents/polmis.php.

28. Police Executive Research Forum, *Civil Rights Investigations of Local Police: Lessons Learned*, Critical Issues in Policing Series (Washington, DC: Police Executive Research Forum, 2013), http://www.policeforum.org/assets/docs/Critical_Issues_Se ries/civil%20rights%20investigations%20of%20local%20police%20-%20lessons%20 learned%202013.pdf.

29. See Oliver Balch, "Corporate Initiative Can Play a Major Role in Anti-Trafficking Movement: The Global Business Coalition against Human Trafficking Needs Support from More Big Brands to Make a Truly Global Impact," *Guardian*, April 3, 2013, http://www.theguardian.com/global-development-professionals -network/2013/apr/03/human-trafficking-global-business-coalition.

30. For an excellent typology of faith-based organizations and a brief overview of ways that faith-based organizations both leverage social capital and build the social capital of their geographic communities, see the introduction chapter by Julie Adkins, Laurie Occhipinti, and Tara Hefferan, "Social Services, Social Justice, and Faith-Based Organizations in the United States: An Introduction," in *Not by Faith Alone: Social Services, Social Justice, and Faith-Based Organizations in the United States*, ed. Julie Adkins, Laurie Occhipinti, and Tara Hefferan (Lanham, MD: Lexington Books, 2010), 1–32.

31. Thomas F. Gieryn, "Boundary-Work and the Demarcation of Science from Non-Science: Strains and Interests in Professional Ideologies of Scientists," *American Sociological Review* 48 (1983): 781–95.

32. Quoted from https://www.ovcttac.gov/views/TrainingMaterials/dspLeader shipVictimServices.cfm.

33. For more information about the National Advocate Credentialing Program, see http://www.trynova.org/help-crime-victim/nacp. For information on OVC NVAA training, see https://www.ovcttac.gov/views/TrainingMaterials/dspNVAA.cfm.

34. Quoted from http://www.trauma-informedtraining.com/level-1-certification -program.html.

35. A national survey of social workers in 2004 found that 79 percent hold MSW degrees, and an additional 2 percent hold doctoral degrees (see Center for Health Workforce Studies and National Association of Social Workers Center for Workforce Studies, "Licensed Social Workers in the United States, 2004," Center for Health Workforce Studies, March 2006, http://workforce.socialworkers.org/studies/intro0806.pdf.) Mental health professionals are likely to have similarly high levels of education.

36. See http://ovc.ncjrs.gov/ovcproviderforum/asp/Transcript.asp?Topic_ID=76.

37. Pippa Hall, "Interprofessional Teamwork: Professional Cultures as Barriers," *Journal of Interprofessional Care* 19, no. S1 (May 2005): 188–96.

38. Jodi Sandfort and H. Brinton Milward, "Collaborative Service Provision in the Public Sector," in *The Oxford Handbook of Inter-Organizational Relations*, ed. Steve Cropper et al. (New York: Oxford University Press, 2008), 147–74.

39. For an overview of social service provision in the United States, see Steven Rathgeb Smith, "Social Services," ed. Lester Salamon, *The State of Nonprofit America* (Washington, DC: Brookings Institution Press, in cooperation with the Aspen Institute, 2002), http://www.aspeninstitute.org/sites/default/files/content/docs/psi/SOS_-_Chapter_4_Highlights_Social_Services.pdf. For analyses and case studies of government-funded social service provision by faith-based organizations, see Julie Adkins, Laurie Occhipinti, and Tara Hefferan, eds., *Not by Faith Alone: Social Services, Social Justice, and Faith-Based Organizations in the United States* (Lanham, MD: Lexington Books, 2010); and Wolfgang Bielefeld and William Suhs Cleveland, "Faith-Based Organizations as Service Providers and Their Relationship to Government," *Nonprofit and Voluntary Sector Quarterly* 42, no. 3 (2013).

40. See Jason D. Scott, "Private-Sector Contributions to Faith-Based Social Service: The Policies and Giving Patterns of Private Foundations," Roundtable on Religion and Social Welfare Policy, 2003.

41. Institute for Illinois' Fiscal Stability at the Civic Federation, "Social Impact Funding through Pay for Success Contracts in Illinois," Civic Federation, September 11, 2014, http://www.civicfed.org/iifs/blog/social-impact-funding-through-pay-success-contracts-illinois.

42. Third Sector Capital Partners, "Massachusetts Launches Landmark Initiative to Reduce Recidivism Among At-Risk Youth," http://www.thirdsectorcap.org/our-work/massachusetts-juvenile-justice-pfs/.

43. By the end of 2014, three SIBs had been launched in the United States to fund reentry employment services to formerly incarcerated individuals (in NY), reduce male juvenile recidivism (in MA), and provide services for youth involved in both the child welfare and juvenile justice systems (in IL).

CHAPTER 3: LEADERSHIP STRATEGIES AND POWER DYNAMICS

1. For a good overview of anti-trafficking efforts by businesses circa 2012, see Technology and Human Trafficking, "Private-Sector Initiatives," University of Southern California Center on Communication Leadership and Policy, https://technologyandtrafficking.usc.edu/private-sector-initiatives/.

2. Alice Korngold, *A Better World, Inc.: How Companies Profit by Solving Global Problems . . . Where Governments Cannot* (New York: Palgrave Macmillan, 2014), 134.

3. Ibid., 137.

4. For more information about the Athens Ethical Principles and the Manpower Group's leadership in recruiting corporate signees, see http://www.manpowergroup .com/wps/wcm/connect/manpowergroup-en/home/newsroom/news-releases/man power+inc.+calls+on+1000+of+the+worlds+leading+corporations+to+join+the+ fight+to+end+human+trafficking+now!+-+video+available#.VLVZiHsSNuo.

5. Quoted from the global Business Coalition Against Trafficking, http://www .gbcat.org/#about.

6. Jonathan Ewing, "This Hotel Is Fighting Human Trafficking Like People's Lives Are Depending on It," U.S. Global Leadership Coalition, March 8, 2014, http:// www.usglc.org/2014/03/08/this-hotel-is-fighting-human-trafficking-like-peoples -lives-are-depending-on-it/.

7. Ibid.

8. See http://www.carlson.com/news-and-media/news-releases.do?article= 6733463.

9. Quoted from Ewing, "This Hotel Is Fighting Human Trafficking Like People's Lives Are Depending on It."

10. See http://www.lexisnexis.com/en-us/about-us/corporate-responsibility/state -dept-report.page.

11. See http://www.ungift.org/knowledgehub/stories/august2012/lexisnexis -launches-human-trafficking-awareness-index.html.

12. See Chris Johnson and Judy McKee, "Giving Voice to the Voiceless: 'Pillars of Hope' Presidential Initiative to Tackle Human Trafficking," National Association of Attorneys General, http://www.naag.org/giving-a-voice-to-the-voiceless-pillars-of -hope-presidential-initiative-to-tackle-human-trafficking.php.

13. For analyses of the ways digital technologies are used by traffickers and law enforcement, see Mark Latonero et al., *Technology and Human Trafficking: The Rise of Mobile and the Diffusion of Technology-Facilitated Trafficking*, Research Series on Technology and Human Trafficking (Los Angeles: University of Southern California, 2012), https://technologyandtrafficking.usc.edu/2012-report/; Jennifer Musto and danah boyd, "The Trafficking-Technology Nexus," *Social Policy*, 2014, doi:10.1093/ sp/jxu018, http://sp.oxfordjournals.org/content/early/2014/08/26/sp.jxu018.full .pdf+html; and Siddartha Sarkar, "Use of Technology in Human Trafficking Networks and Sexual Exploitation: A Cross-Sectional Multi-Country Study," *Transnational Social Review: A Social Work Journal* (2015).

14. See http://www.microsoft.com/about/corporatecitizenship/en-us/working -responsibly/principled-business-practices/HumanRightsCenter.aspx.

15. See http://news.microsoft.com/presskits/photodna.

16. For a summary of all six projects funded via this initiative, see http://research .microsoft.com/en-us/collaboration/focus/education/human-trafficking-rfp.aspx.

17. See http://blogs.msdn.com/b/msr_er/archive/2012/06/12/new-research -grants-aim-at-combating-human-trafficking.aspx and http://www.zephoria.org/ thoughts/archives/2012/06/13/research-human-trafficking.html.

18. See http://blogs.msdn.com/b/msr_er/archive/2012/10/11/efforts-to-combat -human-trafficking-honored-at-white-house.aspx.

19. Quotes in this paragraph are from Balch, "Corporate Initiative Can Play a Major Role in Anti-Trafficking Movement: The Global Business Coalition against Human Trafficking Needs Support from More Big Brands to Make a Truly Global Impact."

20. Many books about interorganizational collaboration mention power dynamics in collaboration structures, but few provide both in-depth explanations and helpful suggestions. One outstanding source on both is Huxham and Vangen, *Managing to Collaborate: The Theory and Practice of Collaborative Advantage.*

21. See Johnson and McKee, "Giving Voice to the Voiceless: 'Pillars of Hope' Presidential Initiative to Tackle Human Trafficking."

22. Minh Dang, in the foreword of Laura T. Murphy, ed., *Survivors of Slavery: Modern-Day Slave Narratives* (New York: Columbia University Press, 2014), xvii.

23. Quoted from U.S. Government, "Coordination, Collaboration, Capacity: Federal Strategic Action Plan on Services for Victims of Human Trafficking in the United States, 2013–2017," 12.

24. Quoted from Office for Victims of Crime, "OVC Announces Multiple Events for National Slavery and Human Trafficking Prevention Month," http://www.ovc .gov/news/HumanTraffickingPreventionMonth/.

25. Barack Obama, "Remarks by the President to the Clinton Global Initiative," White House Office of the Press Secretary, September 25, 2012, http:// www.whitehouse.gov/the-press-office/2012/09/25/remarks-president-clinton-global -initiative; Joye E. Frost, "Improving Services for Victims of Human Trafficking," *Justice Blogs*, January 16, 2014, http://www.justice.gov/opa/blog/improving-services -victims-human-trafficking.

26. Information about survivor-activists' policy recommendations is drawn from Cassie Ann Hodges, "Slavery Survivors Brief U.S. Senate," *FTS Blog: Free the Slaves*, January 27, 2014, http://ftsblog.net/2014/01/27/slavery-survivors-brief-u-s-senate/.

27. Bukola Oriola, "A Forum and Listening Session Indeed!," January 20, 2014, http://bukolaoriola.com/2014/01/20/a-forum-and-listening-session-indeed/.

28. Harold D'Souza, "USA: Harold D'Souza Honored at 'Survivor Forum'—the White House," *Mangalorean.com*, 2014, http://www.mangalorean.com/specials/spe cialnews.php?newsid=454031&newstype=local.

29. See http://www.castla.org/caucus-of-survivors for more information about the Survivor Advisory Caucus.

30. See http://nationalsurvivornetwork.org/.

31. Quoted from http://www.castla.org/nsn.

32. Anne Johnston, Barbara Friedman, and Autumn Shafer, "Framing the Problem of Sex Trafficking: Whose Problem? What Remedy?," *Feminist Media Studies* 14, no. 3 (2012): 419–36.

33. Office for Victims of Crime Training and Technical Assistance Center, "Human Trafficking Task Force e-Guide: Strengthening Collaborative Responses."

34. Keyton, Ford, and Smith, "A Mesolevel Communicative Model of Collaboration."

35. Quoted from http://nationalsurvivornetwork.org/.

CHAPTER 4: RACE AND GENDER IN MULTISECTOR ANTI-TRAFFICKING EFFORTS

1. To gain a better understanding of how individual and group identities intersect in interorganizational collaboration, see chapter 11 in Huxham and Vangen, *Managing to Collaborate: The Theory and Practice of Collaborative Advantage*.

2. Seminal studies of class, gender, and race in regard to work and organizations from before 2000 include: Rosabeth M. Kanter, *Men and Women of the Corporation* (New York: Basic Books, 1977); Joan Acker, "Hierarchies, Jobs, Bodies: A Theory of Gendered Organizations," *Gender and Society* 4 (1990): 139–58; Ronald A. Burt, "The Gender of Social Capital," *Rationality and Society* 10 (1998): 5–46. Some of the landmark studies since 2000 include: Linwood H. Cousins et al., "Race and Class Challenges in Community Collaboration for Educational Change," *School Community Journal* 18, no. 2 (2008): 29–52; Fisher and Shragge, "Challenging Community Organizing: Facing the 21st Century"; James R. Elliot and Ryan A. Smith, "Race, Gender, and Workplace Power," *American Sociological Review* 69, no. 3 (2004): 365–86; Adia Harvey Wingfield, "Are Some Emotions Marked 'Whites Only'? Racialized Feeling Rules in Professional Workplaces," *Social Problems* 57 (2010): 251–68; Gail G. McGuire, "Gender, Race, and the Shadow Structure: A Study of Informal Networks and Inequality in a Work Organization," *Gender and Society* 16, no. 3 (2002): 303–22; Christine L. Williams, Chandra Muller, and Kristine Kilanski, "Gendered Organizations in the New Economy," *Gender and Society* 26 (August 2012): 549–73; Ella L. J. Bell and Stella M. Nkomo, *Our Separate Ways: Black and White Women and the Struggle for Professional Identity* (Boston: Harvard Business School Press, 2001); Ann

V. Bell, Barret Michalec, and Christine Arenson, "The (Stalled) Progress of Interprofessional Collaboration: The Role of Gender," *Journal of Interprofessional Care* 28, no. 2 (2014): 98–102; and Hall, "Interprofessional Teamwork: Professional Cultures as Barriers." Particular attention should be paid to a seminal, but largely overlooked, study published in 1981 by Jon Miller and his coauthors that demonstrated stratification by race and gender among members in six multiagency "systems" for social service provision. See Jon Miller, James R. Lincoln, and Jon Olsen, "Rationality and Equity in Professional Networks: Gender and Race as Factors in the Stratification of Interorganizational Systems," *American Journal of Sociology* 87, no. 2 (1981): 308–35.

3. My method of assessing gender and race was very simplistic; therefore my findings are merely suggestive rather than definitive. Markers of gender were facial appearance and clothing (which depends on cultural contexts to interpret). Markers of race were racially phenotypical features such as hair and skin tone. Such markers are difficult to interpret with people who appear to be either mixed gender or mixed race. For these reasons, I used simple binary ratios, that is, the proportion of women to men and the proportion of whites to nonwhites.

4. Center for Health Workforce Studies and Studies and National Association of Social Workers Center for Workforce Studies, "Licensed Social Workers in the United States, 2004."

5. Brian A. Reaves, "Federal Law Enforcement Officers, 2008" (Washington, DC: U.S. Department of Justice, Office of Justice Programs, Bureau of Justice Statistics, 2012); Curtis Crooke, "Women in Law Enforcement," *Community Policing Dispatch* 6, no. 7 (July 2013), http://cops.usdoj.gov/html/dispatch/07-2013/women_in_law _enforcement.asp.

6. Reaves, "Federal Law Enforcement Officers, 2008."

7. Jeremy Ashkenas and Haeyoun Park, "The Race Gap in America's Police Departments," *New York Times on the Web* (2014), http://www.nytimes.com/interactive/2014/09/03/us/the-race-gap-in-americas-police-departments.html?_r=0.

8. See, for example, National Crime Justice Reference Service, "Statistical Overviews: Human Trafficking."

9. Ibid.

10. Ibid., 24; Michelle Lillie, "Human Trafficking: Not All Black or White," *Human Trafficking Search: The Global Resource and Database* (blog), April 30, 2014, http://humantraffickingsearch.net/wp/human-trafficking-not-all-black-or-white/. Note that although Lillie's summary of the 2013 National Crime Victims' Rights Week data report assigns the victim percentages to minors, the original report does not differentiate between adult and minor victims.

11. U.S. Equal Employment Opportunity Commission, "Human Trafficking," http://www.eeoc.gov/eeoc/interagency/trafficking.cfm.

12. See http://warn-trafficking.org.

13. The account to which I refer is in Mira Sorvino's foreword to Holly Austin Smith, *Walking Prey: How America's Youth are Vulnerable to Sex Slavery* (New York: Palgrave Macmillan, 2014).

14. Ibid., v.

15. Paraphrased from http://smallbusiness.chron.com/difference-between-busi ness-casual-business-attire-24536.html.

16. Peter Glick et al., "Evaluations of Sexy Women In Low- and High-Status Jobs," *Psychology of Women Quarterly* 29, no. 4 (2005): 389–95; Melissa L. Wookey, Nell A. Graves, and J. Corey Butler, "Effects of a Sexy Appearance on Perceived Competence of Women," *Journal of Social Psychology* 149, no. 1 (2009): 116–18.

17. Seminal texts on intersectionality include Kimberle Crenshaw, "Demarginal-izing the Intersection of Race and Sex: A Black Feminist Critique of Antidiscrimina-tion Doctrine, Feminist Theory and Antiracist Politics," *University of Chicago Legal Forum* (1989): 139–68; Kimberle Crenshaw, "Mapping the Margins: Intersectionality, Identity Politics, and Violence against Women of Color," *Stanford Law Review* 43, no. 6 (1991): 1241–99; and Patricia Hill Collins, "Toward a New Vision: Race, Class, and Gender as Categories of Analysis and Connection," *Race, Sex and Class* 1, no. 1 (1993): 25–45. I find the ideas of Ivy Ken particularly useful in unpacking how intersectionality functions. In her amusingly titled book, *Digesting Race, Class, and Gender: Sugar as a Metaphor*, Ken likens race, class, and gender to foods that are in dynamic relationships with each other, which have implications for the shape of our social order. Ken, *Digesting Race, Class, and Gender: Sugar as a Metaphor*.

18. Johnson and McKee, "Giving Voice to the Voiceless: 'Pillars of Hope' Presiden-tial Initiative to Tackle Human Trafficking."

19. Melissa Farley et al., "Comparing Buyers of Sex with Men Who Don't Buy Sex," presented at Psychologists for Social Responsibility Annual Conference, Boston, MA, July 15, 2011, http://www.catwinternational.org/content/images/ar ticle/212/attachment.pdf.

20. For more information about male victims and the dearth of services available to them, see U.S. Department of State Office to Monitor and Combat Trafficking in Persons, "Male Trafficking Victims," June 1, 2013, http://www.state.gov/j/tip/rls/ fs/2013/211624.htm; and Yu Sun Chin, "Trafficked Boys Overlooked," *Juvenile Justice Information Exchange*, April 14, 2014, http://jjie.org/trafficked-boys-overlooked-underrepresented/.

21. The OVC's "Faces of Human Trafficking" PSA is available at https://www.youtube.com/watch?v=NxBilNt-PiU.

22. Meredith F. Small, *Our Babies, Ourselves: How Biology and Culture Shape the Way We Parent* (New York: Doubleday, 1998).

23. Brian Amble, "Collaboration and Gender," http://www.management-issues.com/news/6495/collaboration-and-gender/. The countries included in this survey were not specified; if most respondents were from Western or global north countries, results could be culturally skewed to those regions.

24. Acker, "Hierarchies, Jobs, Bodies: A Theory of Gendered Organizations."

25. Williams, Muller, and Kilanski, "Gendered Organizations in the New Economy."

26. Ibid.; Bell, Michalec, and Arenson, "The (Stalled) Progress of Interprofessional Collaboration: The Role of Gender."

27. Harvey Wingfield, "Are Some Emotions Marked 'Whites Only'? Racialized Feeling Rules in Professional Workplaces," 253.

28. Ibid.

29. Leslie Kwoh, "Picking Someone for a Project? Chances Are, He'll Look Like You," *Wall Street Journal at Work*, June 4, 2012, http://blogs.wsj.com/atwork/2012/06/04/picking-someone-for-a-project-chances-are-hell-look-like-you/.

30. Amble, "Collaboration and Gender."

31. Christine Graef, "Bakken Region Tribes Fight Back against Human Trafficking," http://www.mintpressnews.com/bakken-region-tribes-fight-back-human-trafficking/199156/.

32. Polaris, "Mission and Values," http://www.polarisproject.org/about-us/overview/mission-and-values.

CHAPTER 5: WHY BELIEFS, VALUES, AND PRIORITIES ARE HARD TO ALIGN

1. Huxham and Vangen, *Managing to Collaborate: The Theory and Practice of Collaborative Advantage*, 83.

2. Ibid., 85.

3. Laboratory to Combat Human Trafficking, "Our Values," http://www.combathumantrafficking.org/who-we-are/our-values.

4. Paraphrased from online statements by Polaris; see Polaris, "Mission and Values," http://www.polarisproject.org/about-us/overview/mission-and-values.

5. Paraphrased from online statements by United Against Human Trafficking; see http://www.houstonrr.org/about-us/mission-vision-values/ and http://www.houstonrr.org/about-us/coalition-member-list/.

6. Paraphrased from online statements by the Global Alliance Against Trafficking in Women; see http://www.gaatw.org/about-us/basic-principles.

7. See Kirsten A. Foot, "Cultural-Historical Activity Theory: Exploring a Theory to Inform Practice and Research," *Journal of Human Behavior in the Social Environment* 24, no. 3 (2014): 329–47. The theory of collaborative advantage explicated by Chris Huxham and Siv Vangen is also useful for probing systemic tensions and contradictions in collaboration: see Chris Huxham and Siv Vangen, "Doing Things Collaboratively: Realizing the Advantage or Succumbing to Inertia," *Organizational Dynamics* 33, no. 2 (2004): 190–201; Huxham and Vangen, *Managing to Collaborate: The Theory and Practice of Collaborative Advantage*; Huxham and Vangen, "Leadership in the Shaping and Implementation of Collaboration Agendas: How Things Happen in a (Not Quite) Joined-Up World."

8. U.S. Government, "Coordination, Collaboration, Capacity: Federal Strategic Action Plan on Services for Victims of Human Trafficking in the United States, 2013–2017," 10, http://www.ovc.gov/pubs/FederalHumanTraffickingStrategicPlan.pdf.

9. U.S. Department of Homeland Security, "About the Blue Campaign," April 23, 2015, http://www.dhs.gov/blue-campaign/about-blue-campaign.

10. A majority of victim service providers work for NGOs, not law enforcement agencies. However, since the 1980s, some US federal, state, county, and municipal law enforcement agencies have hired victim specialists to support victims during an initial "recovery" period and sometimes for the duration of an investigation and legal proceedings. For instance, as of 2014, the FBI employed 122 victim specialists stationed around the United States via its Field Office Victim Assistance Program. See http://www.fbi.gov/stats-services/victim_assistance/overview/field-office-victim-assistance-program. People in such positions work in close coordination with investigators. They often accompany investigators during operations, are present during victim interviews, and accompany victims to access medical care, therapies, legal services, and so forth.

11. International Association of Chiefs of Police, *Backing the Badge: Working Effectively with Law Enforcement: Police-Based Victim Services*, http://www.theiacp.org/Portals/0/pdfs/responsetovictims/RESOURCES_DOCUMENTS/TS_Links/9_BackingtheBadge.pdf.

12. Office for Victims of Crime Training and Technical Assistance Center, "Human Trafficking Task Force e-Guide: Strengthening Collaborative Responses," https://www.ovcttac.gov/taskforceguide/eguide/1-understanding-human-trafficking/13-victim-centered-approach/.

13. Washington Anti-Trafficking Response Network, "Collaborating with WARN."

14. Office for Victims of Crime Training and Technical Assistance Center, "Human Trafficking Task Force e-Guide: Strengthening Collaborative Responses," https://www.ovcttac.gov/taskforceguide/eguide/3-operating-a-task-force/31-task-force-membership-and-management/committees/victim-services-committee.

15. Global Freedom Network, "About the Global Freedom Network," http://www.globalfreedomnetwork.org/about/.

16. This phenomenon has been well documented. For a detailed and generally positive analysis of why and how religious leaders, in collaboration with human rights and feminist leaders, exerted significant influence on US anti-trafficking policy and efforts from the mid-1990s through 2003, see Hertzke, *Freeing God's Children: The Unlikely Alliance for Global Human Rights*. For a less detailed, critical, theological analysis of why evangelical Protestants emphasized sex trafficking and garnered the support of the Bush administration, and the broadening of that emphasis during the first half of Obama's administration, see Zimmerman, *Other Dreams of Freedom: Religion, Sex, and Human Trafficking*.

17. Examples of Jewish anti-trafficking organizations include the following: T'ruah: The Rabbinic Call for Human Rights, "Slavery and Human Trafficking," http://www.truah.org/issuescampaigns/slavery-a-human-trafficking-50094.html; Jews Against Human Trafficking, "What's Happening," http://jewsagainsthumantrafficking.org/; and International Council of Jewish Women, "Trafficking of Women and Girls," http://icjw.org/gen.aspx?page=trafficking.

18. Zimmerman, *Other Dreams of Freedom: Religion, Sex, and Human Trafficking*; and Jo Anne Lyon, "The Evolution of Anti-Trafficking Campaigns in the Church," *On Faith: Faith Street,* May 2, 2014, http://www.faithstreet.com/onfaith/2014/05/02/evolution-of-anti-trafficking-campaigns-in-the-church/31942.

19. Hertzke, *Freeing God's Children: The Unlikely Alliance for Global Human Rights*; and Zimmerman, *Other Dreams of Freedom: Religion, Sex, and Human Trafficking*.

20. Wesleyan Holiness Consortium Freedom Network, "Declaration for Freedom," http://holinessandunity.wikispaces.com/file/view/Declaration+for+Freedom.pdf/480446278/Declaration%20for%20Freedom.pdf.

21. Faith Alliance Against Slavery and Trafficking, "Take Action: Immigration," http://www.faastinternational.org/#/take-action/immigration.

22. Ibid.

23. Other types of nongovernmental and nonprofit organizations involved in anti-trafficking efforts in the United States include immigrant and women's rights organizations, labor unions, private foundations, civic organizations, business associations, research centers, universities, and hospitals. Typically, counter-trafficking work is

just one aspect of the aims or programs of these kinds of organizations, in contrast to trafficking-centered MANGOs and VSPs.

24. This e-mail was sent by a leader of an areligious MANGO who is very open about his faith. He sent it from his personal account (that is, not the MANGO's account) to an undisclosed list of recipients. One of the recipients was a Buddhist volunteer for the MANGO. He shared with me that he wondered whether the leader was presumptuous in assuming he was a Christian, or insensitive to the exclusion that he—and any other non-Christians who received that e-mail from this well-known anti-trafficking leader—would feel getting sent the announcement-invitation for an event to which they were not actually invited, even though it was not sent via the MANGO. "Being a non-Christian in this predominantly Christian society is tough. I have talked to my own religious leaders about how this is a constant trial of my faith, but I am thankful for the opportunity for that to happen," he said.

25. Butler, *Well Connected: Releasing Power, Restoring Hope through Kingdom Partnerships.*

26. Sec. 2000e-1 [Section 702] of Title VII of the Civil Rights Act of 1964, available at http://www.eeoc.gov/laws/statutes/titlevii.cfm.

27. For a thoughtful analysis of how religious faith is sometimes expressed in and between anti-trafficking organizations, see Koschmann, "Integrating Religious Faith in Human Rights Collaborations."

28. Pauley Johnson et al., "Interagency and Interprofessional Collaboration in Community Care: The Interdependence of Structures and Values," *Journal of Interprofessional Care* 17, no. 1 (2003): 82.

29. Polaris, "Mission and Values."

30. Hall, "Interprofessional Teamwork: Professional Cultures as Barriers," 191.

CHAPTER 6: THE PERFECT STORM AND PATHS THROUGH IT

1. Minh Dang, Foreword to Murphy, *Survivors of Slavery: Modern-Day Slave Narratives*, xvii.

2. Straus, *How to Make Collaboration Work: Powerful Ways to Build Consensus, Solve Problems, and Make Decisions*, 126.

3. AnnJanette Alejano-Steele, "Reflections on the Colorado Project to Comprehensively Combat Human Trafficking" (Denver: Laboratory to Combat Human Trafficking, 2015).

4. Office for Victims of Crime Training and Technical Assistance Center, "Human Trafficking Task Force e-Guide: Strengthening Collaborative Responses." Quotation from https://www.ovcttac.gov/taskforceguide/eguide/3-operating-a-task-force/34

-addressing-common-operational-challenges/sustainability/limited-resources-personnel-turnover.

5. Chris Huxham and Siv Vangen, "Managing Inter-Organizational Relationships," in *Managing in the Voluntary Sector*, ed. Stephen P. Osborne (London: International Thompson Business Press, 1996), 212. As quoted in Huxham and Vangen (2005), 35.

6. Huxham and Vangen, *Managing to Collaborate: The Theory and Practice of Collaborative Advantage*, 67.

7. Ibid., 68.

8. Office for Victims of Crime Training and Technical Assistance Center, "Human Trafficking Task Force e-Guide: Strengthening Collaborative Responses." Source URL for quote: https://www.ovcttac.gov/taskforceguide/eguide/3-operating-a-task -force/34-addressing-common-operational-challenges/managing-conflict/.

9. Alejano-Steele, "Reflections on the Colorado Project to Comprehensively Combat Human Trafficking."

10. See, for example, Andrew Jones, Rhonda Schlangen, and Rhodora Bucoy, "An Evaluation of the International Justice Mission's 'Project Lantern': Assessment of Five-Year Impact and Change in the Public Justice System," International Justice Mission, October 21, 2010, https://www.ijm.org/sites/default/files/download/ resources/120610-Project-Lantern-Impact-Assessment-AJ.pdf.

11. Researchers from the University of Washington School of Social Work and Businesses Ending Slavery and Trafficking, "BEST Businesses Ending Slavery and Trafficking: Inhospitable to Human Trafficking Program Evaluation," Businesses Ending Slavery and Trafficking, July 2014, http://bestalliance.org/wp-content/up loads/2014/07/ITT-Program-Evaluation-wo-appendix-2.pdf.

12. Giorgio Algeri, "Impact Evaluation of Chab Dai Coalition and Its Role within the Anti-Human Trafficking Sector in Cambodia," Chab Dai, 2010, http://chabdai .org/download_files/Giorgio%20Eval%20Report.pdf.

13. Laboratory to Combat Human Trafficking, *The Colorado Project: National Survey Report*, 2013.

14. William Haskins, "Do You Suffer from Collaboration Fatigue?," *Wainhouse Research Blog: News and Views on Unified Communications and Collaboration*, May 28, 2014, http://cp.wainhouse.com/blog/2014/05/28/do-you-suffer-collabora tion-fatigue. See also Huxham and Vangen, *Managing to Collaborate: The Theory and Practice of Collaborative Advantage*, 39, 69–72.

15. See http://www.seattleagainstslavery.org/no-one-should-be-forced/campaign -posters.

16. Legislature of the State of Idaho, *Construction and Maintenance of Information Centers*, Sixty-third legislature, HB 183, March 2015, http://www.legislature.idaho .gov/legislation/2015/H0183.pdf.

17. Washington Legislature, *Concerning the Trafficking of Persons*, http://apps.leg .wa.gov/billinfo/summary.aspx?bill=5884&year=2015#documents.

18. Fisher and Shragge, "Challenging Community Organizing: Facing the 21st Century."

Bibliography

Acker, Joan. "Hierarchies, Jobs, Bodies: A Theory of Gendered Organizations." *Gender abd Society* 4 (1990): 139–58.

Adkins, Julie, Laurie Occhipinti, and Tara Hefferan, eds. *Not by Faith Alone: Social Services, Social Justice, and Faith-Based Organizations in the United States*. Lanham, MD: Lexington Books, 2010.

———. "Social Services, Social Justice, and Faith-Based Organizations in the United States: An Introduction." In *Not by Faith Alone: Social Services, Social Justice, and Faith-Based Organizations in the United States*, edited by Julie Adkins, Laurie Occhipinti, and Tara Hefferan, 1–32. Lanham, MD: Lexington Books, 2010.

Alejano-Steele, AnnJanette. "Reflections on the Colorado Project to Comprehensively Combat Human Trafficking." Denver: Laboratory to Combat Human Trafficking, 2015.

Algeri, Giorgio. *Impact Evaluation of Chab Dai Coalition and Its Role within the Anti-Human Trafficking Sector in Cambodia*. Phnom Penh: Chab Dai Coalition, 2012. http://chabdai.org/download_files/Giorgio%20Eval%20Report.pdf.

Alliance to End Slavery and Trafficking. "About ATEST." http://www.endslaveryandtrafficking.org.

Amble, Brian. "Collaboration and Gender." June 1, 2012. http://www.management-issues.com/news/6495/collaboration-and-gender/.

Ashkenas, Jeremy, and Haeyoun Park. "The Race Gap in America's Police Departments." *New York Times on the Web*. September 4, 2014. http://www.nytimes.com/interactive/2014/09/03/us/the-race-gap-in-americas-police-departments.html?_r=0.

Austin, James E. *The Collaboration Challenge: How Nonprofits and Businesses Succeed through Strategic Alliances*. San Francisco: Jossey-Bass, 2000.

Austin, James E., and M. May Seitanidi. *Creating Value in Nonprofit-Business Collaborations: New Thinking and Practice*. San Francisco: Jossey-Bass, 2014.

Austin Smith, Holly. *Walking Prey: How America's Youth Are Vulnerable to Sex Slavery*. New York: Palgrave Macmillan, 2014.

Balch, Oliver. "Corporate Initiative Can Play a Major Role in Anti-Trafficking Movement: The Global Business Coalition against Human Trafficking Needs Support from More Big Brands to Make a Truly Global Impact." *Guardian*. April 3, 2013. http://www.theguardian.com/global-development-professionals-network/2013/apr/03/human-trafficking-global-business-coalition.

Bales, Kevin, and Zoe Trodd, eds. *To Plead Our Own Cause: Personal Stories by Today's Slaves*. Ithaca, NY: Cornell University Press, 2008.

Banks, Duren, and Tracey Kyckelhahn. "Characteristics of Suspected Human Trafficking Incidents, 2008–2010." Washington, DC: Bureau of Justice Statistics, Office of Justice Programs, U.S. Department of Justice, 2011. http://www.bjs.gov/content/pub/pdf/cshti0810.pdf.

Bell, Ann V., Barret Michalec, and Christine Arenson. "The (Stalled) Progress of Interprofessional Collaboration: The Role of Gender." *Journal of Interprofessional Care* 28, no. 2 (2014): 98–102.

Bell, Ella L. J., and Stella M. Nkomo. *Our Separate Ways: Black and White Women and the Struggle for Professional Identity*. Boston: Harvard Business School Press, 2001.

Bielefeld, Wolfgang, and William Suhs Cleveland. "Faith-Based Organizations as Service Providers and Their Relationship to Government." *Nonprofit and Voluntary Sector Quarterly* 42, no. 3 (2013): 468–94.

Bloom, Sandra L., and Brian Farragher. *Destroying Sanctuary: The Crisis in Human Service Delivery Systems*. New York: Oxford University Press, 2010.

Boris, Elizabeth T., and C. Eugene Steuerle, eds. *Nonprofits and Government: Collaboration and Conflict*. Washington, DC: Urban Institute Press, 1998.

Brennan, Denise. *Life Interrupted: Trafficking into Forced Labor in the United States*. Durham, NC: Duke University Press, 2014.

Burt, Ronald A. "The Gender of Social Capital." *Rationality and Society* 10 (1998): 5–46.

Bush, George W. "Address to the United Nations General Assembly." United Nations. September 23, 2003. http://www.un.org/webcast/ga/58/statements/usaeng030923.htm.

Butler, Phillip. *Well Connected: Releasing Power, Restoring Hope through Kingdom Partnerships*. Colorado Springs, CO: Authentic Publishing, 2006.

Center for Health Workforce Studies and National Association of Social Workers Center for Workforce Studies. "Licensed Social Workers in the United States, 2004." March 2006. http://workforce.socialworkers.org/studies/intro0806.pdf.

Chin, Yu Sun. "Trafficked Boys Overlooked." *Juvenile Justice Information Exchange.* April 14, 2014. http://jjie.org/trafficked-boys-overlooked-underrepresented/.

Colorado Legislature. *Concerning Human Trafficking.* 69th General Assembly, Second Regular Session, HB 14-1273. July 1, 2014. http://www.leg.state.co.us/clics/clics2014a/csl.nsf/fsbillcont2/0E5766A9A4ACD1F387257C300005Fa09/$FILE/1273_01.pdf.

Cooper, Katherine R. "Exploring Stakeholder Participation in Nonprofit Collaboration." PhD diss., University of Illinois at Urbana-Champaign, 2014.

Cousins, Linwood H., Roslyn A. Mickelson, Brian Williams, and Anne Velasco. "Race and Class Challenges in Community Collaboration for Educational Change." *School Community Journal* 18, no. 2 (2008): 29–52.

Crawford, Karin. *Interprofessional Collaboration in Social Work Practice.* Thousand Oaks, CA: Sage Publications, 2012.

Crenshaw, Kimberle. "Demarginalizing the Intersection of Race and Sex: A Black Feminist Critique of Antidiscrimination Doctrine, Feminist Theory and Antiracist Politics." *University of Chicago Legal Forum* (1989): 139–68.

———. "Mapping the Margins: Intersectionality, Identity Politics, and Violence against Women of Color." *Stanford Law Review* 43, no. 6 (July 1991): 1241–99.

Crooke, Curtis. "Women in Law Enforcement." *Community Policing Dispatch* 6, no. 7 (July 2013). http://cops.usdoj.gov/html/dispatch/07-2013/women_in_law_enforcement.asp.

D'Souza, Harold. "USA: Harold D'Souza Honored at 'Survivor Forum'—the White House." *Mangalorean.com.* 2014. http://www.mangalorean.com/specials/special news.php?newsid=454031&newstype=local.

Elliot, James R., and Ryan A. Smith. "Race, Gender, and Workplace Power." *American Sociological Review* 69, no. 3 (2004): 365–86.

Embrey Family Foundation. "Mission without Borders Guidelines." http://www.embreyfdn.org/embrey/index.php?option=com_content&view=category&id=37&layout=blog&Itemid=37.

Ewing, Jonathan. "This Hotel Is Fighting Human Trafficking Like People's Lives Are Depending on It." U.S. Global Leadership Coalition. March 8, 2014. http://www.usglc.org/2014/03/08/this-hotel-is-fighting-human-trafficking-like-peoples-lives-are-depending-on-it/.

Faith Alliance Against Slavery and Trafficking. "Take Action: Immigration." http://www.faastinternational.org/#/take-action/immigration.

Farley, Melissa, Emily Schuckman, Jacqueline M. Golding, Laura Jarrett, Peter Qualliotine, and Michele Decker. "Comparing Buyers of Sex with Men Who Don't Buy Sex." Presented at Psychologists for Social Responsibility Annual Conference,

Boston, MA. July 15, 2011. http://www.catwinternational.org/content/images/article/212/attachment.pdf.

Fisher, R., and E. Shragge. "Challenging Community Organizing: Facing the 21st Century." *Journal of Community Practice* 8, no. 3 (2000): 1–19.

Foot, Kirsten A. "Actors and Activities in the Anti-Human Trafficking Movement." In *The Dark Side of Globalization*, edited by R. Thakur and J. Heine. 249–65. New York: United Nations University Press, 2011.

———. "Cultural-Historical Activity Theory: Exploring a Theory to Inform Practice and Research." *Journal of Human Behavior in the Social Environment* 24, no. 3 (2014): 329–47.

Foot, Kirsten A., Amoshaun Toft, and Nina Cesare. "Developments in Anti-Trafficking Efforts: 2008–2011." *Journal of Human Trafficking* 1, no. 2 (July 2015).

Foot, Kirsten A., and John Vanek. "Toward Constructive Engagement between Local Law Enforcement and Mobilization and Advocacy Nongovernmental Organizations about Human Trafficking: Recommendations for Law Enforcement Executives." *Law Enforcement Executive Forum* 12, no. 1 (March 2012): 1–11.

The Freedom Fund. "About Us." http://www.freedomfund.org/about-us/.

Frost, Joye E. "Improving Services for Victims of Human Trafficking." *Justice Blogs.* January 16, 2014. http://www.justice.gov/opa/blog/improving-services-victims-human-trafficking.

Gieryn, Thomas F. "Boundary-Work and the Demarcation of Science from Non-Science: Strains and Interests in Professional Ideologies of Scientists." *American Sociological Review* 48 (1983): 781–95.

Glick, Peter, Sadie Larsen, Cathryn Johnson, and Heather Branstiter. "Evaluations of Sexy Women in Low- and High-Status Jobs." *Psychology of Women Quarterly* 29, no. 4 (December 2005): 389–95.

Global Freedom Network. "About the Global Freedom Network." http://www.globalfreedomnetwork.org/about/.

Graef, Christine. "Bakken Region Tribes Fight Back against Human Trafficking." http://www.mintpressnews.com/bakken-region-tribes-fight-back-human-trafficking/199156/.

Hall, Pippa. "Interprofessional Teamwork: Professional Cultures as Barriers." *Journal of Interprofessional Care* 19, no. S1 (May 2005): 188–96.

Hardy, Brian, Bob Hudson, and Eileen Waddington. *What Makes a Good Partnership?: A Partnership Assessment Tool.* Edited by Strategic Partnering Task Force. Leeds, UK: Nuffield Institute for Health, Community Care Division, 2000. https://www.conservationgateway.org/ConservationPlanning/partnering/cpc/Documents/AssessingStrategicPartnership.pdf.

Hardy, Cynthia, and Nelson Phillips. "Strategies of Engagement: Lessons from the Critical Examination of Collaboration and Conflict in an Interorganizational Domain." *Organization Science* 9, no. 2 (1998): 217–30.

Harvey Wingfield, Adia. "Are Some Emotions Marked 'Whites Only'? Racialized Feeling Rules in Professional Workplaces." *Social Problems* 57 (2010): 251–68.

Haskins, William. "Do You Suffer from Collaboration Fatigue?" *Wainhouse Research Blog: News and Views on Unified Communications & Collaboration.* May 28, 2014. http://cp.wainhouse.com/blog/2014/05/28/do-you-suffer-collaboration-fatigue.

Hertzke, Allen D. *Freeing God's Children: The Unlikely Alliance for Global Human Rights.* Lanham, MD: Rowman & Littlefield Publishers, 2004.

Hill Collins, Patricia. "Toward a New Vision: Race, Class, and Gender as Categories of Analysis and Connection." *Race, Sex and Class* 1, no. 1 (1993): 25–45.

Hodges, Cassie Ann. "Slavery Survivors Brief U.S. Senate." *FTS Blog*: Free the Slaves. January 27, 2014. http://www.freetheslaves.net/slavery-survivors-brief-u-s-senate/.

Huxham, Chris, and Siv Vangen. "Doing Things Collaboratively: Realizing the Advantage or Succumbing to Inertia." *Organizational Dynamics* 33, no. 2 (2004): 190–201.

———. "Leadership in the Shaping and Implementation of Collaboration Agendas: How Things Happen in a (Not Quite) Joined-Up World." *Academy of Management Journal* 43, no. 6 (2000): 1159–75.

———. "Managing Inter-Organizational Relationships." In *Managing in the Voluntary Sector*, edited by Stephen P. Osborne. 202–16. London: International Thomson Business Press, 1996.

———. *Managing to Collaborate: The Theory and Practice of Collaborative Advantage.* New York: Routledge, 2005.

Imago Dei Fund. "Grant Application Form." http://www.imagodeifund.org/application.html.

Institute for Illinois' Fiscal Stability at the Civic Federation. "Social Impact Funding through Pay for Success Contracts in Illinois." Civic Federation. September 11, 2014. http://www.civicfed.org/iifs/blog/social-impact-funding-through-pay-success-contracts-illinois

International Association of Chiefs of Police. *Backing the Badge: Working Effectively with Law Enforcement: Police-Based Victim Services.* Alexandria, VA: International Association of Chiefs of Police. http://www.theiacp.org/Portals/0/pdfs/responsetovictims/RESOURCES_DOCUMENTS/TS_Links/9_BackingtheBadge.pdf.

International Council of Jewish Women. "Trafficking of Women and Girls." http://icjw.org/gen.aspx?page=trafficking.

Jews Against Human Trafficking. "What's Happening." http://jewsagainsthumantrafficking.org/.

Johnson, Chris, and Judy McKee. "Giving Voice to the Voiceless: 'Pillars of Hope' Presidential Initiative to Tackle Human Trafficking." National Association of Attorneys General. 2011. http://www.naag.org/giving-a-voice-to-the-voiceless -pillars-of-hope-presidential-initiative-to-tackle-human-trafficking.php.

Johnson, Pauley, Gerald Wistow, Rockwell Schulz, and Brian Hardy. "Interagency and Interprofessional Collaboration in Community Care: The Interdependence of Structures and Values." *Journal of Interprofessional Care* 17, no. 1 (2003): 69–82.

Johnston, Anne, Barbara Friedman, and Autumn Shafer. "Framing the Problem of Sex Trafficking: Whose Problem? What Remedy?" *Feminist Media Studies* 14, no. 3 (2012): 419–36.

Jones, Andrew, Rhonda Schlangen, and Rhodora Bucoy. *An Evaluation of the International Justice Mission's "Project Lantern": Assessment of Five-Year Impact and Change in the Public Justice System.* International Justice Mission. October 21, 2010. https://www.ijm.org/sites/default/files/download/resources/120610-Project -Lantern-Impact-Assessment-AJ.pdf.

Justice and Mercy Philanthropy Forum. "About Us." http://justicemercyforum.home stead.com/about.html.

Kamensky, John M., and Thomas J. Burlin, eds. *Collaboration: Using Networks and Partnerships.* IBM Center for the Business of Government Book Series, edited by Mark A. Abramson and Paul R. Lawrence. Lanham, MD: Rowman & Littlefield Publishers, 2004.

Kanter, Rosabeth M. *Men and Women of the Corporation.* New York: Basic Books, 1977.

Ken, Ivy. *Digesting Race, Class, and Gender: Sugar as a Metaphor.* New York: Palgrave Macmillan, 2010.

Keyton, Joann, Debra J. Ford, and Faye I. Smith. "A Mesolevel Communicative Model of Collaboration." *Communication Theory* 18, no. 3 (2008): 376–406.

Konrad, Helga. "The Fight against Trafficking in Human Beings from the European Perspective." In *Trafficking in Human$: Social, Cultural and Political Dimensions,* edited by Sally Cameron and Edward Newman. 161–80. New York: United Nations University Press, 2008.

Korngold, Alice. *A Better World, Inc.: How Companies Profit by Solving Global Problems . . . Where Governments Cannot.* New York: Palgrave Macmillan, 2014.

Koschmann, Matt. "Integrating Religious Faith in Human Rights Collaborations." *Journal of Communication and Religion* 36, no. 2 (2013): 1–27.

Kwoh, Leslie. "Picking Someone for a Project? Chances Are, He'll Look Like You." *Wall Street Journal at Work*. June 4, 2012. http://blogs.wsj.com/atwork/2012/06/04/picking-someone-for-a-project-chances-are-hell-look-like-you/.

Laboratory to Combat Human Trafficking. "About the Colorado Project to Comprehensively Combat Human Trafficking." http://lcht.hotpressplatform.com/about/theproject.

————. *The Colorado Project: National Survey Report*. Denver: Laboratory to Combat Human Trafficking, 2013.

————. "Our Values." http://www.combathumantrafficking.org/who-we-are/our-values.

Latonero, Mark, Jennifer Musto, Zhaleh Boyd, Ev Boyle, Amber Bissel, Kari Gibson, and Joanne Kim. *Technology and Human Trafficking: The Rise of Mobile and the Diffusion of Technology-Facilitated Trafficking*. Research Series on Technology and Human Trafficking. Los Angeles: University of Southern California, 2012. https://technologyandtrafficking.usc.edu/2012-report/.

Leathard, Audrey, ed. *Interprofessional Collaboration: From Policy to Practice in Health and Social Care*. New York: Brunner-Routledge, 2003.

Legislature of the State of Idaho. *Construction and Maintenance of Information Centers*. Sixty-third legislature, HB 183. March 2015. http://www.legislature.idaho.gov/legislation/2015/H0183.pdf.

Lewis, Laurie K., Matthew G. Isbell, and Matt Koschmann. "Collaborative Tensions: Practitioners' Experiences of Interorganizational Relationships." *Communication Monographs* 77, no. 4 (2010): 460–79.

Lillie, Michelle. "Human Trafficking: Not All Black or White." *Human Trafficking Search: The Global Resource and Database*. April 30, 2014. http://humantraffickingsearch.net/wp/human-trafficking-not-all-black-or-white/

Limanowska, Barbara, and Helga Konrad. "Problems of Anti-Trafficking Cooperation." In *Strategies against Human Trafficking: The Role of the Security Sector*, edited by Cornelius Friesendorf. 427–58. Vienna and Geneva: National Defence Academy and Austrian Ministry of Defence and Sports, 2009.

Lotia, Nuzhat, and Cynthia Hardy. "Critical Perspectives on Collaboration." In *The Oxford Handbook on Inter-Organizational Relations*, edited by Steve Cropper, Mark Ebers, Chris Huxham, and Peter Smith Ring. 366–89. New York: Oxford University Press, 2008.

Lyon, Jo Anne. "The Evolution of Anti-Trafficking Campaigns in the Church." *On Faith: Faith Street*. May 2, 2014. http://www.faithstreet.com/onfaith/2014/05/02/evolution-of-anti-trafficking-campaigns-in-the-church/31942.

Mattesich, Paul W., Marta Murray-Close, and Barbara R. Monsey. *Collaboration: What Makes It Work: A Review of Research Literature on Factors Influencing*

Successful Collaboration. 2nd ed. St. Paul, MN: Amherst H. Wilder Foundation, 2001.

McGuire, Gail G. "Gender, Race, and the Shadow Structure: A Study of Informal Networks and Inequality in a Work Organization." *Gender and Society* 16, no. 3 (June 2002): 303–22.

McTaggartt, Robin. "Is Validity Really an Issue for Participatory Action Research?" *Studies in Cultures, Organizations, and Societies* 4, no. 2 (1998): 211–36.

Miller, Jon, James R. Lincoln, and Jon Olsen. "Rationality and Equity in Professional Networks: Gender and Race as Factors in the Stratification of Interorganizational Systems." *American Journal of Sociology* 87, no. 2 (1981): 308–35.

Murphy, Laura T., ed. *Survivors of Slavery: Modern-Day Slave Narratives.* New York: Columbia University Press, 2014.

Musto, Jennifer, and danah boyd. "The Trafficking-Technology Nexus." *Social Policy* (2014). doi:10.1093/sp/jxu018. http://sp.oxfordjournals.org/content/early/2014/08/26/sp.jxu018.full.pdf+html.

Nagel, Thomas. *The View from Nowhere.* New York: Oxford University Press, 1989.

National Crime Justice Reference Service. "Crime and Victimization in the United States: Statistical Overviews." Washington, DC: Office of Justice Programs, U.S. Department of Justice, 2014. https://www.ncjrs.gov/ovc_archives/ncvrw/2014/pdf/StatisticalOverviews.pdf.

———. "Statistical Overviews: Human Trafficking." Washington, DC: Office of Justice Programs, U.S. Department of Justice, 2013. https://www.ncjrs.gov/ovc_archives/ncvrw/2013/pdf/StatisticalOverviews.pdf.

Obama, Barack. "Fact Sheet: The Obama Administration Announces Efforts to Combat Human Trafficking at Home and Abroad." White House Office of the Press Secretary. September 25, 2012. http://www.whitehouse.gov/the-press-office/2012/09/25/fact-sheet-obama-administration-announces-efforts-combat-human-trafficki.

———. "Remarks by the President to the Clinton Global Initiative." White House Office of the Press Secretary. September 25, 2012. http://www.whitehouse.gov/the-press-office/2012/09/25/remarks-president-clinton-global-initiative.

———. "Statement by the President on the Meeting of the Interagency Task Force to Monitor and Combat Trafficking in Persons." White House Office of the Press Secretary. March 15, 2012. http://www.whitehouse.gov/the-press-office/2012/03/15/statement-president-meeting-interagency-task-force-monitor-and-combat-tr.

Office for Victims of Crime. "OVC Initiatives to Expand Services to Human Trafficking Victims." Office of Justice Programs, U.S. Department of Justice. http://www.ovc.gov/news/human_trafficking.html.

Office for Victims of Crime Training and Technical Assistance Center. "Human Trafficking Task Force e-Guide: Strengthening Collaborative Responses." Department of Justice: Office of Justice Programs: Office for Victims of Crime. https://www.ovcttac.gov/taskforceguide/eguide/.

Oriola, Bukola. "A Forum and Listening Session Indeed!" January 20, 2014. http://bukolaoriola.com/2014/01/20/a-forum-and-listening-session-indeed/.

———. *Imprisoned: The Travails of a Trafficked Victim.* Spring Lake Park, MN: Bukola Publishing, 2012.

Papa, Michael J., Arvind Singhal, and Wendy H. Papa. *Organizing for Social Change: A Dialectic Journey of Theory and Praxis.* New Delhi: Sage Publications, 2006.

Partnership for Freedom. "About Us." http://www.partnershipforfreedom.org/about/.

Polaris. "Mission and Values." http://www.polarisproject.org/about-us/overview/mission-and-values.

Police Executive Research Forum. *Civil Rights Investigations of Local Police: Lessons Learned.* Critical Issues in Policing Series. Washington, DC: Police Executive Research Forum, 2013. http://www.policeforum.org/assets/docs/Critical_Issues_Series/civil%20rights%20investigations%20of%20local%20police%20-%20lessons%20learned%202013.pdf.

Purdy, Jill M. "A Framework for Assessing Power in Collaborative Governance Processes." *Public Administration Review* 72, no. 3 (2012): 409–17.

Reaves, Brian A. "Federal Law Enforcement Officers, 2008." Washington, DC: U.S. Department of Justice, Office of Justice Programs, Bureau of Justice Statistics, 2012.

Researchers from the University of Washington School of Social Work and Businesses Ending Slavery and Trafficking. "BEST Businesses Ending Slavery and Trafficking: Inhospitable to Human Trafficking Program Evaluation." Businesses Ending Slavery and Trafficking. July 2014. http://bestalliance.org/wp-content/uploads/2014/07/ITT-Program-Evaluation-wo-appendix-2.pdf.

Research Network on the Legal Parameters of Slavery. "Bellagio-Harvard Guidelines on the Legal Parameters of Slavery." Queen's University Belfast School of Law. 2012. http://www.law.qub.ac.uk/schools/SchoolofLaw/Research/HumanRightsCentre/Resources/Bellagio-HarvardGuidelinesontheLegalParametersofSlavery.

Sandfort, Jodi, and H. Brinton Milward. "Collaborative Service Provision in the Public Sector." In *The Oxford Handbook of Inter-Organizational Relations*, edited by Steve Cropper, Mark Ebers, Chris Huxham, and Peter Smith Ring. 147–74. New York: Oxford University Press, 2008.

Sarkar, Siddartha. "Use of Technology in Human Trafficking Networks and Sexual Exploitation: A Cross-Sectional Multi-Country Study." *Transnational Social Review: A Social Work Journal* (2015).

Scott, Jason D. "Private-Sector Contributions to Faith-Based Social Service: The Policies and Giving Patterns of Private Foundations." Roundtable on Religion and Social Welfare Policy, 2003.

Seattle Times Staff. "Help Vulnerable Girls and Women Leave Prostitution." *Seattle Times*, December 20, 2009. http://www.seattletimes.com/opinion/help-vulnerable -girls-and-women-leave-prostitution.

Small, Meredith F. *Our Babies, Ourselves: How Biology and Culture Shape the Way We Parent*. New York: Doubleday, 1998.

Smith, Steven Rathgeb. "Social Services." In *The State of Nonprofit America,* edited by Lester Salamon. Washington, DC: Brookings Institution Press, in cooperation with the Aspen Institute, 2002. http://www.aspeninstitute.org/sites/default/files/ content/docs/psi/SOS_-_Chapter_4_Highlights_Social_Services.pdf.

Straus, David. *How to Make Collaboration Work: Powerful Ways to Build Consensus, Solve Problems, and Make Decisions*. San Francisco: Berrett-Koehler Publishers, 2002.

Technology and Human Trafficking. "Private-Sector Initiatives." University of Southern California Center on Communication Leadership and Policy. https://technology andtrafficking.usc.edu/private-sector-initiatives/.

Third Sector Capital Partners. "Massachusetts Launches Landmark Initiative to Reduce Recidivism among At-Risk Youth." December 16, 2014. http://www.thirdsec torcap.org/our-work/massachusetts-juvenile-justice-pfs/.

T'ruah: The Rabbinic Call for Human Rights. "Slavery and Human Trafficking." http://www.truah.org/issuescampaigns/slavery-a-human-trafficking-50094.html.

U.S. Department of Homeland Security, "About the Blue Campaign," http://www .dhs.gov/blue-campaign/about-blue-campaign.

U.S. Department of Justice. "Bush Administration Hosts First National Training Conference to Combat Human Trafficking: President George W. Bush and Attorney General John Ashcroft Address Conference." Department of Justice. July 16, 2004. http://www.justice.gov/archive/opa/pr/2004/July/04_ag_489.htm.

U.S. Department of State Office to Monitor and Combat Trafficking in Persons. "Male Trafficking Victims." June 1, 2013. http://www.state.gov/j/tip/rls/fs/2013/211624 .htm.

———. *Trafficking in Persons Report*. 10th ed. U.S. Department of State. June 2010. http://www.state.gov/documents/organization/142979.pdf.

U.S. Department of State, Office to Monitor and Combat Trafficking in Persons. "The 3Ps: Prevention, Protection, and Prosecution." U.S. Department of State, Democracy and Global Affairs. June 2011. http://www.state.gov/documents/orga nization/167334.pdf.

U.S. Equal Employment Opportunity Commission. "Human Trafficking." http://www.eeoc.gov/eeoc/interagency/trafficking.cfm.

U.S. Government. "Coordination, Collaboration, Capacity: Federal Strategic Action Plan on Services for Victims of Human Trafficking in the United States, 2013–2017." Office for Victims of Crimes. January 2014. http://www.ovc.gov/pubs/FederalHumanTraffickingStrategicPlan.pdf.

Vanek, John. "Human Trafficking: Building an Agency's Social Capital through a Social Justice Response." *Police Chief* 81 (July 2014): 48–54. http://www.policechief magazine.org/magazine/index.cfm?fuseaction=display&article_id=3414&issue _id=72014.

Washington Anti-Trafficking Response Network. "Collaborating with WARN." Available from https://www.ovcttac.gov/taskforceguide/eguide/3-operating-a -task-force/resources-34-addressing-common-operational-challenges/.

Washington Legislature. *Concerning the Trafficking of Persons.* 64th Legislature, SB 5884. March 2015. http://apps.leg.wa.gov/billinfo/summary.aspx?bill=5884&year =2015#documents.

Watson, E., and P. G. Foster-Fishman. "The Exchange Boundary Framework: Understanding the Evolution of Power within Collaborative Decision-Making Settings." *American Journal of Community Psychology* (2012): 1–13.

Wesleyan Holiness Consortium Freedom Network. "Declaration for Freedom." http://holinessandunity.wikispaces.com/file/view/Declaration+for+Freedom .pdf/480446278/Declaration%20for%20Freedom.pdf.

Williams, Christine L., Chandra Muller, and Kristine Kilanski. "Gendered Organizations in the New Economy." *Gender and Society* 26 (August 2012): 549–73.

Wookey, Melissa L., Nell A. Graves, and J. Corey Butler. "Effects of a Sexy Appearance on Perceived Competence of Women." *Journal of Social Psychology* 149, no. 1 (2009): 116–18.

YouthCare. "The Bridge Continuum of Services for Sexually Exploited Youth." http://www.youthcare.org/our-programs/services-sexually-exploited-youth#.VQ9P dOESNuo.

Zimmerman, Yvonne C. *Other Dreams of Freedom: Religion, Sex, and Human Trafficking.* New York: Oxford University Press, 2013.

Index

Acknowledgments

I am immensely grateful to each person who invested time during the course of my research for this book to talk with me about their anti-trafficking work and their experiences in interorganizational collaboration. I am also grateful to the coalition and task force leaders in every city who permitted me to conduct participant observation during their meetings, and trusted me to take notes during sometimes-difficult discussions. I have written this book with them and for them, as well as about them.

Amoshaun Toft and Nina Cesare worked with me good-naturedly over several years, analyzing data on global anti-trafficking efforts that form part of the context of this book. The Department of Communication at the University of Washington provided research funds and other forms of material support throughout the course of this project. I have particularly appreciated the enthusiastic support of my department chair, David Domke, all along the way. Grants from Microsoft Research, the Imago Dei Fund, and the Namaste Foundation, combined with donations designated to anti-trafficking research at University of Washington enabled me to have course releases in order to focus on writing this book. Kathie and Greg Burnside, Jennifer and Bob Doede, Ginny and Bob Foot, Jill and Tim Griffin, Karen Grigsby, Amy and Bob Sheehy, and Jun Young of Zum Communications encouraged me greatly through their support of this research.

I am grateful to Leanne Silverman, my editor at Rowman & Littlefield, for championing this book by an academic for diverse audiences of nonacademics, and for her insightful guidance through the final phases of the writing process. Our phone conversations about the manuscript at key junctions were invaluable. This book also benefited tremendously from the feedback offered by people (from many sectors!) on earlier versions of part or all of the manuscript. I am indebted to each of these thoughtful reviewers: AnnJanette Alejano-Steele, Megan Bruneau, Kathie Burnside, Robert Beiser, Mar Brettmann, Minh Dang, Jeremy Floyd, Sheila Houston, Kathleen Morris, Emily Nielsen-Jones, Brenda Oliver, Nancy Pham, Rane Stempson-Johnson, Maria Trujillo, Sandra Morgan, and several others who prefer to remain anonymous. Nancy Bixler devoted her 2015 spring break to giving this manuscript her amazingly thorough and powerful argument-editing treatment. Any remaining blunders, errors, or oversights in this book are my own.

I have been blessed by many forms of support from friends and family members during the research and writing of this book. To each of my dear ones—and especially to my mother, my husband, and my daughter—thank you. Your companionship means more than I can say.

About the Author

Kirsten Foot is professor of communication at the University of Washington, and adjunct faculty in UW's Information School and Jackson School of International Studies. She has published extensively on organizing processes, digital media, and practice-based theory and research. She is the lead author of *Web Campaigning*, which received the 2008 Doris Graber Award from the Political Communication division of the American Political Science Association, and a coeditor of *The Internet and National Elections: A Comparative Study of Web Campaigning* and *Media Technologies: Essays on Communication, Materiality, and Society*. She has been studying anti–human trafficking efforts both in the United States and internationally since 2007, and she advises several multisector counter-trafficking initiatives under way at city, state, and national levels.